The Sea King

The Sea King

The Life of James Iredell Waddell

Gary McKay

BIRLINN

First published in 2009 by
Birlinn Limited
West Newington House
10 Newington Road
Edinburgh
EH9 1QS

www.birlinn.co.uk

ISBN: 978 1 84341 046 1

British Library Cataloguing-in-Publication Data
A catalogue record for this book is available from the British Library

Designed and typeset by Carolyn Griffiths
Printed and bound by CPI Cox & Wyman, Reading

CONTENTS

Pardon
– a warrant granting release from punishment for an offense.

'The President shall be Commander in Chief of the Army and Navy of the United States, and of the Militia of the several States, when called into the actual Service of the United States; he may require the Opinion, in writing, of the principal Officer in each of the executive Departments, upon any subject relating to the Duties of their respective Offices, and he shall have Power to Grant Reprieves and Pardons for Offenses against the United States, except in Cases of Impeachment.'
– Constitution of the United States of America, Article 2, Section 2

'Humanity and good policy conspire to dictate, that the benign prerogative of pardoning should be as little as possible fettered or embarrassed.'
– Alexander Hamilton, in the *Federalist Papers,* published on 25 March 1788

'I come from the South. I know at the end of the War Between the States, there was a sense of forgiveness for those who had been not loyal to our country in the past, and this same thing occurred after other wars as well.'
– James Earl Carter, 39th President of the United States of America, commenting upon his general pardon to draft-evaders of the Vietnam War

1

After action

Late on the afternoon of 2 August 1865, two vessels, one a large
three-masted sail steamship and the other a small three-masted
bark, met in the Pacific Ocean a thousand miles south-west of
the city of San Francisco, California. As the large, black-painted
steamship lowered away a boat to row to the small bark, neither
crew of either vessel could have imagined the tremendous gulf in
time, distance and experiences that separated them.

The smaller vessel had been at sea for several days out of San
Francisco and was making slow progress across the Pacific
Ocean due to her sailing into the dominant westerly winds. The
dark brooding mass of the steamship, if it could have been
clearly seen by the crew of the bark, was scarred by weather and
ice. Her bottom, originally covered entirely by copper, had been
ravaged by ice in the Bering Sea, coral in the South Pacific, and
barnacles as well as seaweed in both the Atlantic and the Indian
Ocean. She was in the process of completing a circumnavigation
of the globe, though at this moment, in the last, languid minutes
of a hot August day, neither her crew nor her captain knew this.

On the bark her master patiently awaited the arrival of the

steamship's boat. Vessels commonly flagged or hailed each other down at sea, particularly if one had been at sea for a great length of time. It was a chance to exchange the news of the day, to pass on newspapers that had already been well read by the outgoing vessel and, perchance, for the inbound vessel to warn of weather or other dangers ahead for the outward bound ship.

The captain and his ship were a proud product of the greatest maritime nation in the world, Great Britain. As the away boat from the black steamship grew closer, those aboard the bark could faintly hear voices speaking with English, Scottish and American intonations. There was nothing to fear here, as they had been hailed originally by a good strong English accent from the great steamer – and was there not an English pennant floating listlessly from her stern? Finally, it was evident to all aboard that she had been built in that great birthplace of the world's finest ships, Glasgow. Liverpool could build fine vessels, but a Glasgow-built clipper or steamer had a line to it that brought a twinkle to the eye of any sailor of the time.

The rowers on the small boat that had launched from the black steamship had almost reached the bark. Their parent vessel was a product of Glasgow, for sure, but it was owned by a nation that no longer existed. The pennant that hung astern was for show only, for her true flag stayed hidden, unless needing to be displayed for her mortal enemy, the United States of America. She was no pirate, at least in the eyes of her crew, for had not the world's greatest maritime power, Britain, asserted that her country was a legal belligerent?

Atop the quarter-deck of the black steamship, her captain peered impatiently towards the sleek sailing ship, sliding his ship's telescope in and out slowly, waiting for the signal from the boarding party's leading officer that he had arrived safely, and without suspicion. The bark's crew may have believed that the black steam-sail ship was merely paying a courtesy call, but for the strangely silent boarding party this was not only business, but also potentially another act in the war that they had been carrying out around the world's oceans.

The boarding party's gig boat having reached the rope ladder of the bark, the seemingly friendly, but determined faces looked up into the eyes of the inquiring faces aboard the bark as the mooring lines were tied up. The leading officer from the boarding party, with a wave back towards the great black steamship, leapt for a rung of the ladder, and, followed closely and quickly by other members of the party, lightly climbed the ship's side and stepped aboard the main deck of the bark.

Met by the captain of the bark with an outstretched hand, the leading officer of the boarding party was informed that he was welcomed aboard the *Barracouta*, originally out of Liverpool. The officer from the black steamship responded in a soft but firm southern American accent that he was Ship's Master Bulloch from the Confederate States Navy warship *Shenandoah* and could he see the *Barracouta*'s papers, please. The flabbergasted captain of the *Barracouta*, looking beyond the cluster of swarthy fierce-eyed men who had boarded his vessel, would have seen the distant black-hulled ship in her true colours, hidden cannon ports flung aside and the 'white flag' naval ensign of the Confederate States Navy flapping quietly from her sternpost mast. Eyes locked upon the css *Shenandoah*, the captain of the *Barracouta* may have replied in an equally polite but knowledgeable voice, that 'the Civil War has been over four months now!'.

Mutual astonishment must have silenced both crews for a few moments, if not minutes, before an avalanche of questions poured out – but not before maritime protocol was completely satisfied. The boarding crew of the CSS *Shenandoah* had seen, heard and experienced every form of maritime subterfuge during their cruise against commerce owned by the United States of America; false owner papers and false-flags were a routine occurrence. Before any further discussions could take place and before any friendly conversation could carry on, *bona fides* had to be established to Master Bulloch's satisfaction.

As soon as a careful examination of the ship's papers and cargo manifest had been completed, questions flew as fast as the newspapers aboard could be flung open to show the now stateless Confederates what had transpired during their voyage to the edges of the world. As the doctor of the *Shenandoah* related many years later in a newspaper interview for the *Atlanta Journal-Constitution*, 'Her captain informed our boarding officer that the war was over, and produced New York and San Francisco papers, telling us for the first time of the great and closing scenes of the fearful drama: the surrender of Lee; the capture of Richmond; the assassination of Lincoln; and the final collapse of the Confederacy.'

However, back on the *Barracouta* on that hot August day in 1865, the *Shenandoah*'s doctor, as well as her impatient captain, had no idea òf the news that their boarding party would be bringing back to them. Maybe the slow pull on the oars of the small gig boat as it made its way back to the *Shenandoah* gave something away, or possibly Ship's Master Bulloch shouted the news once they were within earshot; time has carried away that detail and it matters not. What is certain is that the man most affected by the news and who had ventured most in his career as a professional naval officer was the CSS *Shenandoah*'s captain, Lt. Commanding James Iredell Waddell of the Confederate States Navy, formerly a lieutenant in the United States Navy.

We don't have to imagine Waddell's reaction to the news for we have it in his own words from a lengthy memoir he penned years later, originally for his family (and since published in an edited form). Waddell noted that, 'My life had been chequered from the dawn of my naval career and I had believed myself schooled to every sort of disappointment, but the dreadful issue of that sanguinary struggle was the bitterest blow, because unexpected. . . It cast a gloom over the whole ship and did occupy my thoughts. I had, however, a responsibility of the highest nature resting upon me in deciding the course we should pursue, which involved not only our personal honour, but the honour of the flag entrusted to us which had walked the waters fearlessly and in triumph.'

Waddell would have known that the US Navy was searching for him, which was part of the cat-and-mouse game that had begun with his original cruise. Waddell also knew that his depredations against the US merchant marine since the formal end of the Civil War made him a virtual pirate. What Waddell didn't know, at least not on 2 August 1865, was that President Andrew Johnson had declared him to be a pirate and that his wife, Anne Iglehart Waddell had been arrested under order from President Abraham Lincoln and Secretary of War Edwin M. Stanton – and this had taken place while he was in the South Atlantic months before!

President Andrew Johnson's declaration that Waddell was to be considered a pirate elevated him to the status of 'enemy of the state' insofar as the government of the United States was concerned. To be called a 'pirate' in the mid nineteenth century anywhere in the world carried the same terrible connotation as 'terrorist' does now in the twenty-first century. What had Waddell done that surpassed all other 'rebels'?

Some explanation can be found in Waddell's own proud words from his memoirs, 'The *Shenandoah* was actually cruising eight months in search of the property of the enemy, during which time she made 38 captures, of which she released six on bond and destroyed 32 of them. She was the only vessel which carried the flag of the South around the world.' Waddell went on to say, 'She carried it six months after the war was over and she was surrendered to the British nation. The last gun in defence of the South was fired from her deck, and that gun was fired by South Carolina's gallant son, Lt. John Grimball. She ran a distance of 58,000 miles and met with no serious injury during a cruise of 13 months. Her anchors were on her bows for eight months. She never abandoned a chase and was second to no other cruiser, not excepting the celebrated *Alabama*.'

The *Shenandoah* destroyed only 32 vessels in comparison to the *Alabama's* tally of 64, yet the US government would prosecute Waddell in a manner that, astonishingly, would not officially end until the last three years of his life. But governmental fury went far beyond even this. Waddell's naval compatriot, Rafael Semmes, had made his way back to the United States from Europe – via Mexico nonetheless – to continue to fight for the Confederacy in its last desperate days and for his efforts had been captured, to the great delight of Secretary of the Navy Gideon Welles, who had a particular, almost insane hatred, of those officers who had abandoned the

Union Navy for the upstart 'rebel' navy. Why? Semmes of the *Alabama*, Maffit of the *Florida* and Waddell and his *Shenandoah* had virtually driven the US merchant navy from the world's seas – in the decade preceding the American Civil War, 67 per cent of all shipping tonnage coming to America was carried by American-owned ships; after the war the percentage was a mere 39 per cent. The American shipping industry would not recover from this debacle until World War II, three-quarters of a century in the future.

The American shipping insurance industry was also in disarray as a result of the Confederate Navy's campaign of commercial destruction; rates rose stratospherically during the depredations of the *Florida* and the *Alabama*. The capture of the *Florida* in Brazil and the destruction of the *Alabama* in a naval duel with the uss *Kearsage* off Cherbourg, France, temporarily gave hope to the Yankee sailing industry that relief was finally at hand.

Then came news that a new raider had been launched by the Confederacy, a vessel built in Glasgow and originally designed for the Far East tea trade. Experienced sailors knew what this meant. With the latest advances in steam propulsion she would be fast under sail and her hull would be designed so she could sail long distances quickly with the need for far fewer coal stops. Her capabilities were even greater than the merchant sailors knew, for the vessel had been built originally to a specification for the British government in order to transport members of the military to India rapidly. When it was eventually discovered that the vessel, originally named the *Sea King*, had only made one trip to India before being sold to the Confederacy, the white-hot suspicion that the British government had been trying to destroy the Union all along – while pretending to be a great and benign friend – would acquire the ring of truth for the American public.

Great Britain may have been the world's greatest mistress of the waves and empress of the lands bordering the seas, but she also peeked over her shoulder at the Yankee damsel fast catching up with her; in the power politics of the day, if America could be divided, that threat could be diminished. British government policy, until the third year of the American Civil War, was to turn a very generous, blind eye to the activities of Confederate naval officers and civilians in their attempts – often successful – at building and buying vessels in order to attack US merchant ships or run the US Navy's tenuous blockade. Only in the last year and a half of the conflict, with the North becoming the obvious victor, did the British government begin seriously to clamp down on the covert shipbuilding and buying consortium created by the Confederacy. But this was too little and too late, as far as the people and politicians of the newly re-forged United States of America were concerned. Serious financial compensation would have to be made by the British government to the American people, or the arrogant British would discover that while the American merchant navy had declined, the world's mightiest navy and army now belonged to America. The pockets of the Yankee merchants had been emptied and somebody was going to have to pay – either with gold or with blood – but satisfaction would be had either way. Waddell was an instrument of the British in a tenuous way, so he became the lightning rod for the anger of the American government, which was fuelled by the failure of the US Navy to capture him. Waddell's great crime, in truth, was that he had not been captured.

So, on 2 August 1865, as the away boat of the *Shenandoah*

began to pull alongside her mother ship, the shouts of 'The war is over!' would have reached the ears of Waddell well before Bulloch could have gained the deck. We know what Waddell would write in the future of his thoughts on receiving that news, but in the actual moment he must have maintained a remarkable degree of outward equanimity, while his mind raced to come to terms with the situation that now faced him, his crew and his ship. The newspapers that Master Bulloch would have placed before him, along with the information gleaned from a careful interrogation of the *Barracouta*'s captain would have told him in no uncertain terms that, as far as maritime law was concerned, they were at that moment pirates – a thought that would have terrified him, not only in a personal, but in a professional way. What Waddell could not have known was the depth of the enmity and hatred that the US government and public had for him and his crew, not to mention the *Shenandoah*.

As far as nineteenthth-century Washington, DC, was concerned, the issues that excited and aggravated the American body politic were no different then than they are today in the twenty-first century. The spectre of organised terrorism (in the form of piracy), covertly financed from abroad (Britain, France and others), supplied with foreign arms, including what could be termed weapons of mass destruction (British rifle manufacturers and British shipbuilders constructed raiders, ironclads and even torpedoes, all happily built to order), with tacit foreign governmental support (from the British) and with the goal of the dismemberment of the United States of America in order to clear the way for another power to gain global dominance (in the nineteenth century, of course, it was Britain's overriding ambition to remain the world's pre-eminent power), was just as dominant then as it is today. If one substitutes nineteenth-century Britain's actions and interests for those of China or sundry terrorist organisations in the twenty-first century, the basic schema of things remains the same. Fortunately for history, the right man at the right time once again appeared on stage.

The decisions that Waddell would make in the dying moments of that early August day of 1865 would have repercussions far beyond those felt by him and his crew. His careful course of action, a credit to his 20 years as a member of the United States Navy in voyages around the world, and his experiences as a commanding officer of the Confederate States Navy aboard the CSS *Shenandoah*, were about to shape future US and UK relations, the course of European history (and by default world history) and, beyond doubt, international law. His actions, which in the short term would engender him no goodwill, would, in the long term, turn opinions of him to the point where he was recognised as one of the greatest fighting sailors America ever produced. In fact, in 1964, a century after the beginning of the cruise of the CSS *Shenandoah*, the United States Navy built, commissioned and launched a guided missile destroyer named the USS *Waddell* in honour of his exceptional achievements as a sailor's sailor. It would be hard to imagine America honouring a modern-day 'enemy of the state' in such a manner; as will be seen, the long-term economic damage to America caused by Waddell and his fellow Confederate raiders was equal to, if not greater than, that inflicted by modern-day 'terrorists'.

All this was in the future though. As the *Shenandoah* sailed away, the crewmen of the *Barracouta* shouted and waved their best wishes to the disconsolate, and now stateless, crew of the former Confederate warship. For Waddell, the immediate concern on 2 August 1865 was rapidly to make his warship as inconspicuous as possible. Now Waddell's professionalism and adherence to the letter of maritime law took over and he made the following entry into the logbook, recorded by Lt. Dabney M. Scales, Watch Officer: 'Having received by the British bark *Barracouta* the sad intelligence of the overthrow of the Confederate Government, all attempts to destroy the shipping or property of the United States will cease from this date, in accordance with which the First Lieutenant William C. Whittle Jr., received an order from the Commander to strike below the battery and disarm the ship and crew.'

With this order, Waddell had rendered the *Shenandoah* defenceless against the searching forces of the US Navy, or any other nation's navy that chose to treat the ship and her crew as a pirate force. Waddell, however, could not afford to show any emotions at the moment, for as an experienced commander he knew that a ship's crew with low morale was the greatest challenge that a captain could face. His immediate act to disarm the ship was both a legal formality and an attempt to keep his crew employed at some work that would occupy both their time and their minds, while he considered his options.

What Waddell chose to do would not only astonish the British Empire and the wider world, but would also represent the pinnacle of all his years as a professional mariner. It would be the point at which his redemption from being classed by Americans as a pirate and 'enemy of the state', to achieving the status of honourable and heroic warrior, would begin. In the end, Waddell would become a true 'Sea King', much as the original name of the *Shenandoah* had suggested.

Who was James Iredell Waddell, and how did he acquire the

necessary skills to accomplish this epic undertaking? His story begins far away from the sea, in the rolling foothills of Appalachia in the state of North Carolina.

2

A *new and interesting world*

In the year 1824, the United States of America consisted of 24 states and was situated, for the most part, along the Atlantic Ocean. The 'West' still began at the Mississippi River. The year of 1824 was also the last year of a period in American history dubbed by historians as the 'Era of Good Feelings' (1815–1824). This term was coined due to the demise of the Federalist Party, which had campaigned vigorously for a strong, centralised government controlled from Washington, DC. With the Federalist cause losing out, the individual states developed of their own accord, creating specialised economies along the way, but conversely becoming interdependent upon one another. This helped to create a national economy, but also created conflicts between different sections of the country and in particular, between the North and the South.

One state in particular had a long-running political and legal feud with any form of centralised government emanating from Washington, DC, that state being North Carolina. The North Carolinian who had the earliest legal influence over the infant American republic was James Iredell. A staunch revolutionist, James Iredell was famous throughout the state as a jurist, a fact recognised by President George Washington when he nominated him to the US Supreme Court as one of its original justices. Iredell, uniquely for the time, held a strong anti-slavery position, and, contrary to other prominent North Carolinians, had urged that his state ratify the Constitution.

Iredell was a bit of a legal prodigy, even for the age. In 1767, aged 17, he had emigrated from Lewes, England, to North Carolina to take up a colonial office position arranged for him by his relatives as a comptroller for the Port of Edenton. Iredell, as was common for lawyers of the age, read, or was apprenticed, under Samuel Johnston, who later became governor of North Carolina. By 1771, at the age of 19, Iredell had begun practicing on his own and by 1779 was Attorney General for the State of North Carolina. When George Washington and the US Congress elevated him to Associate Justice on 12 February 1790, Iredell was the youngest member of the original Supreme Court, aged 38.

James Iredell's rapid rise to the summit of the new US legal system had gained him many friends, possibly due to his amiable personality, which made him seem less threatening. But his intellect was formidable and his closest friends both respected and admired his opinions. One of his best friends was Alfred Moore, who had also served as Attorney General for North Carolina. When James Iredell died while serving on the bench of the US Supreme Court in 1799, Alfred Moore replaced him as Associate Supreme Court Justice. Alfred Moore's son, Alfred Jr. (1782–1837), followed in his father's footsteps and became a lawyer as well.

Alfred Moore Jr.'s daughter, Elizabeth Davis Moore, married Francis Nash Waddell, a lawyer, on 30 April 1822, in St James

Church, Wilmington, North Carolina. This marriage cemented the relations between three families that had directly influenced the history of America in its pre-revolutionary and revolutionary period, the Nash, Moore and Waddell clans; Francis Nash Waddell could claim Colonel Hugh Waddell, who had served in the French and Indian War (1754–1763) as an ancestor on his paternal side, and on his maternal side, Francis Nash Waddell could claim Brigadier General Francis Nash, who served under George Washington at the Battle of Germantown, Pennsylvania (4 October 1777), where he died. Waddell's marriage to Elizabeth Davis Moore meant that two North Carolina families with significant military experience were now intertwined with the state's best-known family of legal minds. The Waddells were truly a nexus of North Carolina's political and legal culture, as well as military history.

On 13 July 1824, James Iredell Waddell was born to Francis and Elizabeth Waddell in Pittsboro, North Carolina. James Iredell was not their first child, but only the second that had survived. After the birth of James Iredell, four younger brothers would be born, along with two younger sisters. The riskiness of childbirth in this era is harshly reflected in this bald telling of Francis and Elizabeth Waddell's aspirations for a family, but it also shows the remarkable fortitude and hope that they had in persevering after the loss of their first two children. It may be that some of this indefinable quality of fortitude passed into James Iredell. It may also be that James Iredell's physical size at birth kept him from being taken into the next world before proceeding through this one. Later in life many remarked on his height and imposing physique.

Besides his parents, Francis and Elizabeth, one constant

through James Iredell's early life was his nurse, an African-American woman named Mammy Sue. Mammy Sue served as both midwife and family nurse for the Waddell family until 1857. It is likely that Mammy Sue was a slave, though the census data concerning her status is unclear.

James Iredell's father, Francis Nash Waddell, was embarked upon a legal career that coincided with a key period in American history, one which would only later be recognised as the beginning of the tectonic political shifts that would lead to the American Civil War. As previously mentioned, the year in which James Iredell was born, 1824, was the last year of the 'Era of Good Feelings'. The Federalist cause having declined to the point of non-existence, and the individual states going their own way, conflicts between different sections of the country were becoming more and more pronounced, particularly between the North and the South.

During James Waddell's youth, North Carolina had both tobacco and cotton plantations, and he would have known one hard and fast rule, that when a man invests his money, he expects to get returns, and North Carolinians, like the rest of the South, expected that their investment in slavery would continue to reap financial benefits, irrespective of what the rest of the nation, or other nations, thought. This economic system constructed on slavery was nothing less than a keg of gunpowder set atop a pile of kindling wood, ready to explode.

In 1819, only five years before James Iredell Waddell's birth, the Missouri territory applied for statehood as a slave state. A Democratic representative from the state of New York, James Tallmadge, pushed for an amendment to Missouri's statehood bill that would make slavery illegal in the new state. For the first time in American history, the issue of slavery exploded into the national consciousness. Vitriolic debate ensued, but a compromise was created whereby the Maine territory would enter the United States as a 'free' state and Missouri would enter the Union a 'slave' state. Slavery would be declared illegal in any new states created in the Louisiana Purchase territories north of 36° 30'. Forty years before the outbreak of the American Civil War, the first crack in the Union had developed.

These then were the issues that men such as Francis Nash Waddell, his fellow jurists, and well-connected families of North Carolina would have discussed and debated in both a polite and, at times, heated manner. But, for young James, these were matters of little concern to a little boy, who, by his own account, was often up to 'deviltry'.

Pittsboro, North Carolina, where Waddell spent his earliest years, lay virtually halfway across the state's lengthwise mass. The town, described by him in his memoirs as being a 'hamlet', lay upon the rolling hills of Chatham County that stretched away into the west until they built up into the Appalachian Mountains, which were essentially the geographic boundary of the United States. At some point during Waddell's youngest years, his father Francis and mother Elizabeth moved to Louisiana, where Francis took over as manager of the St Maurice Plantation, a good example of the Waddells' ability to position themselves optimally for the time, for the plantation sat astride the 'El Camino Real', or Old San Antonio Road, that ran from San Antonio, Texas, to Natchitoches, Louisiana, with other spurs of the road leading further eastward. Among a few of the more famous Americans who stayed at St Maurice Plantation were General Sam Houston, co-founder of the Republic of

Texas, and a young Lt. Ulysses Samuel Grant, who would become the Union's greatest military hero in the American Civil War as General 'US' Grant.

Waddell missed out on meeting any of the famous personages who visited St Maurice Plantation, for his parents had decided that it was best that he stay in North Carolina and be educated there. Why this decision was made is not known, but his paternal grandmother Sarah took him on and arranged for him to be enrolled in a private school. Sarah's grandson would later humorously note that he was 'taught the rudiments of education' while still maintaining a reputation for 'deviltry', as any 'committed in and about the hamlet was laid at my door'. Pittsboro would have been a typical, idyllic settlement in early America for a little boy with a rambunctious streak, with plenty of hills, streams and fields to explore – as well as farmers and merchants to tease. This early character trait would come to the surface again in Waddell as an adult, but would express itself in a much more serious manner.

In 1837, Waddell's grandmother Sarah became seriously ill and was no longer able to care for him. By now, he would have been 13 years of age, and if he had retained his impish traits he would have been a handful even for a grandmother in good health. But if stern measures had not already been taken at school and at home, they were going to be applied now, for James' maternal grandfather, Alfred Moore, was about to take over. Family lore has it that Alfred Moore was the one who had the young Waddell named for the illustrious US Supreme Court justice, James Iredell, but he must have questioned that decision when faced with the behaviour of the 'young' James Iredell Waddell.

Since Alfred Moore's home was in Orange County, North Carolina, James had to leave Pittsboro behind. He may have been wistful about leaving the place of his birth and childhood ramblings, but it is also likely that more than a few neighbours of Grandmother Sarah slept more peacefully at night with the boy's departure. Grandfather Alfred would ensure that James' penchant for naughty behaviour did not follow on in Orange County and nipped any hopes in the youngster's mind that he would be able to tear away over hill and stream by enrolling him in Bingham's School. The reputation of the school was such that it must have struck fear in the heart of any recalcitrant youngster, and smug confidence in the hearts of the parents who sent their children there. Bingham's School was located in Hillsborough, North Carolina, and was a noted classical school based on the educational principles espoused by the Scottish Age of Enlightenment. By the time Waddell had entered the US Naval School, later to be known as the US Naval Academy, his former alma mater of Bingham's was regarded as the finest preparatory school in the United States, charging over $150 a year in tuition, or about $2,500 in today's money. Bingham's was a serious investment and it shows how serious the Waddell and Moore families were about education.

While Waddell was having his rapscallion ways curbed by Grandfather Alfred – under the steely gaze of W.J. Bingham – the wild and exuberant young Republic of America was itself experiencing growing pains, with the wiser politicians trying to instil some sense of national discipline and direction. The political manifestos of the entire period from Waddell's birth until the beginning of the Civil War proclaimed that it was an 'age for the common man', though that should be qualified for the times, for it meant that women, freed slaves, slaves and Indians were generally excluded from this great 'commonality'. Moreover, while the politicos may have proclaimed an era of infinite possibilities for everyone as the young republic expanded, in reality, the economic disparity between the industrialising North and the agrarian West and South expanded greatly between 1828 and 1860. One fact brings the economic inequality into sharp relief: by 1860 the upper 10 per cent of the American population owned 70 per cent of the nation's wealth.

While internal relations between the states of America became increasingly strained, those between America and its mother country, Britain, had been slowly improving as small grievances and arguments that remained from the blood-soaked family row of the War of Independence were resolved. The first substantial step forward was the Webster-Ashburton Treaty of 1842, which smoothed differences that had been simmering since the Treaty of Paris in 1783, which gave America its independence. The conclusion of this treaty opened a new age for Anglo-American relations and made the forthcoming discussions about the 'Far West' (i.e. the Pacific Northwest) far easier.

By the time the Webster-Ashburton Treaty had been concluded in 1842, young Waddell had begun the career that would effectively dominate his entire life. The lingering effects of the depression of 1819 and the dramatic changes in the economic landscape of North Carolina meant that the conclusion of his education at Bingham's School saw him launching into an uncertain world. Connections and education were necessary for any young man growing up in the newly emerging business world of America, unless one fell back into the traditional careers of the adventure-seeking, the military or the church.

Once again, Grandfather Alfred had a weather-eye on the situation, and recognised that while his grandson may have received an education, he needed a career with discipline, combined with adventure. It would be the military for Waddell, specifically, the United States Navy.

The series of influential connections and friends that the Nash, Moore and Waddell families had cultivated over the years now came up trumps for young James. Alfred Moore knew the Secretary of the Navy, George E. Badger, who himself hailed from New Bern, North Carolina, and on 10 September 1841 Waddell became Acting Midshipman Waddell USN.

Waddell was ordered to report to the USS *Pennsylvania* at Norfolk, Virginia, doing so on 15 December 1841. When Waddell first crossed her deck, he could not have known that he was walking across a vessel that had been dreamed of by the Father of the US Navy, John Paul Jones, as one of America's most powerful naval deterrents, and was now languishing as a mere training ship. If he had known how low an ebb the US Navy had reached in 1842, one wonders if he would have entered the service, but his boyish enthusiasm for what the future might hold shines through in comments from his memoirs when he describes his first moments aboard the *Pennsylvania*, noting that he had entered 'a new and interesting world'.

Thrust directly into the duties of standing watch and other menial tasks, which in the naval world meant a working day that went around the clock in shifts, Waddell commented in his memoirs that he was reminded of his duty to the ship early on. Finding himself tired of pacing a prescribed route about the ship's deck while on watch, a superior officer called down to him, sharply emphasising 'Mister', and carefully enunciating

'Wad-dell', before reminding him that he was on watch and to keep a sharp eye out. Suitably admonished, it was a lesson learned early that remained with him throughout his naval life – and one memorable enough to be subsequently recounted in his memoirs.

Waddell made his way through this strange new world of naval customs and work schedules until May 1842 when he was insulted by another midshipman, Archibald Waring. Anecdotes relate that Waring was older than Waddell, but was his junior in rank, by date of commissioning. Waring obtained his commission on 19 October 1841, while Waddell's commission was given to him on 10 September 1841. In an age when the rules of courtesy and gentlemanliness still counted for everything, and particularly for a Southerner such as Waddell, Waring may have spoken 'down' to Waddell, forgetting that in the US Navy rank and due respect to more senior officers was the driving force. Another possibility is that a young lady was involved, as one historian has speculated. For whatever reason, both midshipmen lived in an age when, at least in America, duelling was still considered to be an acceptable way to deal with arguments and perceived insults to a gentleman's honour. On 27 May 1842, the two young midshipmen carried out their duel. It is not recorded what injuries were sustained by Midshipman Waring, but Waddell suffered a wound to his hip that was so serious that he was on sick leave for the next 11 months. He was in the Gosport Naval Hospital at Norfolk until 21 September 1842, when he received permission to leave the hospital to visit family and friends. From then until 18 March 1843, he was apparently at his family's home in North Carolina, as on this date he posted a letter to the Navy Department stating that he 'was restored and ready for duty'. He must have thought that his naval career was ended before it began, as he waited anxiously for the reply from both the navy surgeons and the Navy Department. The legacy of the duel was a pronounced limp for the rest of his life, but it didn't stop him from serving in many ships and on many oceans.

In early 1846, more vessels of the US Navy began to patrol off the coast of Mexico, particularly in the Gulf of Mexico, including the USS *Somers*, on which Waddell was serving. Meanwhile, President Polk also ordered General Zachary Taylor to move US Army units to the Rio Grande River to protect Texas from the expected invasion by the Mexican army. On 24 April 1846, 2,000 Mexican cavalrymen attacked a US Army detachment of 63 men north of the Rio Grande River, killing 11 American soldiers. Events escalated and on 11 May 1846, a joint session of the US Congress declared war on Mexico. Waddell found himself involved in his first war. California was to be taken as well, in order to deny any aspirations that Britain might have there.

The war progressed in fits and starts, with successes by the Americans on the one hand counterbalanced by disasters on the other hand. On the Pacific coast of California, Admiral Stoat sailed into Monterey harbour on 7 July and 'took possession of California' with no opposition. On the eastern side of Mexico, Waddell and the USS *Somers* participated in an ongoing blockade of the Mexican ports, the *Somers* leaving station only to return to naval station Pensacola, Florida, for supplies when necessary. Waddell would observe the weapons, men and supplies moving off to war, but apparently he saw no combat.

A few short weeks after the Battle of Monterey, on 6 October

1846, Waddell received orders posting him to the new US Naval School at Annapolis, Maryland. He immediately crossed over to the first ship headed to the eastern United States, the supply ship USS *Relief*. It may have been a normal supply run for the crew of the *Relief* as it made its way to Pensacola, Florida, but for Waddell it was another chance to gain valuable information and experience from sailors who had been around Cape Horn and into the Pacific Ocean, an area he had no knowledge of as yet.

Arriving at Pensacola, Waddell would have found a naval station bustling with activity as it tried to support the war farther west, and to a lesser degree, a regional port that served as a base for fishermen, the timber trade and other cargo carriers. Railroads were still in the future for Pensacola, so its Spanish name, translated into English as 'trail's end', meant that it was still a largely land-locked, sleepy backwater. Waddell arrived at Pensacola in October, and headed north across country to Annapolis, reaching there on 28 November 1846. He reported to the US Naval School on 2 December.

January 1847 was the harbinger of a tumultuous year for America. Mexican forces in California surrendered on 13 January and barely a month later, on 22–23 February, the Battle of Buena Vista was barely won by US forces, largely due to heroics of the future President of the Confederate States of America, Jefferson Davis. Only a few weeks later on 9 March, the US Navy and Marine Corps conducted the first true amphibious operation in the history of the naval service with its landing at Vera Cruz. By early April, the Battle of Cerro Gordo, with the famed General Santa Anna of the early Mexican–Texan War of Independence commanding Mexican forces again, was under way on the mountain passes to Mexico City. Again, a future personality of the American Civil War influenced the outcome of the battle, as Captain Robert Edward Lee flanked Santa Anna's blocking forces via a hidden track. After bloody fighting, Santa Anna's forces retreated, leaving the field to the advancing American army. Attempts at negotiating an end to the war were made by the US but collapsed; the war slogged on.

As these events dominated the headlines of America's newspapers, Waddell was being rushed off his feet into the educational and social world of the US Naval School. After six years of various services in the fleet, a return to a strict educational environment may have been a shock to his system, but his previous rigorous training and discipline at Bingham's School would have come to his rescue. Though he may have hated his time there, James may have secretly thought that the teachers of the Naval School seemed easy-going by comparison.

Antebellum Annapolis was a world that Waddell had never experienced, one awash with commercial growth that supported an expanding merchant class who were inclined to spend their wealth on an ever-increasing variety of social functions. The proximity of Annapolis to Washington, DC, brought the main influence, as far as society and politics were concerned, but the new Naval School further enhanced the city's stature and provided another subtle form of patronage. Since midshipmen were appointed by US senators, it was assumed by astute businessmen and politicians that cultivating personal relationships could be good for future military contracts or information on naval affairs. The fact that there was now a never-ending supply of young, ambitious and presumably well-educated men on their doorstep must have seemed a gift from heaven for ambitious fathers who had daughters in need of husbands; the fact that these men might have influence in the future if their careers progressed was just the icing on the cake.

If the scene outside the gates of the Naval School seemed to be one of constant social whirl – and maybe inside as well, since the naval ball had occurred just as Waddell arrived to take his place – the daily schedule inside the grounds of the young training academy must have seemed mind-numbing to the midshipman. For 'middies' such as Waddell, whose internal clocks were set to the schedule and custom of a ship at sea, there must have been a disdain for knowledge that wasn't of practical naval use. But the inclusion of mandatory subjects such as chemistry, English, French, gunnery and steam, mathematics and navigation, as well as natural philosophy, was highly pragmatic. James would discover that he had a penchant for mathematics and navigation that would prove useful in the near term for his career, and life-saving in the future. But first, he had to master the subjects that Bingham's School had not prepared him for, such as gunnery and steam, which today's midshipmen would recognise as the sciences of ballistics and physics.

Although James had not seen combat in the Mexican–American War, which was now coming to an end (2 February 1848), he had been close enough to the smell of gunpowder to have a whiff of it about him, and this, coupled with a strong physical presence and a handsome face, made him an irresistible source of attraction to the young ladies of Annapolis. While a painting held by the North Carolina State Museum shows Waddell in the prime of life, and a truly handsome man by any standards, he may have regarded himself as less attractive to the young ladies about him due to his physical infirmity – the permanent limp gained in his duel with Archibald Waring. But in an age when 'dangerous' men were romanticised in literature (Sir Walter Scott's novels had been extraordinarily successful in America), James would been assured by the young ladies who fluttered about him that he was evidently a man of 'honour and purpose', and not to be trifled with.

Sometime in 1848, Waddell met Anne Sellman Iglehart, the daughter of James Iglehart, a member of Annapolis' successful merchant class. There are no records of the circumstances of their first meeting in either Waddell's memoirs, or Anne's letters, but James was totally smitten by the petite Anne, whose photograph shows a handsome woman with dark hair, for he pursued her without rest or care. Later comments by friends in letters mention that they were considered to be one of, if not the most handsome couple in Annapolis. Interestingly, James may have been a bit of a musician, for the Museum of Orange County, North Carolina, has his guitar, which has a maker's certificate inside indicating it was made in Havana, Cuba in 1841. In the highly romantic Antebellum period, it is not hard to imagine the tall, handsome and 'dangerous' James Waddell serenading Anne Iglehart in the sitting room of her father's house.

James, knowing the life of a professional naval officer, must have been driven by two thoughts during his courtship of Anne. First, and obviously, he was deeply in love with her, and second, that his time at the Naval School might end with a posting to the far side of the world. Anne, seeing beyond James' slight physical impediment, had the emotional make-up that James knew was desirable in a relationship that might be stretched not only over time, but distance. At this moment in their lives when the heady mix of love, youth and parties seemed to indicate nothing but a lifetime of happiness, they could not have imagined that at the end of their lives, they would become the living embodiment of the 'Odyssey'.

On 16 November 1848, James Iredell Waddell and Anne Sellman Iglehart were married in Annapolis, Maryland, and established a home there. Waddell's progress at the Naval School kept pace with the success of his personal life, as just before his marriage, on 12 October 1848, he was posted (while still an 'unpassed' midshipman) to the US Naval Observatory, then known as the National Observatory. Waddell's mathematical and navigational skills were already known to be exceptional and while on temporary duty there he was tasked with studying winds and currents. If the paltry records are to be believed, after completing his duty at the Naval Observatory he returned to the Naval School where he became a navigation instructor. If this is true, then Waddell was an extraordinary talent. For a normally conservative naval bureaucracy to award such an important training position to an 'unpassed' midshipman (though of course by now he had almost eight years of naval service) was unheard of at the time.

Apparently James Waddell held his position as a navigation instructor throughout the greater portion of 1849, for he was graduated as a passed midshipman on 29 September 1849. For some reason, his date of rank was then back-dated to 10 August 1847. Why this date was chosen is a mystery, as he had arrived at the Naval School in January 1847 (and received his 'warrant' still earlier in 1843). But its importance to Waddell is that it would be used to determine his selection over his fellow officers of equal rank in the years to come, for among equals in the military, the officer with the earliest 'date of rank' is the senior officer, and considered to be the one with the most experience.

Under military protocol, that officer would normally be the one chosen for more challenging positions of duty, barring the obvious politics that would sometimes intervene. In Waddell's case, though he would never reach a high rank (by the standards of today's navy), his early date of rank and long experience would, in the future, mean that he was in the right place at the right time to assume command and assiduously carry out his orders to their fullest extent. His instructors at the Naval School could never have imagined, in 1849, that one of their star pupils would in the future use the skills honed at their institution against their own nation's ships. But that would be said about many of Waddell's fellow Southern naval officers.

The short and happy interlude that James and Anne Waddell had experienced in Annapolis was now to be ended by Waddell's first set of 'blue-water' orders since 1845. On 30 May 1849, he was sent to the USS *Independence*, a ship that was part of the Mediterranean Squadron. This fleet was an active reminder of the US Navy's wars against the 'Barbary pirates' after the War of 1812. It is interesting to note that Waddell stayed for only a short while before receiving a set of orders posting him back to the now renamed Naval School – the United States Naval Academy, on 5 September 1851.

Waddell was now a full-fledged instructor at the academy, responsible for training incoming midshipmen aboard the USS *Preble*, a practice ship. He would remain in this position until late 1853, when he received orders to the USS *Germantown* on 27 October 1853. Waddell had an ironic meeting with his own family's history with this posting, as his grandfather General Francis Nash had been killed at the Battle of Germantown during the American War of Independence. For Anne Waddell though, it was the part of life that a naval officer's wife dreaded most, a long period of separation and the uncertainty about her husband's safety. But America was not at war, nor was there an indication of a foreign threat, so at least on that count Anne did not have to worry. However, as the *Germantown* was being recommissioned for her new duties, the seismic political forces that were moving beneath the American republic were gathering strength, creating subtle new stress fractures that were weakening the Union.

Only 11 days before the Treaty of Hidalgo (2 February 1848) had been signed, ending the bloody and costly war between Mexico and America, gold was discovered in California. While the US government paid Mexico some $15 million for the disputed Rio Grande area, California and New Mexico – and assumed all the debts that the Mexican government owed to US citizens – the discovery of gold in California would make this expenditure look like one of the great investments of all time. In the ten years after the discovery, over half a billion dollars in gold was extracted, or nearly 37 times the cost to the US taxpayer. While this catapulted the US government into solvency *extraordinaire*, it also presented a problem to Congress. How would these areas be brought into the Union, as slave territories or free territories? One representative had already tried to attach a rider to a congressional bill that funded the Mexican–American War, which would make it unlawful to hold slaves in any land captured from Mexico. The attempt was thwarted when the bill went to the US Senate, as half the senators were from the South. The last newspapers that James Waddell would read while at the New York Naval Yard, before setting sail on the uss *Germantown,* would have been filled with political commentary concerning the anti-slavery movement and counter-actions by Southern spokesmen and politicians.

The *Germantown* would prove to be a lucky ship for James Waddell, once he joined her in October of 1853, for he had been selected to be the vessel's navigator. For the next two years the *Germantown*, along with the USS *Dale* and *John Adams*, as well as the brigs *Perry* and *Porpoise*, would cruise the South Atlantic to St Helena, and east along the African coast from Cape Mesurado to Loando in Portuguese West Africa. The *Germantown* was relieved by 'Old Ironsides', the USS *Constitution*, while on station, and she sailed for America from Porto Praya on 4 March 1853. Her destination was now the Boston Naval Yard and as she made her way home across the Atlantic, her crew collected wind and current information for Lt. Matthew Maury's global wind and current survey. The *Germantown* was recommissioned to service on 23 November 1853, with Commander W.F. Lynch as her captain. Her new assignment was to join Commodore W.D. Salter's Brazil Squadron operating off the coast of South America.

As 1854 flowed into 1855, Waddell and the *Germantown* found themselves off Montevideo, Uruguay, where political disturbances and civil disorder surrounding a revolution threatened the lives and property of not only American citizens, but other foreign nationals. Unfortunately, in the middle of 1855, as at many other periods in Waddell's life, his circumstances become unclear. According to his memoirs, he served three and a half years aboard the *Germantown*, and returned to the United States aboard her. If so, then his time on board would have ended in the middle of 1855 and it is known that he was promoted to 2nd Lieutenant on 10 September of that year. On 23 October he was also warranted to be Master of the Ship, a considerable achievement. US Naval historical records indicate that the *Germantown* did not return to the United States until 9 February 1857, and if this is true, Waddell's memory may have suffered a lapse while writing his memoirs. Still, the South American cruise with the *Germantown* had given him new responsibilities as an active navigator, and exposed him to the use of naval vessels in foreign diplomacy, and critically for the future, to the location and characteristics of key anchorages across the South Atlantic. The knowledge gained on this voyage would have incalculable value in the future.

The *Germantown,* as noted above, made landfall off Hampton Roads, Virginia, on 9 February 1857, taking almost exactly a month to transit from Bahia, Brazil. The *Germantown* was decommissioned three days later, for repairs and refitting. Waddell walked down the gangway on 14 February 1853, with three months of leave in his uniform pocket.

Picking back up on Waddell's notes, which seem to come back into line with the known ship movement reports, he says that he was given three months' leave, before receiving orders to the USS *Release*, a supply ship destined for Panama. Naval records show that on 6 May 1857 he received orders to the *Release,* which was about to set sail with supplies for the Pacific Fleet.

On paper, the voyage of the *Release* should have been a straightforward affair. Tasked with transporting supplies to the US Navy depot at Aspinwall (Colón), Panama, the *Release* was making a standard run that would give Waddell plenty of time in port to explore the area around Aspinwall. The outward voyage went well apparently, as Waddell made no mention of any unusual event in his memoirs.

Arriving in Aspinwall, the *Release* went about her standard routine of transferring cargo and other stores ashore. While the quartermasters and supply clerks compared lists and checked the off-loaded supplies, Waddell made his way ashore to tour Panama. Somehow he made the acquaintance of the project's chief engineer, a man named Fulton, who had been involved in the great construction project of the time, the Panama Isthmus railroad.

When news of the discovery of gold in California reached New York, the ticket offices of the Pacific Mail Steamship Company were the scenes of riots as gold-seekers fought to obtain passage aboard its next vessel to Panama, hoping to then catch a vessel north to California. When the businessman William Aspinwall and his investors realised that if they could drive a railroad through the mosquito-infested jungles and reduce transit time to the Pacific anchorage – and of course charge a hefty fee – they would literally have a 'golden pipeline' that would pour endless funds into their pockets. But it would be a dangerous project. When Ulysses S. Grant crossed the Isthmus in 1852 with several hundred soldiers on their way to California, 250 men died and until his death he remarked that it was more horrible than anything he witnessed in the Civil War.

What Waddell saw in 1857 was the result of possibly 10,000 deaths and heroic engineering efforts that built bridges over mile after mile of malarial swamp. Fulton related that they had recruited men from the Caribbean islands in the hope that their African heritage would make them more suitable to the work – they died in the same numbers as the Irish, the Chinese, the Polish, and every other nationality unfortunate enough to turn its hand on the project. Waddell came away suitably impressed, and possibly somewhat humbled by what he saw and heard. While he didn't know it at the time, the epic feats performed in crossing the Isthmus by rail paved the way for the future Panama Canal, as without the rail line it would have been near impossible to build it.

Unfortunately for Waddell, he came away from Panama with a personal experience of the price paid by the builders of the Isthmus railroad. Just before departing Aspinwall, he came down with yellow fever. Even today the disease commonly known as 'yellow jack' kills tens of thousands of people every year around the world. In 1857 it was the bane of ships operating in tropical and semi-tropical climates.

Waddell would have suffered the classic symptoms of the disease which include fever, chills, headache, backache, nausea, and vomiting. Jaundice can also occur, and in its most serious state, the disease can affect the blood, liver, and kidneys. In the 1850s, the only positive aspect to the disease was that if one caught it, and survived its onslaught, one would not catch it again.

Two days after Waddell was confined to his bed aboard the *Release*, she weighed anchor to return home. Whether the ship's commander, Captain Brasher, decided to get under way because he feared that a yellow fever epidemic was breaking out, or he was ordered off by the Customs and Health Officer at Aspinwall, is not known, but over the next few days the *Release* would become a 'hell ship'.

As Waddell's bone-shaking fever began to subside and his condition improve, his fellow shipmates succumbed one after another, until only one seaman and the ship's boy were healthy. Waddell, realising that the vessel had to have an able pilot, got out of his sickbed to assume temporary command of the *Release*. Deciding that the ship needed to reach a harbour where they could get both medical help and supplies, James directed the vessel towards Matanzas, Cuba.

Arriving off Matanzas harbour, the local pilot came out to board the *Release* and bring her into port. Discovering that the *Release* was full of sailors ill with yellow jack, the pilot refused to take her into port and abandoned the vessel to its fate. Waddell displayed his iron will and navigational skills by bringing the *Release* into Matanzas harbour on his own, a considerable feat with an entire crew on hand, an extraordinary feat with a three-man crew!

The *Release* remained in Matanzas harbour for five days to allow more men to recover before attempting to weigh anchor and set sail for home port. The original orders for the *Release* were for her to return to Boston Naval Yard. However, after a few days at sea, the condition of the men who had returned to duty was found not to be as good as had been hoped – the ship's captain and most of the ship's officers had still not recovered. Still, the vessel had made such quick time heading northwards that Captain Brasher issued a letter to the rest of the ship's officers from his sickbed asking for their opinion as to whether they should sail the vessel into New York, rather than Boston, and whether the circumstances warranted such a deviation from his orders.

For the second time during his voyage aboard the *Release*, James Waddell exhibited his fierce determination to follow naval regulations. He must have made an impassioned argument in his reply to Brasher's letter requesting the officer's opinions on their course of action, as the rest of the officers recommended turning into the New York Naval Yard and Waddell, alone, recommended returning to Boston Naval Yard. Brasher, swayed by Waddell's arguments, which were probably based on his quoting naval legal precedent regarding the carrying out of lawful orders, directed the vessel be taken to Boston.

Upon reaching Boston, the crew of the *Release* was detached and she was laid up for future refit, but before Lt. Waddell was detached on 14 August 1857, a grateful Captain Brasher, realising that Waddell's wise counsel may have aided his naval career, wrote a special commendation for Waddell. This may be the document that gave James his next career boost, for his next orders were to report to the receiving ship for new naval trainees at Annapolis as its executive officer.

Commanded by Robert F. Pinkney (who would also serve in the Confederate Navy as a commander, and as captain of the CSS *Savannah*, a crude ironclad), the Annapolis receiving ship (the USS *Allegheny* at the time) was a taste of shipboard life to new naval trainees, midshipmen and young officers. For Waddell, it was a chance to return to the vibrant social life of Annapolis and the academy, and even more importantly, to resume some form of home life again with Anne. As 1857 turned into 1858, Waddell received yet another posting that would seem to be a return to an earlier point in his career, as an instructor at the Naval Academy on 9 January 1858.

James Waddell's position at the Naval Academy in 1858 was not only a step upwards in his career, but as before, it gave him a teaching position that would give him the responsibility for shaping the minds of the future leaders of the US Navy. The tremendous respect and admiration that he inspired at the end of his life in many US Navy personnel, even after his notoriety as a commander of a Confederate commerce-raider, was born out of the natural affections that all pupils have for their favourite teachers.

His initial duties were as Assistant Instructor of Seamanship, Naval Tactics and Practical Gunnery, and it appears that he became an Assistant Professor of Navigation as well. Before 1858 was over, Waddell found himself promoted to full lieutenant, the highest rank he ever achieved in the US Navy, and by the time 1859 had rolled in he found himself detailed to be the Assistant to the Commandant of the Midshipmen under Commander Thomas T. Craven.

And while his professional life flourished, so too did his personal life. On 9 February 1859 a baby girl, named Anne Harwood Waddell, was born to James and Anne. These would be the days the Waddells remembered as the happiest of their lives. Companions and friends described James as having 'a noble bearing and an intelligent manner about him', both 'gracious and courtly' and 'always thought to be kind', while Anne was noted as being a 'lovely and affectionate woman'. (Waddell, in turn, said his fellow officers were, '. . . as companionable gentlemen as the sunlight ever shone upon'.)

James and Anne were only able to enjoy their time together with their new daughter, Annie, until 11 July 1859, when James received orders to report to a vessel under construction in San Francisco, the USS *Saginaw*. Although Waddell followed his orders without hesitation in reporting to the *Saginaw*, he was furious at what confronted him – an unfinished vessel unsuited for any form of sailing in the near future. For the first time in his naval career he had a family, and he was obviously keen to be a doting father while he had the opportunity. He complained bitterly to Anne of the enforced separation when they could have all been together. He reckoned it would be six more months before the *Saginaw* would be ready for her cruise and duty station with the Pacific Fleet.

Waddell was not far off his prediction, as the *Saginaw* was finally ready in early spring of 1860, and with Commander J.F. Schenck in command, departed Mare Island, California for the western Pacific. Reaching Shanghai, China, on 12 May 1860, she took up her duty station with the US East India Squadron, whose duties were largely to cruise along the Chinese coast and protect American citizens and their commerce ashore while hunting for pirates. While this duty was certainly mundane, the journey across the Pacific and the exposure to the unique maritime culture of Asia were experiences that would not be lost on Waddell. The military experiences were not lessons forgotten by Waddell either, as when the *Saginaw* entered the Gulf of Bahai he witnessed a combined operation by French and English forces on Chinese fortifications, which was part of a greater European stratagem to destabilise the country and bring it under European control.

A trip in November 1860 to Japan was surely a highlight for Waddell. Although open to foreign trade for almost a decade now, Japan was still largely unknown and the mystique surrounding its land and people had yet to fade away in Western imaginations. The *Saginaw* apparently made for Hong Kong after her visit to Japan, as Waddell reports in his memoirs that upon reaching there he found orders waiting on him that instructed him to transfer back to New York aboard the USS *John Adams* on 15 December 1860.

The last three years had been eventful for Waddell. He had led a disease-plagued vessel safely into port and had been meritoriously commended, promoted to full lieutenant, and served as the Assistant Commandant of the US Naval Academy – and enjoyed the personal joy of having a daughter born to him. For the American republic, however, the years from 1857–1860 were the years that sealed the country's fate.

On 6 March 1857, a decision by the US Supreme Court stated that popular sovereignty, as a means whereby states or territories could decide for or against slavery, was not legal. Any future political or legal compromise would now be impossible. The Supreme Court then went on to say that Congress could not deny the entry of slaves to any state in the Union, since this would deprive citizens of their rights to transfer, or transport, their property wherever they chose within the United States. The Abolitionists exploded with rage, while Southerners celebrated, believing they could carry on the slave trade everywhere in the United States. The Northern states essentially ignored the Supreme Court after this decision.

After the famous abolitionist John Brown was hanged, the American republic began to tear itself apart and die. As the body of John Brown lay 'a-mouldering in the ground', the presidential election campaign of 1860 began. All through the spring, summer and fall, fractious political speeches, rallies and conventions were held. In the end, after the presidential election was held in November, the winner was Abraham Lincoln of the new Republican Party, winning with just 39 per cent of the popular vote, but 180 electoral college votes. America's culture, economics, and now its political structure, were separated into two distinct and adversarial groups. Meanwhile, in 1861, Waddell sailed away from Japan aboard the *John Adams*, not knowing the Union was beginning its disintegration.

In America, with the election of Abraham Lincoln on 6 November 1860, the fuse to the political charge that would blow the republic apart was lit on 20 December, when the state of South Carolina seceded from the Union. By the end of February 1861, the states of Mississippi, Florida, Alabama, Georgia, Louisiana and Texas had followed suit. The Confederate States of America came into being on 9 February with Jefferson Davis, graduate of the US Army's West Point Academy and hero of the Mexican–American War, as President. On 4 March, Abraham Lincoln was sworn in as President of the United States of America, or at least President of those states still choosing to be united. On 12 April, Gen. Beauregard of the South Carolina militia followed his orders and directed his artillery batteries to open fire on Fort Sumter. The bloodiest war in American history had begun.

President Lincoln reacted quickly, issuing a proclamation on 15 April that called for 75,000 militiamen to be inducted in the Federal Army, and for a special session of the joint Congress to be held on 4 July. Meanwhile, on 17 April, Virginia seceded from the Union, to be followed over the next few months by Arkansas, Tennessee and finally, North Carolina. By May the Confederate States of America had gained all its members. It had a population of 9 million in 11 states, while the Union would have 21 states and over 20 million in population.

On 19 April 1861 Lincoln issued his Proclamation of Blockade against the Southern ports. This issue backfired on the Union almost immediately, due to a lack of foresight by both the State Department and the US Navy in failing to sign the Treaty of Paris in 1856. The treaty stated in clear and simple terms that:

1. Privateering is, and remains, abolished;

2. The neutral flag covers enemy's goods, with the exception of contraband of war;

3. Neutral goods, with the exception of contraband of war, are not liable to capture under enemy's flag;

4. Blockades, in order to be binding, must be effective, that is to say, maintained by a force sufficient really to prevent access to the coast of the enemy.

The United States had failed to sign the treaty, whose signatories were, among others, Britain, France, and the German Confederation, as well as non-European powers such as Argentina, Brazil and Uruguay, because President Buchanan knew that the US Navy was too weak (due to tight-fisted congressional funding) and that the United States had raised its naval forces in the past by issuing letters of marque, creating privateers. Buchanan didn't want to lose the capacity for the rapid expansion of the navy because of international law.

Unfortunately, President Lincoln, in trying to re-attach the wayward states of the South to the Union, didn't just raise the issue, but pitched it headlong into the international arena with the declaration of blockade. This threatened Britain, the world's supreme empire, both militarily and economically, since loss of access to the Southern cotton fields meant the potential collapse of its textile trade. At the moment that Lincoln issued the blockade proclamation, British newspapers scoffed, as they were convinced that the US Navy was incapable of sealing 3,000 miles of southern coastline.

While the international community – and its navies – digested this news, events continued to unfold in America. On 20 April 1861, Colonel Robert E. Lee resigned from the US Army, eloquently stating his reasons in a manner that would be echoed by thousands of other Southern military officers by saying, 'I cannot raise my hand against my birthplace, my home, my children'. Lee went to Richmond, Virginia, where he was offered command of Virginia's military forces, including all her naval assets.

A false calm prevailed on both sides of the Mason-Dixon line. Lincoln's speech before the joint session of Congress on 4 July 1861 thundered like the sermon of a Biblical prophet from the rostrum of the speaker's platform. Lincoln elevated the war to a quixotic level, saying that it was '. . . a People's contest. . . a struggle for maintaining in the world, that form, and substance of government, whose leading object is, to elevate the condition of men. . .' Congress roared its approval and voted to raise a massive army of 500,000 men. The Southern leadership was stunned and realised it would have to move quickly before the North's population and industrial might could be brought to bear against it.

On 21 July 1861, Union forces under General Irvin McDowell clashed with Confederate forces under the command of Generals Joseph P. Johnston and P.G.T. Beauregard at Manassas Junction, Virginia. After some initial success by Union soldiers, the Confederate line, solidified by General Thomas 'Stonewall'

Jackson's brigade and his morale-raising refusal to withdraw, surged forward, causing the inexperienced Federal 'blues' to fall back, then break and run. Some fled all the way into Washington DC. Lincoln sadly observed that 'it's damn bad'.

The *John Adams* had swung her bow westwards towards the Indian Ocean and home on 6 July 1861, carrying a box with two royal letters from the king of Siam to President Lincoln, a pair of elephant tusks, and a ceremonial sword. We have no record of what Waddell thought of his time in the East Indies or the Andaman Sea, but it is hard to imagine that he would not have been fascinated by all that he saw. But in the back of his mind must have been thoughts of his wife Anne, and his little girl Annie, who was by now nearly two and a half years old – she was learning to walk and talk, having never really known her father.

In November of 1861, having rounded the Cape of Good Hope, the USS *John Adams* made for St Helena Island in the South Atlantic, stopping for fresh water, fresh food and fresh news. The news would be deeply unsettling for those officers and ratings from the South. Waddell could not have imagined the Ulysses-like course his life would now take. He would earn a naval fame that many an admiral would admire in the future, but not in the navy he had loved, nor under the flag he had served – and it would come at a terrible personal price.

3

War is a trade

In 1861, Glasgow was near the apogee of its power as the great industrial heart of the British Empire. The city was arguably the nexus of advanced industrial technology for the entire world at that time, with shipbuilding, railway-related engineering, heavy industrial engineering such as cranes, foundry fittings, bridge-building equipment and more, issuing forth from its port area in a virtually inexhaustible stream. This industrial strength was further underpinned by financial power, most of which emanated from the city of Glasgow bank and the numerous finance houses involved in foreign trade.

With their near global reach, Glasgow's industrial and financial institutions could hardly be expected to escape the effects of the American Civil War, nor in return, could they fail to affect the war. In fact, the effects of the conflict on Glasgow, its extensive shipbuilding area along the River Clyde (known as Clydeside), and the rest of Scotland, were tremendous. The struggling Confederate States of America were desperate for a wide variety of manufactured goods that the largely agricultural South either did not or could not produce. Moreover, for these goods to reach the Confederacy, they would have to be shipped across an increasingly hostile Atlantic Ocean that was patrolled by roving Union warships that were suspicious of any British-flagged vessel sailing for North America. The Union vessels that roamed the Atlantic Ocean formed the outer 'picket line' for the dense Union naval blockade that lay across the entire southern coastline. The vessels that undertook the dangerous task of shipping goods into the Confederacy through the ever-tightening Union blockade came to be known as 'blockade-runners'. The activities of the blockade-runners have come to be highly romanticised with the passage of time, but the story of their construction, financing and voyages, which either brought fantastic fortunes to their backers or complete ruin to both backers and ship's crew, is one that reveals numerous connections between Glasgow and the Confederacy.

How Glasgow came to be directly linked with the American Civil War and the career of James Iredell Waddell is extra-ordinary in that it can be traced to one man, James Dunwoody Bulloch, a native of the state of Georgia, and a future uncle of a president of the United States of America, Theodore Roosevelt Jr.

The head of the Confederacy's secret naval programme in Britain was Commander James D. Bulloch. He was dispatched to Great Britain in 1861, not long after the war began, with a mission to procure ironclad vessels, coordinate the purchase and shipping of critical technology such as mines and gun cotton, and pursue a programme for the covert construction or purchase of vessels for the purpose of commerce-raiding against Union-registered vessels. A mission of such broad scope would be a challenge for an entire naval staff, let alone one individual, but Bulloch was a man who combined extensive maritime knowledge with considerable organisational skill.

Prior to the outbreak of war in 1861, Bulloch had served 14 years in the US Navy before becoming a civilian captain of both cargo and passenger steamers. When war began, Bulloch immediately wrote a letter to Judah P. Benjamin, then Attorney General of the new Confederate States of America, offering his services to the Confederate government. However, Bulloch, like Waddell, had an intense sense of duty that had been ingrained from years of US naval service. When members of Louisiana's Confederate Board of War attempted to secure the USS *Bienville* by purchase, then by subtle threat of governmental seizure, Bulloch responded that he still had a duty to the owners and the passengers to return the vessel to New York City and would not consider surrendering the vessel. Bulloch quietly made the *Bienville* ready for quick sailing by rigging her mooring lines so they could be slipped from the vessel, allowing the current of the spring-flooding Mississippi River to rapidly swing the vessel's prow out and away for escape. Fortunately, Bulloch received a letter the following morning from the Confederate Board of War allowing him to sail without fear of seizure. This would be the first of many hair-raising near catastrophes that Bulloch would escape from during the next four years. Yet Bulloch's response to the potential seizure of his vessel, and the possible disruption of his assigned mission was something that he could not, would not let happen, as it transgressed a core naval value of duty. This is the same reaction that Waddell had when he discovered that the stricken captain and crew of the USS *Release* wanted to take the disease-plagued ship into New York, instead of its original ordered destination of Boston Naval Yard. Waddell won his argument, just as Bulloch had, by justifying his actions according to naval duty and naval law.

One other personality trait was shared by Bulloch and Waddell. Like Waddell, who had spent years in blue-water operations with the US Navy around the world, Bulloch had few Southern connections when the Civil War began, due to his years of sailing with his New York-based shipping firm. Bulloch himself said that his personal sympathies were with the South, while his personal and professional relationships were in the North, while Waddell noted that blue-water sailors of the US Navy tended to view their allegiances as belonging to the deck they stood upon, the crew around them and the flag that flew above them – and that regional discords read about in the newspapers that reached them on faraway voyages seemed to have little meaning. Yet, for both Bulloch and Waddell, the familial relationships and the sense of belonging to a particular landscape, or homeland, would prove to be the very things that brought them 'south' to join the Confederate Navy, as it did for so many others.

Bulloch got the USS *Bienville* to New York on 22 April 1861, after a voyage from New Orleans to Havana, Cuba. Finding upon arrival that the ship was being chartered by the Union government to take troops south to Washington, DC, Bulloch informed the director of the company that he could not go on that voyage, as he would not help to bear arms against his own people.

The next morning, Bulloch discovered that a letter had arrived from Attorney General Benjamin telling him that the new Confederate Secretary of the Navy, Stephen Mallory, desired to talk with him immediately. At nearly midnight on 7 May 1861, after several close calls, Bulloch arrived in Montgomery, Alabama, then the capital of the Confederate republic. Early on the morning of 8 May, he was at the office of Confederate Secretary of the Navy, Stephen Mallory. There they had one of the shortest, and possibly most important, conversations of the American Civil War. Mallory simply stated that he wanted Bulloch to go to Europe and asked when he could start. Bulloch was stunned as he assumed that his advice on more prosaic naval matters, such as the sea defence of New Orleans, was being sought, but Mallory has already sized up Bulloch's real capabilities before his arrival. Mallory knew that Bulloch's considerable commercial shipping background, coupled with his US Navy experience, made him the right man at the right time for the maritime strategy that Mallory envisaged. Mallory wanted Confederate cruisers at sea as soon as possible to destroy Union commerce, to draw away ships that might be used for blockade duty, and to get, by purchase or construction, blockade-runners for the transport of critical naval stores. After this short statement, Mallory told Bulloch to make notes as necessary to memorise their whole conversation, then to destroy them, as Bulloch would have to travel north through Union territory to reach Canada where he could catch a steamship for England. Mallory then told Bulloch to visit him again the following morning.

On 9 May, Mallory questioned Bulloch over all that they had discussed the day before, then moved on to the subtle international legal issues that would surround their naval stratagem. At this point in the early days of the American Civil War, the Confederate government believed that they would be recognised as a legitimate government by the great European nations because of the world's dependency on the South's cotton for the textile trade. However, Mallory was more pragmatic and believed that until a significant military victory had been achieved no European country of significance would recognise the Confederate States. Mallory therefore advised Bulloch that he would have to be very cautious and prudent in his financial and contractual deals for ships and supplies. If Bulloch had wondered which European country would be the base for their covert naval programme, Mallory's comment that he should become familiar with the Foreign Enlistment Act of Great Britain and the Queen's Proclamation on Neutrality, ended that speculation. Britain, the world's greatest power by virtually every means of measure, would be their organisational nexus. Mallory then reverted to his priority mission for Bulloch: to get vessels capable of cruising against Union commerce as quickly as possible, with the subsidiary mission of getting naval supplies of all kinds as quickly as possible through the developing Union blockade.

Bulloch queried Mallory as to how he would obtain funds to procure the desired ships and supplies. Mallory then disclosed that Fraser, Trenholm & Co. of Liverpool were functioning as the Confederacy's bankers and that Bulloch should conduct all his financial affairs through them. Mallory then directed Bulloch to proceed immediately to Britain by the fastest means available so that he could begin his mission. Bulloch evaded Union inspectors, travelled north to Michigan and on into Canada, where he obtained passage on the Allan Line steamer *North American*, which landed him in Liverpool on 4 June 1861, just shy of a month from his meeting with Stephen Mallory.

Many Europeans today believe that Americans have no knowledge of or interest in world affairs, nor have they had so in the past. Yet, in a land-locked city in the deep south of the former American republic, a naval strategy was conceived that would in a few years bring Great Britain and the United States to the brink of a war potentially involving France, Spain, Denmark and even Egypt – to name but a few nations affected – and bring about the first-ever international reparations tribunal. But for now this was in the unknown future for James Dunwoody Bulloch as he searched for lodging on an early summer's night in the port of Liverpool.

The following morning, 5 June, Bulloch called upon the offices of Fraser, Trenholm & Co., establishing his *bona fides* and in return receiving the utmost support from Charles K. Prioleau, one of the firm's managers. Prioleau told Bulloch to order what items he thought were of critical importance to the Confederacy and to refer the financial arrangements back to the company. With this *carte blanche* financial support in hand, Bulloch had free rein to pursue his agenda in the foremost shipbuilding country of the world, Great Britain. The fact that his headquarters would be in Liverpool, which along with Glasgow were the two major centres of ship construction, only made his job that much easier.

On the afternoon of 5 June 1861, however, Bulloch was not ordering naval supplies, but heading for London to meet the Confederate commissioners, William Yancey and Dudley Mann. Bulloch needed to size up the political lay of the land before he could put into action the strategy he and Mallory had agreed upon in Montgomery. Once in London, Bulloch met with Yancey and Mann who immediately confirmed the suspicions of Confederate Secretary of the Navy Stephen Mallory; they had not yet been officially received by Her Majesty's Secretary of State for Foreign Affairs, a signal that the Confederate cause was in some doubt as far as the British government was concerned, and that they themselves did not think the Confederacy would be recognised until a major military victory occurred. However, both Yancey and Mann noted that the European powers had recognised that their 'country' was a major, organised government capable of raising military forces, taxes and such, and that they thought the Confederacy could purchase military supplies just as any other recognised belligerent. Yancey and Mann also advised Bulloch that he would have to work with caution and prudence, for the Union government was conducting a heavy surveillance and intelligence operation via the US consular offices to Britain.

Bulloch now knew the obstacles he would face in constructing from scratch a blue-water navy for the Confederacy that would be capable of raiding Union commerce and weakening the blockade of the Southern ports. He returned to Liverpool immediately to get matters in hand and get his naval programme under way.

By the end of June 1861, Bulloch had already had the keel of his first commerce-raiding vessel laid. This was the first foreign-built Confederate naval cruiser and, thanks to the support of Fraser, Trenholm & Co., was partially framed up before the Confederate Naval Department was able to transfer funds to pay for her construction. This vessel was built under the name *Oreto,* and was ostensibly for Italian trade. Her real name was the *Confederate States Steamship Florida,* or CSS *Florida.*

As if Bulloch was not busy enough already, even while negotiations were under way for the construction of the CSS *Florida*, he began dealings with the famous Laird & Son at Birkenhead for the construction of yet another commerce-raider.

Here, in order to evade any prying eyes of the Union intelligence effort, Bulloch signed in his own name a private contract with the firm to build a vessel that would exceed the quality and construction of a Royal Navy vessel. Interestingly, at a time when most of the world's navies were ceasing to have vessels of wood constructed, Bulloch went to great trouble to ensure quality wood could be found, knowing that any Confederate cruiser would have to be capable of being repaired at any point in the world. The name of the Laird vessel would remain cloaked in secrecy until she was completed, sea-trialled and accepted by Bulloch; for now, she would be called *No. 290*. After Bulloch accepted her and she was safely at sea and being commissioned under her 'true' flag, she would become famous as the greatest Confederate raider of them all, the CSS *Alabama*.

Bulloch hid his dealings on behalf of the Confederate government from the prying eyes of the Union agents employed by the US consuls, but in one key area he operated in plain view, and that was in the British legal system. On top of all the frenzied shipbuilding contracts, naval supply ordering and organising of personnel, Bulloch found time to consult British solicitors on how he could safely navigate the intricacies of the Foreign Enlistment Act. In Mr F.S. Hull of Liverpool, Bulloch found a solicitor of extreme shrewdness and capability.

Hull drew up a test legal case which explored whether, under the Foreign Enlistment Act, Bulloch could legally construct his vessels without Her Majesty's government intervening or seizing his vessels. The test case was returned from counsel with a successful result for the Confederate commander. In a nutshell, Bulloch could get firms such as Laird to build his vessels as long as they did not fit them out with weapons or equipment that could conceivably be used for military purposes, nor have anything to do with Bulloch's activities for the Confederate government, either in Great Britain (to include the whole Empire) or in the rest of the world.

The legal advice gained by Hull gave Bulloch the last piece of help he needed to create an operative 'shadow' navy for the government of the Confederate States of America. As long as he kept his head down and his business circumspect, the eyes of the British legal system would be averted. This legal advice came just in time, for by 27 July 1861, the css *Florida* was partly framed, the plans and specifications of *No. 290* (the css *Alabama*) were done and a contract was to be signed with Laird & Son on 1 August. Bulloch and his diligent, discreet clerk (he had somehow found time to acquire one) had become a two-person naval department. Their headquarters were established within the offices of Fraser, Trenholm & Co., probably due to the insistent persuasion of Charles K. Prioleau. Early on, Bulloch and Prioleau had come to admire each other's business skills. This undoubtedly made it much easier for Bulloch to keep tabs on financial matters, but it also gave Prioleau and his partners influence on Confederate naval matters. Fraser, Trenholm & Co. probably strongly endorsed Bulloch's attitude that the Confederate government must establish a flotilla of blockade-runners under its own control in order to guarantee the shipment of war materiel, but more importantly for the export of cotton to the European markets. The company realised more than any Confederate government official that cotton was money, and money was needed to fund a victorious war against the Union.

With this in mind, while the shipyards of Liverpool were hard at work constructing two of the Confederacy's first commerce-raiders, Bulloch decided to purchase a vessel capable of functioning as a blockade-runner. He had an extensive list of naval stores on order throughout Britain that needed shipping back to the Confederacy. Bulloch wisely noted that his frenzied activities had already caught the eye of the developing Union intelligence effort and that even at that early stage of the war, he and Fraser, Trenholm & Co. were coming under constant surveillance. There was only one other port that Bulloch knew that would have exactly the kind of vessel he was looking for: Glasgow.

Liverpool may have produced more ships, but Glasgow was second-to-none in quality. Clydeside firms such as Scott & Co., J. & G. Thomson, Kirkpatrick & MacIntyre, William Denny & Bros., W.G. Simons & Co., A.H. Stephens and Thomas Wingate & Co. would produce a great many of the ships that ran the Union blockade, and four ships that would go on to serve in the Confederate Navy. Shipbuilders were not the only group to benefit from the civil conflict, however. Ship owners and blockade-running houses, or partnerships, also made massive profits by running the blockade, shipping in vital goods and luxury merchandise on the inward voyage and bringing out cotton on the return trip, which would then be sold at vastly inflated prices in European markets. But one man and one vessel began it all: James Dunwoody Bulloch and the *Fingal*.

The *Fingal* was a screw-steamship. She was almost brand new when Bulloch purchased her, having previously made only two trips, and she could steam up to 13 knots in good weather. Bulloch noted in an amusing aside that when he purchased her she had a full complement of toddy glasses, complete with ladles for each, and that each of the half-pint glasses was stout enough to serve as a grape-shot in case of need. Bulloch had the *Fingal* put alongside a loading berth at Greenock, just down river from Glasgow, where he immediately began the process of having her loaded, with some goods arriving by rail, others from London by sea. Bulloch's sleight of hand was necessary as US consular spies were by now constantly sending reports to their respective chief consuls, who were bombarding the British foreign secretary with complaints. If the Union was complaining at this early stage about Bulloch and the Confederate Navy's activities, before any commerce-raiding had even begun, they would be positively howling in a few years when the css *Florida, Alabama* and *Shenandoah* had finished their depredations. For the moment though, Bulloch was intent on getting away with his critically needed munitions for the war effort.

All through August and September Bulloch loaded the *Fingal*, to the point where it must have been thought that she would founder at the pier. The ship was loaded with 15,000 rifles, many of them the latest Enfield models, the finest of the day; over a million ball cartridges; two million percussion caps; 3,000 cavalry sabres; 500 revolvers; two 4½-inch rifled guns, with carriages; two 2½-inch rifled guns and over 400 barrels of gunpowder. Finally, there was an enormous quantity of material for uniforms and a large supply of medical equipment. This was the first vessel to run the blockade under direct Confederate government command and the first Clyde-built vessel to operate under Confederate naval command. This would also be the single largest consignment of military materiel to reach the Confederate States of America for the entire war. Bulloch had surpassed himself.

There were other firsts as well when the *Fingal* sailed from Greenock on 8 October 1861. Bulloch put into action the strategy and tactics that he would employ for virtually every ship that he constructed or bought hereafter for the purposes of blockade-running or commerce-raiding. In order to adhere strictly to the British Foreign Enlistment Act, Bulloch kept the vessel under a British flag and used a British captain holding a Board of Trade licence. This cleared the *Fingal* to sail under the regulations laid down by the Merchant Shipping Act. To maintain the appearance of non-involvement with the sailing of the vessel, Bulloch himself did not travel on the *Fingal*, but instructed the captain to call at Holyhead, an important ferry and shipping port in north-west Wales commonly used for transit to Ireland at the time. The calling in of the *Fingal* at such a busy port would have elicited little attention, and Bulloch himself noted that shortly after the vessel sailed from Greenock, a tremendous gale that lasted for several days sprang up in the Irish Sea. As Bulloch and other Confederate officials anxiously awaited news of the ship in Holyhead, knowing Union agents would be on the outlook for their whereabouts as well, nearly a week passed before the *Fingal* made port in Holyhead. If Bulloch thought the gale had made things close-run from the start, the story the captain had to tell must have raised the hairs on the back of his head.

The *Fingal* was carefully slipping around the outer breakwater at Holyhead harbour just before dawn on 15 October 1861 when she ran down a brig that was anchored with no lights upon her. The *Fingal* attempted to change course, but at such a slow speed steering was sluggish; her rakish prow stove in the brig's starboard quarter, or right front side. With only a desultory shout from the unfortunately unlit craft, the mortally damaged vessel sank directly down. Hearing this more than unsatisfactory news, and realising that every moment they delayed sailing from Holyhead invited the unwanted attentions of British customs authorities and reports to the US consul (from both British officials and Union agents on their trail), Bulloch ordered everyone aboard for immediate sailing. Wishing to keep the incident as quiet as possible, Bulloch hastily dashed off a letter to Fraser, Trenholm and Co., asking them to look into it and to make the necessary financial reparations with the least amount of discussion or reports. Bulloch and his associates would hear more later, but for now, the *Fingal* was away into the rapidly rising dawn.

The first few days of the Atlantic crossing were uneventful, but on 19 October 1861 another gale bore down upon the *Fingal*. The crew now discovered how heavily loaded the vessel was as she could barely make nine knots in good weather; in gale conditions they barely made headway. But the stout Clyde-built vessel showed her pedigree and rode the weather into the Azores. After resupplying, the steamship made her way to Bermuda, arriving there on 2 November.

One of the great ironies of the war occurred while Bulloch and the *Fingal* were in Bermuda. Also anchored there at the time was the first Confederate commerce-raider, a rather slow and ungainly paddle-wheeler named the CSS *Nashville*. The *Nashville* had already captured and destroyed a Union ship. She would sail on to Britain and become something of a celebrity to the British public, being, as it were, the first visible example of Confederate nationhood. The US consuls were, of course, not amused by this at all and produced considerable paperwork complaining about the *Nashville*. For Bulloch, however, it was a chance to confer with ingoing and outgoing persons from the Confederacy who had news of the war and other activities.

Bermuda acted as a Confederate blockade-running depot and de facto consular station for most of the war. Bulloch obtained message traffic for himself pertaining to the *Florida* and *Shenandoah*. Confederate Secretary of the Navy Mallory had approved all of Bulloch's contracts for the vessels, plus other naval stores, as well as the voyage which Bulloch was now making in the *Fingal*. Still, the Union intelligence effort did not let up, even in Bermuda, a British dominion. The US representative dogged the Confederate vessel's attempts to leave, and it was not until 9 November 1861 that the *Fingal* ventured forth to vault her last hurdle, the running of the Union blockade into Savannah, Georgia.

Bulloch maintained his operational secrecy until the last with the British authorities, stating that the next port of call for the *Fingal* would be Nassau. Meanwhile, he checked with the chief engineer, a Scotsman by the name of McNair (who later served as engineer on the CSS *Alabama*) into the state of the vessel's engines. McNair reported that with a good scouring out of the vessel's flues he'd be able to gain a few more knots above her normal speed. McNair had apparently suspected what was afoot, as he had stashed a few tons of good, clean coal for just such an occasion.

On 10 November 1861, Bulloch finally told the entire crew that they were not sailing for Nassau, and revealed their true mission. As could be expected in those early days of the war, when few battles had yet been fought and very few lives lost, an air of adventure prevailed. The entire crew volunteered for the race through the blockade.

Early in the first hours of 12 November, the *Fingal* reached waters shallow enough to take soundings inside the Gulf Stream; engineer McNair had finished cleaning his flues just before midnight. Taking advantage of a steadily thickening fog that would mask their approach, the *Fingal* slowly made her way towards the mouth of the Savannah River. They were in a perfect place for a sprint into the river mouth before being noticed by the blockading Union ships. All of a sudden, a shrill shriek from a rooster brought aboard in Bermuda broke the silence, stunning the Confederates. A desperate scramble broke out amongst the sailors to reach the on-deck coop and wring the neck of the offender; in the deep fog, a chicken was grabbed and its neck wrung, but the shrieking continued. The wrong chicken had been killed. The noise-maker was finally caught and dispatched, but not before many a nerve had been frayed to the edge.

As the dawn rose, the crew of the *Fingal* realised they were directly opposite Warsaw Sound, but the normal buoys that marked this course into the Savannah River had been taken up by the Union vessels. It was decided to take advantage of the fog, which still remained heavy to seaward, and make a dash for the main Savannah River mouth, some 17 miles northeast. Soon they spotted the immense brickworks of Fort Pulaski, which guarded the main route up the Savannah River estuary to the city itself. The *Fingal* raised her Confederate flag and fired a signal gun to salute the fort and to alert them of her presence as a Confederate vessel. More of Bulloch's extraordinary luck came into play again shortly thereafter, for while the Union Navy had sunk several vessels in an attempt to block the main river channel used by Confederate shipping, Bulloch's astute choice of the *Fingal* meant that her relatively shallow draught would allow her to pass unhindered. Moreover, the expected Union ships had been moved away north to the Port Royal, South Carolina, area while Union forces attacked the Confederate positions there.

On 12 November 1861 Bulloch and the first Confederate government blockade-runner, the CSS *Fingal* laid anchor off the wharf of Savannah, Georgia. Bulloch telegraphed Mallory that same afternoon and received an immediate reply to come north to Richmond, Virginia, now the capital of the Confederacy. Bulloch had come nearly full circle in less than six months, from New York, to Alabama to Canada, then to England, and now back to Georgia, his home state. He had almost single-handedly begun the construction of a blue-water Confederate naval flotilla capable of commerce-raiding, managed to find legal loopholes in the British Foreign Enlistment Act that the Confederacy could exploit and, finally, proved that large amounts of military stores could be shipped through the Union blockade if the right type of vessels were used.

At almost the same time as the *Fingal* was discharging her cargo of Confederate war materiel in Savannah, far out in the South Atlantic Ocean the USS *John Adams,* with Lt. James Iredell Waddell aboard, was reaching St Helena Island. Stopping in for supplies and the most recent communications on her way back from a patrol in the Far Pacific, the officers and men of the *John Adams* would have been intensely interested in news of hostilities in America. Waddell received a letter from home that laid out the news of the Battle of Bull Run, Virginia. On 20 November 1861, with a heavy heart, Waddell wrote out his resignation letter. Waddell's resignation could not take effect, however, until the *John Adams* reached port in New York. As ever, Waddell continued to do his duty in a fit and proper manner, though some of his inner turmoil was apparent in his resignation letter to Sec. Welles when he said that, 'separating myself from associations which I have cherished for twenty years, I wish it to be understood that no doctrine of the right of secession, no wish for disunion of the States impel me, but simply because, my home is the home of my people in the South, and I cannot bear arms against it or them'. This sad resignation letter, probably not unlike many received from other naval officers of the US Navy who hailed from Southern states, carries with it a common theme: that at that moment in American history, politics still did not supersede the powerful link between homeland and family. It would take many years after the resolution of the American Civil War for this essential attribute of Southern culture to be obscured within the national body politic.

Meanwhile, Bulloch made his way north to Richmond by rail, where he conferred with Secretary Mallory for several days concerning the needs of the Confederate Navy, Bulloch's needs in Britain, and the needs of the Confederacy in general, as they related to blockade-running. With new orders in hand, Bulloch raced south to Savannah again, hoping to fill the cargo holds of the *Fingal* with cotton, run her through the blockade back to Bermuda, and then to Britain. From late November 1861 until mid January of 1862, Bulloch tried to run the *Fingal* out through the Union blockade, but without success.

While Bulloch was being frustrated by Union blockaders on the Savannah River, Waddell was arriving in New York City aboard the USS *John Adams*, his US Navy career at an end with his letter of resignation now in effect. Ironically, even though Waddell had technically resigned from the US Navy, he had been forced to take an oath upon arrival in the New York naval yard that he would not bear arms against the Union. If that did not begin to inflame Waddell's sense of personal honour, then surely the scenes that met him on the streets of New York did. At that early stage of the conflict Waddell witnessed what could only be described as war euphoria. From every direction he heard imprecations against the South, its politicians and its people.

Turning to resolve a more immediate issue of the moment – his pay – Waddell visited the paymaster of the naval yard to get money due to him. The paymaster shocked Waddell by saying that he had received instructions directly from the Department of the Navy that they alone would handle the settlement of Waddell's pay. While Waddell may have carefully and properly handed in his resignation from the US Navy, what he could not know about was the bitter, almost rabid hatred that US Secretary of the Navy Gideon Welles had developed for the South and any suspect US naval officers with Southern backgrounds. But if Welles had thought he could get the better of any of the 'rebel' officers, he certainly could not have reckoned on a man with a towering rage who would literally pursue Union vessels to the ends of the world – and back again.

Waddell's personal honour had now been questioned and his integrity insulted by the leading figure of an organisation that for 20 years had been his professional family, for lack of a better term. Even now though, Waddell's professionalism and decorum as a naval officer meant that he would follow proper channels. So it was that on 18 January 1862, Waddell wrote a letter to President Abraham Lincoln laying out his case in barely controlled rage, describing what, in his mind, was utterly despicable and dishonourable behaviour by the Department of the Navy. Even here, Waddell had the ability to rise above his palpable hatred of Sec. Welles, whom he did not mention by name in the letter, only specifying 'that Department'. This communiqué, more than any other, brought Waddell's name prominently to Welles' attention for the first time, for immediately after it was received by the White House Welles issued a letter acknowledging Waddell's original letter of resignation on 18 January 1862. The letter specified that 'by direction of the President, your name has, this day, been stricken from the rolls'. Welles would not have liked having been called on the carpet for his behaviour by President Lincoln, but he probably let Waddell's name drop from his mind. Welles, however, had begun a fight with a North Carolina 'Tar Heel', and their reputation for sticking to issues, if wronged, was already part of American folklore. Waddell wanted his pay, and he would get it, or Gideon Welles and the US Navy would know the better of it.

As Waddell engaged in a war of words with the US Navy over his withheld pay, Bulloch was contacting Mallory over his inability to run the *Fingal* through the Savannah River blockade, and out to sea. Mallory finally ordered Bulloch to return to England by any means possible and on 5 February he was able to escape through the Union blockade at Wilmington, North Carolina, aboard the *Annie Childs*. After another stormy crossing, (with US consular difficulties in the Azores again, to boot) Bulloch touched land in Ireland, taking the ferry train from Dublin to Holyhead, then on to Liverpool on 10 March. He had arrived back in Liverpool almost five months to the day after he had left. He would find that while he had been gone, almost everything that he had put in motion had ground to a halt.

A letter from the US Treasury Department delivered the final outrageous insult that would push Waddell over the edge to the 'South'. On 21 February 1862, as Bulloch was crossing the stormy and wintry Atlantic Ocean, James Iredell Waddell got a letter directly from US Secretary of the Navy Gideon Welles. In it, Welles acknowledged that Waddell's request for payment from a North Carolina source (as the Treasury Department demanded), and for a military pass, had been received. Welles then went on to say that these would be granted only if Waddell signed a letter, written upon Waddell's word of honour, that he would take no part in the conflict now raging across the country.

Waddell was now incandescent with fury. He had followed the rules of the US Navy for 20 years and had resigned honourably, with no intention of taking up arms on either side. He had been forced to take an oath already, though against his better nature. But Welles' irascibility and wilfulness had now collided with a core personal value of Waddell's, that of due financial reward, a value instilled from the earliest days in any North Carolinian during their Bible studies and at church. Not to be paid one's just rewards was cause for unlimited retribution against the offender.

Waddell began to pack his bags and plan his escape south to join the Confederate Navy. His war was now personal. He would find a ship and a crew, and a way to create the maximum amount of damage possible for Gideon Welles, the navy that had dishonoured him, and the Unionist states that seemed only to worship the god of Mammon.

As fate began to spin Waddell towards the man who would facilitate his retribution against Welles, Bulloch was in Liverpool, trying to get his commerce-raiders afloat and into action. Bulloch had left careful instructions on how the first

commerce-raider, the CSS *Florida*, was to be fitted out, that is, to
have no appearance or equipment that could suggest use as a
vessel of war. Having inspected her himself, Bulloch was
satisfied that she was legal under the terms of the Foreign
Enlistment Act. Following the strategy he employed with the
Fingal, Bulloch found a fully qualified captain and again engaged
a crew in compliance with the Merchant Shipping Act. The
captain and crew signed documents that stipulated they would
be undertaking a voyage from Liverpool to Italy, and possibly
other ports in the Mediterranean or the West Indies, then
finishing the voyage in Great Britain. The contract said the
voyage would not exceed six months. Now all Bulloch had to do
was get a Confederate naval commander, officer staff, and sundry
other specialist crew members for the vessel. This proved to be the
problem, for Bulloch had hoped to get a commander and core
staff from the CSS *Nashville*, which he had hoped would still be in
Great Britain; unfortunately she had already sailed.

Once again Bulloch thought on his feet and called in Lt. John
Low CSN, who had sailed on the *Fingal* with him to America.
Bulloch ordered Low to sail outwards from Liverpool with the
clandestine CSS *Florida* (still known to the British authorities as
the *Oreto*) for Nassau in the Bahamas. Bulloch knew that Lt.
John Maffitt CSN had been sent to Nassau on special duty for
the Confederate Navy, and that Maffitt had the necessary skills
and tenacity to command a commerce-raider. Time was very
critical now, as the Union intelligence effort was in full swing
against Bulloch's covert shipbuilding programme, and the US
consular authorities had begun heated correspondence with the
British Foreign Office over the *Oreto*/CSS *Florida*.

Working at a frenetic pace, and only 12 days after he had

arrived back in Liverpool, on 22 March 1862 Bulloch had the Confederacy's first foreign-built, blue-water commerce-raider, the CSS *Florida,* sailing down the Mersey and off across the Atlantic to the Bahamas. (The honour of being the first armed Confederate commerce-raider belongs to the CSS *Sumter,* commanded by Rafael Semmes, who would gain greater fame as the captain of the CSS *Alabama.*) The *Florida* arrived safely in the Bahamas on 28 April. However, due to the suspicions of the British Crown about the vessel's intended use (provoked, of course, by the US consular officers and intelligence agents), which led to a short legal case to ascertain its 'true' pedigree, the *Florida* was not able to transfer aboard her weapons battery and other military supplies until 9–10 August. While Bulloch could not have known all of these details immediately, due to the communications lag of the day, he would have carefully noted the glitches that had occurred and would adjust his strategy accordingly for the launch of his next commerce-raider, *No. 290,* or the CSS *Alabama.*

While Bulloch was getting his first commerce-raider under way, Waddell, still in a white-hot rage from his treatment by US Secretary of the Navy Welles, was making his arrangements to be smuggled through the Union and Confederate lines by sea from Annapolis. He knew that it was possible that Sec. Welles would have him under surveillance and might attempt to have him arrested. His first attempt to leave by night from Annapolis failed. Next, an associate of Waddell's told him to visit a contact that he knew of in the Marsh Market of Baltimore, Maryland, a fat man who worked in a certain meat shop there. Waddell's friend told him to ask the fat man 'the price of beef'. Waddell did so and the fat butcher asked him if he wished to go south. 'Yes,' muttered Waddell. The fat butcher told Waddell that he would collect him the following evening at about 8 o'clock and take him to Carroll Island, located between Annapolis and Baltimore. A schooner would be waiting there to take him to Virginia.

The following evening, Waddell left his wife Anne and his young daughter Annie to make his attempt to sneak through Union lines. Leaving in a driving rainstorm with another friend who also wished to cross into the Confederacy, Waddell was asked by the driver of the small coach to identify himself. Upon doing so, the driver handed Waddell a small pellet wrapped in tinfoil, with the mysterious instruction to, 'Give that to Mr Benjamin'. Waddell's covert transit was now even more dangerous, as he was obviously carrying information for Confederate Attorney General Judah Benjamin. If he were caught, he would be treated as a spy and either hung or shot before he ever donned a Confederate naval uniform.

Arriving under cover of rain and darkness at Carroll Island just after midnight, Waddell and nine other hopeful Confederates huddled in a small log cabin to await events. Just at daylight, the schooner arrived and the small group boarded the vessel with all speed. Waddell noted with some wryness that the captain of the schooner was a Yankee and doing his smuggling for the love of money rather than the Union. Waddell had paid the fat butcher one hundred dollars US for his and his friend's passage.

The journey was not without some excitement, for as they sailed away under the strengthening light of day, they could see the flotilla of steamships, commanded by McClellan, heading up the Potomac River to Washington, DC. Creeping carefully along in order to avoid attracting the attention of any Union vessels that might be about, they did not approach the Virginia shore until all was clear.

Finally coming close to land, the vessel met a local pilot who told them that a Union patrol had been spotted thereabouts, but that he knew where the schooner could be safely anchored. After following the pilot's instruction to enter a small side creek, Waddell was nominated to go ashore and discover what intelligence he could. He was able to borrow two carriages from an old farmer whose grandson had been mortally wounded in the Battle of Bull Run.

The small party of illegals, led by Waddell, stopped in a village near the Rappahannock River in order to hire a wagon, and send back the farmer's vehicles. The driver of the hired wagon was a Union man, just as the schooner's captain had been, but he had no qualms in taking the fugitives to a ferry crossing over the Rappahannock, controlled by the Confederacy. After being ferried across the river, the group were sequestered by Confederate pickets in a guard house until the commanding officer could be informed. The commander of the guard detail, upon being informed of their arrival, had them brought to a hotel where his quarters were located. There, an enlisted man from a Baltimore artillery unit recognised Waddell and vouched for his identity; with that, they were released.

After taking time for supper, Waddell and his companion continued onwards towards Richmond by wagon. Luckily, they were able to catch a train on the York River Railroad that took them directly into Richmond. That evening they lodged at the Spotswood Hotel, enjoying supper and a well-earned night's rest, but not before Waddell had delivered his secret tinfoil pellet to Attorney General Benjamin.

The following day, Waddell and his associate visited the head of the Confederate Secret Service, General John H. Winder. As Waddell would have known about ship and troop movements from his period at the US Navy Yard in New York, as well as what he had observed before crossing Union lines, he would have been a good source of information for the Confederacy's intelligence chief. More importantly, Winder established James Waddell's *bona fides*, thus vetting him for the Confederate Navy. In fact, Waddell left Winder's office and immediately went to the Confederate Department of the Navy to enter his application for commission in the Navy. Like Bulloch, James Iredell Waddell wasted no time.

On 27 March 1862, Waddell was commissioned as a lieutenant in the Confederate States Navy. On this same day, Union Commodore David G. Farragut began to bring a fleet up the Mississippi River to attack New Orleans. With some 67 vessels of all types making up the attacking Union force, this was the greatest emergency the Confederate Navy had yet faced. Waddell was immediately given orders to report to New Orleans and report to the CSS *Mississippi*. He was about to get his first grazing touch of combat under the Confederate flag.

Meanwhile Bulloch's first commerce-raider, the CSS *Florida,* had sailed only a week before from Liverpool and was still in transit to Nassau in the Bahamas under her British registered name, *Oreto*. Not concerned with what he could not know about the *Florida*, Bulloch turned his energies to getting *No. 290* (CSS *Alabama*) off the slipways of Laird & Son at Birkenhead. All through April 1862, the Laird engineers and workers pressed on with getting *No. 290* completed. Bulloch, ever aware of Union surveillance and suspicions about the vessel, worked through intermediaries and maintained his distance from the Laird shipyard.

Meanwhile, across the Atlantic Ocean in the Gulf of Mexico, Waddell reached New Orleans as the fleet under the command of Commodore David Farragut was beginning its assault. Waddell had been posted to the CSS *Mississippi,* an incomplete ironclad under construction at the Tift Brothers Shipyard. Launched on 17 April 1862, the *Mississippi* was towed to an area just off the shipyard and upstream of New Orleans. A week later, on 25 April, the Union fleet fought its way through the Confederate defences and anchored off the city's main levee. As the Union naval forces appeared ever closer, the crew and workmen at the Tift yards struggled for 24 hours to move the incomplete *Mississippi* upstream with the help of two steamships, but the size of the vessel and the current of the Mississippi River made it impossible; more vessels were needed. Commander Arthur Sinclair, captain of the ironclad, ordered Waddell to stand by on the vessel with orders to burn her if Union forces got too close; Sinclair would try to get into New Orleans to see if he could get more towboats. As Sinclair carefully made his way towards New Orleans, he could see that all was in chaos, with what boats he could see afire, fleeing, or sinking. Turning back north up the river, he could see a pall of smoke from where the *Mississippi* was anchored. Waddell had followed his instructions to the letter.

In his memoirs Waddell noted that all the Confederate naval personnel from the shipyard and the ironclad had been transported upriver to Vicksburg. Once there, Waddell says that he reminded Commander Sinclair that the *Mississippi* could be destroyed to prevent its use by Union forces. Sinclair agreed to

Waddell's proposal. Waddell set off downstream in a small open boat, with one of the Tift yard engineers, a Mr Pierce, to help. Reaching the deserted *Mississippi,* Waddell and Pierce laid charges throughout the vessel's critical points. As they were completing their scuttling mission, five men suddenly appeared on the deck of the vessel, saying they'd come to find the Tift brothers and hang them as traitors. Waddell coolly informed the small lynching party that the vessel was about to blow up, just as Pierce reappeared. The Confederate mob abandoned the vessel quickly as Waddell and Pierce pulled away in their boat to safety up river. The css *Mississippi* exploded with a satisfying roar, denying its use to the Union. Waddell had begun his war in an improbable fashion, scuttling a warship from his own navy, but he had carried out his mission successfully. In today's naval terminology, this adventure was a 'special boat' or 'special warfare' mission.

Shortly after the Confederacy's loss of New Orleans, Waddell was transferred to the naval gun battery at Drewry's Bluff, located in Chesterfield County, Virginia, down river of the Confederate capital at Richmond. The battle of Drewry's Bluff saved Richmond from invasion and helped Waddell's career. His actions during the battle earned him a promotion, in October of 1862, to the rank of 1st Lieutenant in the CSN. This was his first naval promotion of any type since 1855 in the US Navy, seven years before. He settled into garrison duty and obtained occasional news of his wife Anne and daughter Annie from other Confederate officers whose relatives in the North had smuggled letters and notes south through the Union lines. This would be one of the longest periods that Waddell would be stationed ashore and separated from his beloved Anne, during his entire Confederate naval service.

On the far side of the North Atlantic Ocean, on the same day as the Battle of Drewry's Bluff (15 May 1862), James Bulloch saw *No. 290* launched from the Laird shipyards at Birkenhead. The erstwhile Confederate commander proved he had a romantic streak when he had the vessel christened by a lady acquaintance, then went on to name the vessel for her, but using a Spanish language equivalent to help mask her identity further. She was now called the *Enrica*. This meticulous adherence to operational security gave rise to a rumour in the Union that the vessel was meant for either the Spanish government or some Spanish concern. Bulloch would take great delight in the wild rumours that subsequently surrounded the vessel.

Exactly a month later, on 15 June 1862, the *Enrica* (soon to be CSS *Alabama*) was sea-trialled and performed up to the expectations of all concerned. Once more, Bulloch went about his strategy of finding a British certified ship's master/captain, crew and relevant shipping documents. Bulloch also sent out McNair, the Scottish engineer from the *Fingal* voyage, to oversee personally the engineering department of the ship.

The greatest disappointment of Bulloch's naval career now occurred. He had hoped that he would personally command the *Enrica*/CSS *Alabama* himself, but Rafael Semmes' commerce-cruiser, the CSS *Sumter,* had developed engineering and hull problems and was docked in Gibraltar as a result. Semmes and his entire officer staff from the ship had been ordered back to the Confederacy when new orders from Confederate Secretary of the Navy Mallory caught up with them in Nassau. Mallory had ordered Semmes back to England to command the *Alabama*. Semmes promptly telegraphed Bulloch in Liverpool that he was coming there by the first available vessel; this must have doubly added to Bulloch's disappointment, for if any delay had occurred, Bulloch would have probably seized the opportunity to take the *Alabama* out himself. Bulloch was a consummate professional, however, and did not let his personal disappointment affect his work. He rapidly got the *Alabama* provisioned and fuelled with coal, while at the same time he purchased a smaller freight sailing ship that would carry the military stores and weapons to the rendezvous point for the fitting out of the commerce-raider. The support vessel was named the *Agrippina* and she had just finished a British government contract for hauling old weapons and shot from Gibraltar. She was loaded with the military materiel for the *Alabama* on the London docks, with no apparent surveillance from Union intelligence agents.

The Union surveillance effort concerning the *Enrica*, or CSS *Alabama,* was another story. The US consul in Liverpool, Thomas F. Dudley, led a full-scale intelligence effort against all Confederate activities in his area, coordinating his efforts with US Minister to Great Britain, Charles Francis Adams, located in London. Bulloch, who had his own sources high in the British government, learned on Saturday, 26 July 1862, that the US intelligence and diplomatic effort had finally coerced the British government into seizing the vessel in order to inspect it, and Laird's papers, for incriminating evidence that would prove that Bulloch was violating the British Foreign Enlistment Act.

Wasting not a moment, Bulloch made for the Laird yards and requested another sea trial of the *Alabama,* to take place on the following Monday. He then contacted his temporary captain of the vessel, Captain Butcher, and told him to finish loading his stores quickly and to take extra coal aboard. He then quietly told Butcher that the vessel would not be returning. A quick telegraph to the captain of the *Agrippina*, Alexander McQueen, about the necessity for an immediate sailing, was also sent. The pre-arranged rendezvous point was known only to Bulloch, Butcher and McQueen.

Bulloch then surpassed himself in the art of 'hiding it in plain view'. The CSS *Alabama*, still masquerading under the guise of the *Enrica*, sailed away from the Laird yards on 29 July 1862, with bunting and flags, along with a small party of guests. A small steam-tug, named the *Hercules*, also accompanied the vessel out of the yards. To all intents and purposes, they were out for a day-long sea-trial and ship-completion party.

The sense of exhilaration that Bulloch must have felt that fine sunny day would have been tinged with melancholy. The *Alabama* was a vessel that he had designed and built to a better specification than any vessel afloat in the Royal Navy, a vessel that he had hoped to command. Yet the Confederate Department of the Navy needed his organisational skills more ashore. Still, for today, the *Alabama* was his. The vessel raced several times between Bell Buoy and the northwest lightship off Liverpool, reaching speeds of nearly 13 knots. She was superb in every aspect. At three o'clock in the afternoon, Bulloch began to play his hand, asking the Liverpool pilot George Bond if he knew of Moelfra Bay, south-west. Acknowledging that he did, Bulloch directed him to proceed there after he and the invited party had departed via the tug *Hercules*. Bulloch then informed Captain Butcher of his plans and told him to keep the *Alabama* in Moelfra Bay until he returned the following day. Hiring the *Hercules* for the morrow's work as it sailed back towards Liverpool, Bulloch watched the *Alabama* move southwards, wondering if the Union intelligence apparatus had noted her position. If so, they may have already alerted the US consuls and the Union warships that were known to be operating off the south and west coasts of Britain, searching for suspected Confederate vessels.

At dawn on the following day, Bulloch and a crew of seamen that would hopefully be induced to ship aboard the *Alabama,* as well as left-behind miscellanea for the ship, were waiting for the *Hercules* to take them to Moelfra Bay; that is, if no Union warship had discovered her. In another improbable event in Bulloch's covert maritime career, the seamen who came aboard the *Hercules* had their wives and girlfriends with them. The ladies refused to let their male partners aboard, or sign on for a voyage, unless a month's pay was handed over upfront. Bulloch refused, but relented when the captain of the *Hercules* said that it was a case of all or nothing for the crew-starved commerce-raider; with that, they cast off for the *Alabama.*

On reaching the *Alabama* at three o'clock in the afternoon, Bulloch quickly got his 'crew' off the *Hercules.* After feeding the potential crewmen, and 'splicing the mainbrace', that is, passing out a few rounds of grog, Bulloch explained to the assembled men (and women) that the *Alabama*, still known to them as the *Enrica*, would be making a cruise for Havana, with possible intermediary stops. If the vessel did not return to Britain, they would be sent back home free of charge, or have cash put in their hand to their satisfaction. And yes, a month's pay would be laid down now. All but a very few signed on and the ladies were satisfied with the conditions.

Not completing the pay and other arrangements until midnight, Bulloch watched nervously as a southwest gale began to develop. Worried about the whereabouts of the USS *Tuscarora*, which he knew had slipped her anchor at Southampton and was headed somewhere up the Irish Sea, Bulloch gave orders to get the women off the *Alabama* and to get the ship under away. Finally, at two thirty on the morning of 31 July 1862, the *Alabama* was steaming away north, and hopefully away from the *Tuscarora* or any other Union warship that might be looking for her. Bulloch had craftily decided to run the *Alabama* over the top of Ireland, a route that would not be anticipated by Union pursuers.

Flying up the Irish Sea before the ever-increasing gale, the *Alabama* was making 13 knots. By 8 p.m. on 31 July, she was off Rathlin Island and Fair Head. With the weather having cleared, the late sun of the northern summer day would have back-lit the vessel for any curious ship-watchers on the nearby Mull of Kintyre, or even the Isle of Islay, the westernmost extensions of Scotland. Bulloch left his cherished *Alabama* near the Giant's Causeway, along with the Liverpool pilot, George Bond, by signalling a passing fishing boat; the conditions were foul.

Captain Butcher now sailed the *Alabama* on to her pre-determined rendezvous with her support ship, the *Agrippina*. They would meet in the Azores, in Praya Bay, the same bay that Bulloch had observed on his outward-bound voyage in the blockade-runner *Fingal*. Bulloch's second commerce-cruiser was now on her way, and her future was now in the hands of Fate.

On returning to Liverpool, Bulloch telegraphed Mallory about the *Alabama*'s sailing, and the intensifying Union efforts to halt the covert shipbuilding programme. He also received a letter from Rafael Semmes saying that he would arrive in Liverpool within the next few days. Bulloch made immediate arrangements to have the ship that brought Semmes into Britain, the *Bahama*, turn about and sail for the Azores to meet the *Alabama*. Bulloch also managed to find 30 more crewmen, as well as two more 32-pound guns, which were shipped in concealed crates.

Bulloch decided to sail out with the *Bahama*, along with Semmes and other Confederates, in order to oversee any last minute glitches. The *Bahama* sailed for the Azores on 13 August 1862, meeting the *Alabama* on 20 August. On 24 August, the vessel formerly known as the *No. 290*, then *Enrica*, was formally commissioned in a ceremony at sea as the CSS *Alabama*. Bulloch departed the vessel just after midnight and began steaming back to Liverpool with Captain Butcher aboard the *Bahama*. Bulloch undoubtedly hoped for some short respite from his endeavours. Unfortunately, one of the original subsidiary missions assigned to Bulloch by Confederate Secretary of the Navy Mallory had become an immediate necessity: the construction of ironclads. This would also be the point at which Glasgow's renowned shipbuilding technology would become key to the Confederate naval effort.

The Confederate war effort had begun to falter by the spring of 1862. Waddell had taken part in two strategic campaigns, albeit in a minor fashion, but with his knowledge of maritime strategy he would have understood better than most the situation that the Confederacy was beginning to face. From the outset of the war, Confederate Secretary of the Navy Mallory had envisioned an ocean-going ironclad that would sweep the blockading Union squadrons from the Confederacy's coastline. However the Confederate Congress failed to pass the bill to appropriate the naval funds for the purchase of the ironclad. His new orders were to obtain estimates for building such vessels, but to take no further action. He sent Lt. North, who, after a very rough crossing of the Atlantic, reached Liverpool on 25 June

1861. After delivering messages from Secretary Mallory to Bulloch, North found lodging for his family. He departed Liverpool for London the next day with messages for Confederate commissioners Yancey and Mann. Although it first appeared that North would be as energetic as Bulloch in naval matters, almost at once he became the proverbial tourist abroad. From 27 June until 1 August, North and his family visited sights such as Westminster, Madame Tussauds wax museum, even the Queen's stables. While Bulloch was desperately trying to get the *Florida* and *Alabama* projects under way and, in America, Waddell was wondering when he would be able to strike another blow in his personal war against Gideon Welles, Lt. North was being a sightseer.

North finally conducted a few desultory interviews with various shipbuilders, who told him plainly that to purchase, or build, a vessel of the type desired by Mallory would cost several millions, and both England and France would stop at nothing to have them first. North posted off a discouraging note to this effect to Mallory, then proceeded to accept an offer to go yacht racing in the English Channel.

North became involved in setting up house in Paris and then tried to make his own way in the business of quietly getting an ironclad warship built for the Confederacy; he asked for no help from Bulloch. In early October, North discovered, to his surprise, that Bulloch had purchased the *Fingal* and was intending to run her through the Union blockade with a load of war materiel. North dropped all his French projects and dashed north to Liverpool, where he arrived in the middle of the last frantic preparations for the *Fingal*'s voyage, Bulloch having little time for the apparently lackadaisical North.

North immediately went to Bulloch's headquarters and asked to be placed in charge of the *Florida* and *Alabama* while Bulloch was gone. Bulloch refused. Bulloch had no faith in North, and Mallory, equally aware of the lieutenant's shortfalls, had already written new orders instructing North to remain in England and either buy or build an ironclad. An additional admonishment from Mallory was that he was to perform whatever other duties might fall his way until further instruction.

Once North had relocated to Liverpool, he began to undertake visits to British shipbuilders concerning the possibilities of constructing the hoped-for ironclad. He also made the odd visit to the *Florida* to inspect building progress on her, and wrote numerous letters to Secretary Mallory begging for funds with which to build a vessel and to cover his incurred costs.

Bulloch's return to Liverpool in March 1862, preceded by a letter to North from Secretary Mallory informing him that Bulloch had been commissioned a commander, created even more personal animosity between the two Confederate shipbuilders. North posted off an indignant letter to Mallory, while Bulloch tried to soothe the more-than-ruffled feathers of the lieutenant, to the point of offering him the command of the *Florida*. Even when North's rank was increased to commander on 5 May, he was still not satisfied, as he knew his all important 'date of rank' made him junior to the 'civilian' Bulloch. Personal animosity now plagued the Confederate naval programme abroad.

Lt. North, still believing he was being left out of the loop by Bulloch, now stubbornly went back to his original orders from Secretary Mallory, to get an ironclad built in England for the Confederacy. He would show Bulloch that he could not only negotiate a ship contract and get a vessel constructed, but it would be capable of sailing across the Atlantic and confronting the Union Navy head-on in combat. To give North his due, for once his thick-headed behaviour got him somewhere first in his personal competition with Bulloch. Bulloch may have put Glasgow into the history books as being the place where the first Confederate blockade-runner was built, but it was North who got the first true, purpose-built Confederate ironclad built – and it was Clyde-built as well.

On 21 May 1862, six days after Waddell had fought at the Battle of Drewry's Bluff, his compatriot, the newly promoted Commander James North, signed the contract with Thomson's Shipyard to begin construction of the blue-water ironclad. It was to be designated, for the time being, *No. 61*. The specifications, in compliance with the original thoughts of Secretary Mallory that the vessel should be capable of fighting its way through a blockading Union squadron, seemed appropriate. North felt that he had complied with Secretary Mallory's original instructions and his personal animosity with Bulloch was dropped as he asked the more knowledgeable Georgian what he thought of the ship's price and specifications. Bulloch, careful not to upset the volatile North, expressed his concerns that the vessel was too big, too expensive and with too deep a draught for the naval requirements the South now had. Bulloch pointed out that the vessel might be able to slug it out with Union blockaders in deep water, but it would not be able to reach the predominantly riverine ports of the Confederacy: Savannah, New Orleans and Richmond, to name but a few. North took these points well, but he would not be denied now; he had his contract and his ship was being built. He would not change course.

By 15 August 1862, North reported that Thomson yards had half-finished *No. 61*. Two days later, out in the Atlantic Ocean, near Nassau in the Bahamas, the CSS *Florida* was finally commissioned formally into the Confederate Navy under the command of Captain John N. Maffitt. A week after that, the CSS *Alabama* was commissioned under the command of Captain Rafael Semmes. Waddell, however, was still cooling his heels at the Drewry's Bluff naval battery outside Richmond, Virginia. It wouldn't be long, though, before the actions of the *Florida* and the *Alabama* became news not only in the beleaguered Confederacy, but around the world.

The CSS *Florida* had a star-crossed, though successful career as a commerce-raider. Almost immediately after being commissioned, the ship was struck by an outbreak of yellow fever. The situation became so dire that Captain Maffitt tried to run the vessel into Cuba for help, not knowing that a yellow fever epidemic was raging there as well. Maffitt's 16-year-old son, Laurens, died within 24 hours of contracting the disease. At one point, the effective crew on the raider consisted of only ten men, with Maffitt himself near death.

On 1 September 1862, the CSS *Florida* departed Havana, Cuba, with the intention of running the Union blockade into Mobile, Alabama. As Maffitt approached the outer bar, he noted the entrance to Mobile Bay was blocked by three Union cruisers. He raised an English pennant and kept his course. The Union vessels, led by the USS *Oneida* opened fire. Still the *Florida* sailed on, sustaining terrible punishment. The *Florida* was unable to return fire as she had no men for her gun batteries. Sheer speed and determination on the part of Maffitt got the vessel into Mobile. The *Florida* was missing most of her rigging, a fore topmast and fore gaff, one crewman had been killed and seven injured, but she had survived. She would lick her wounds and be re-fitted in Mobile.

Meanwhile, the *Florida* sister raider, the CSS *Alabama*, had begun her career as the most successful Confederate cruiser, in terms of total ships destroyed, on 5 September 1862, with the destruction of the *Ocmulgee* near the Azores. The *Alabama,* commanded by Rafael Semmes, continued to drift slowly north-westwards until early November, before changing course. She had, by now, destroyed 16 vessels. Her new course took her south, paralleling the eastern seaboard of America, where she destroyed another three ships. Veering south-westwards now, before turning back north to enter the Gulf of Mexico proper, Semmes captured and destroyed three more vessels by the end of 1862.

The CSS *Florida* remained in Mobile until 15 January 1863, when she ran the blockade out to Nassau again. It is possible that Maffitt knew the *Alabama* was nearby, for newspaper accounts had reported her destroying a vessel near Cuba on 7 December 1862. The crew of the *Alabama* read of the *Florida*'s successful escape from seized newspapers. For the next six months the *Florida* cruised the Atlantic, destroying 21 vessels. Maffitt transformed three vessels that he captured into commerce-raiders by transferring munitions and crewmen from the *Florida* at sea, thus copying Bulloch's tactics in fitting out the *Florida* and the *Alabama*. These vessels went on to destroy another 14 Union-flagged ships. During this same period Rafael Semmes and the *Alabama* had engaged and destroyed a Union warship off Galveston, Texas, and captured or destroyed 30 more vessels by the time Maffitt and the *Florida* began to look for a port.

With the Union's Atlantic fleet searching for Maffitt and the *Florida* (as well as the *Alabama*) and with both man and ship in need of rest and repair, the Confederate captain took his ship into Brest, France, on 23 August 1863, testing the French nation's policy of neutrality and treatment of belligerents. This presented a diplomatic quandary for the French, as the only harbour facilities at Brest were government-owned. French foreign minister Drouyn de Lhuys decided that the *Florida* was no different from any other vessel of a belligerent nation at war with another and that the ship was eligible to use the port facilities provided she adhered to the declaration of French neutrality. In other words, the *Florida* could make essential repairs, but no improvements to her war-making capability.

Maffitt, knowing that his health was broken by yellow fever and the stress of combat, requested that he be relieved of command, a request supported by his surgeon. Maffitt's request was granted on 11 September 1863, and the vessel passed into the hands of Commander Joseph N. Barney. Barney himself also had to be relieved of command due to ill-health. Meanwhile the *Florida*'s original crew had been disbanded. Union vessels also lurked around Brest monitoring the Confederate raider. On 5 January 1864, Lt. Charles Manigault Morris took the *Florida* out of Brest, escaping Union pursuit, and after obtaining new military stores off Belle Isle, made his way to the West Indies and then north to Bermuda.

While the *Florida* was undergoing this command turmoil and attempts at re-crewing and refitting, the *Alabama* destroyed another seven ships, but was finding the hunting harder going as Union ship owners 're-flagged' their vessels, avoided sailing in areas the raider might be, or simply avoided sailing altogether.

Rafael Semmes wrote on just this subject to Secretary Mallory on 22 December 1863 – from Singapore! He had pursued the hated Yankees to the far side of the world and now began to turn back towards the Atlantic Ocean. The *Alabama* was at the height of its meteoric cruise.

On 10 July 1864, the *Florida* restarted her career as Maffitt had left it, striking terror directly into the hearts of the Union by destroying ships off the coasts of Delaware and Maryland. Recognising that the Union would soon send a squadron of ships after him, Morris wisely withdrew across the Atlantic to Tenerife, before drifting back across the Atlantic to Brazil, landing at Bahia on 4 October 1864. Semmes and the *Alabama* had visited the area to take on coal in May of 1863, before heading to the Far East via the Cape of Good Hope. The Brazilian government acceded to the Confederate commander's request for belligerent status and necessary repairs, giving the *Florida* 48 hours, unless a survey by a marine engineer should find more extenuating circumstances. Meanwhile, Brazilian authorities pointed out the presence of a Union warship, the USS *Wachusett,* in the bay and told Lt. Morris that they had been warned to maintain the neutrality laws.

On the evening of 6 October, a large party of *Florida* crewmen went ashore on leave. Early on the following morning the USS *Wachusett* was spotted under way in the harbour by lookouts on the *Florida*; the Union warship appeared to be heading directly for them. Before the Confederate vessel could hail the Union ship, or the *Florida* could be got under way, the *Wachusett* had struck the *Florida*, opening fire with several batteries of guns and small arms fire. The Confederates never had a chance. The USS *Wachusett* then took the stricken Confederate vessel under tow and proceeded to drag her, in violation of numerous international laws, out of Bahia harbour, with the sleeping Brazilian Navy now becoming roused by the sound of cannon and rifle fire. But the Union warship had her steam up and a considerable lead. The Brazilians attempted to give chase in smaller vessels, but to no avail. The career of the CSS *Florida* had ended. This affair would damage relations between Brazil and the United States, the US being forced to court-martial the Union captain, Collins, for violating the territorial jurisdiction of a neutral government. He was found guilty, but US Secretary of the Navy Gideon Welles showed himself to be above the law by refusing to accept the military court's ruling, an unprecedented act in the history of the US Navy. Welles again demonstrated why Waddell despised him so.

The *Alabama* lay beneath 58 metres of water off the French port of Cherbourg on 7 October 1864. Rafael Semmes, after returning to the Atlantic Ocean in the spring of 1864, had recognised that both he and the crew needed a rest, and the *Alabama* a refit. She had destroyed a total of 64 Union-flagged vessels and one Union warship. The *Alabama* entered Cherbourg harbour on 11 June 1864. Semmes learned that Captain John Winslow and the USS *Kearsage* were at Flushing on the Cornish coast. The *Alabama*, forced to adhere to French laws of neutrality, could do little more than refuel; no fresh gunpowder or crew could be brought on board. Rafael Semmes, flamboyant to the end, informed Captain Winslow, via the US consul, that as soon as the *Alabama* was re-coaled, he would come out and fight. The chivalric era of naval warfare was in its twilight.

On the morning of 19 June 1864, the *Alabama* sailed out of Cherbourg harbour and immediately made for the *Kearsage*. At one mile distant, the *Alabama* turned hard to port and opened fire with her starboard guns. The *Kearsage* continued to come on until she was only 1,000 yards distant. Then she opened fire. The two ships began to circle each other, moving along the coast, pouring shot after shot at each other. The months of cruising told on the *Alabama*, for her gunpowder, not being fresh, made her shot less effective. The *Kearsage* had also draped her sides with iron chains to lessen the effect of cannon shot.

Semmes tried to make for the French coast, but the *Alabama* was sinking faster than her sails could carry her forward. Realising that she was mortally wounded, Semmes struck her famous 'Stainless Banner' and gave orders to abandon ship. He had been wounded during the conflict, but was helped over the side by his redoubtable executive officer, John McIntosh Kell. The *Alabama* had lost nine men in combat, 20 men by drowning and 20 more wounded. Some were picked up by the USS *Kearsage*, some by French fishing boats. Semmes and McIntosh Kell escaped Union capture by being rescued by the English yacht *Deerhound*; they were in Southampton by evening.

The sinking of the *Alabama* was a cause for celebration all over the North, and for near-mourning in the South. The exploits of the Confederate cruiser-raiders were a source of constant morale-boosting in light of the reverses suffered in land battles. Both of Bulloch's prized commerce-raiders had been captured or destroyed within the space of four months. The plight of the Confederacy's blue-water naval policy was now dire.

With orders to join one of the new ironclads, Waddell had left Charleston on 19 March 1863, aboard the blockade-runner *General Beauregard,* bound for Bermuda. Having arrived there a

few days later, Waddell remained in Bermuda for a month before
taking a British packet ship to Halifax, Nova Scotia, where he
landed around the middle of April 1862. Being in Canada, which
like Great Britain regarded all Confederates as lawful
belligerents, he was able to telegraph his wife in Annapolis,
Maryland, with the news that he had passed through the
blockade, and then to Halifax, in safety. The telegraphed reply
he got from his wife Anne broke his heart. Their beloved
daughter, Annie, had ended her journey through life on 16
February 1863, having died from scarlet fever and diphtheria.
James Waddell telegraphed back to his wife, asking her to
come to Canada, and then to Europe with him. Anne crossed
the border from the United States, probably reaching James
sometime in late April. Their joy in being back together
again would have been tempered by sadness over their
daughter's death, and the fact that they would be moving on yet
again. They quickly booked passage on the first steamship to
England.

While the Waddells were en route to England, the CSS *Florida*
and the CSS *Alabama* were coming to the ends of their commerce-
raiding careers. But strangely, in one last ironic twist of fate, a
conflict on the farthest edge of the world's oceans would give the
Confederacy its last and most epic commerce-raider, as well as
Waddell's opportunity to gain his everlasting revenge against
Gideon Welles. And again, not only were Glasgow's Clyde
shipbuilders involved, but one of the foremost naval architects of
the era as well.

In 1863, the British Empire was facing an uprising from the
Maori people in New Zealand. The Waikato war found the British
Army fully stretched with the need to transport troops rapidly

from Britain. Robertsons & Company, a London financier ever keen to cash in where a possible military contract or lease might be concerned, decided to convert a ship that had been originally built to transport tea. This was no ordinary 'tea ship', however. The famous naval architect William Rennie had been commissioned to construct a vessel that could get the first of the season's tea to London faster than any vessel afloat. The ship he created would exceed everyone's wildest dreams in her performance. In her sea trials along the southwest coast of Scotland, the *Sea King* demonstrated stunning speed, displaying a course average of slightly more than 11 knots over the set course, and climbing to a speed of more than 12 knots at one instance during the test.

The *Sea King* dazzled even the most jaded seaman after the results of her first voyage were reported: Britain to Auckland in 74 days. The *Sea King* then turned north to make a run to Shanghai in only 23 days. After placing a cargo of Chinese tea aboard, she proceeded to make for her home port of Deal in Kent, stopping only twice along the way, for a total of five days, to take on coal. She danced her way over the waves to England in 79 days. If there were any doubters as to who built the finest and fastest ships in the world, there were none now, for this new 'Queen of the Seas' had put on a show of Clyde-built quality. But, what had William Rennie done in the design of the *Sea King* that made her that much faster and better than any previous tea ship? In a nutshell, everything.

Rennie's design for the *Sea King* was nothing less than a floating revolution in ship technology. First of all, starting from the bottom up, was the hull. The *Sea King*'s hull was built using an iron frame with rock elm planks for the area beneath the waterline, and six-inch teakwood for the area above the waterline. The use of iron frames meant that more room could be made within the ship's holds for cargo, as well as rendering a lighter overall weight for the hull. A further benefit, harking back to the principles behind the Viking longship, was that the increased hull strength was balanced by greater hull flexibility, thus allowing the vessel to cut through the water at a higher speed.

A second design innovation was the use of Cunningham's patent self-reefing topsails, which meant that sails could be reefed, furled, or taken in without having to send men high into the masts – dangerous on any clear sailing day, potentially deadly on a storm-tossed night. The sails could be operated by as few as three men using a mechanism operated from the deck.

While the *Sea King* was not the first 'auxiliary steamer', that is to say a fully-rigged sailing ship with a steam engine to propel it when the wind was not sufficient, she did incorporate a third innovation on this design idea: a propeller that could be lifted out of the water (termed 'tricing up' in Waddell's day) into a propeller well, or hold, beneath the wheelhouse. This effectively reduced the *Sea King*'s hydro-dynamic drag through the water when she was operating at her highest speed under sail. In complementary fashion, her steam engine's funnel also telescoped downward into itself in order to reduce aerodynamic drag, thus again helping to raise the vessel's speed.

The fourth design innovation that has been overlooked by many who have written about the *Sea King*, in her career as the css *Shenandoah*, was her truly unique maritime first: an on-board water distillation plant capable of producing 500 imperial gallons of water a day. Today's vessels take this capability for granted, but, in 1863, providing fresh water for the crew's consumption and cleaning was still extraordinarily difficult on virtually every ship in the world. The *Sea King*, with her high speed, large holds for large amounts of coal, and the ability to manufacture that most crucial of all resources, water, was a nearly autonomous ship.

The overall dimensions of the *Sea King* made her an elegant sight to behold. She was 220 feet long, with a beam of 36 feet at the widest point. Her maximum depth was 20 feet. On her deck she had a forward deck house, with large windows, for the crew. This also contained a galley. Aft she had a large wardroom, which was housed within a raised stern. The junior officer's spaces occupied the forward part of the wardroom, with the captain's cabin furthest aft. The wardroom had a tremendous skylight that provided an amazing amount of illumination for an area that was normally dark in most vessels. The captain's cabin had the pilot house directly above, meaning the vessel could be steered in all weathers. All this innovation in maritime design was carried in a vessel that weighed only 1,025 tons.

The incredible performance of the *Sea King* was soon common gossip amongst seafarers throughout the world. With the demise of both the CSS *Florida* and *Alabama* in mid 1864, James Dunwoody Bulloch was the recipient of several telegraphs from Confederate Secretary of the Navy Mallory: how soon could he put another commerce-raider into action? Bulloch could not see what value another Confederate commerce-raider could supply to the South's war effort at that moment; he may have been wearied by long hours and few funds, but he was a pragmatic man and knew the intelligence of the South's losses. However, he could see the morale value of flying the stars and bars on the oceans of the world. Fortunately for James Dunwoody Bulloch, out of one catastrophe for the Confederacy came the immediate solution to his current problem – how to find and finance the commerce-cruiser Secretary Mallory so desperately wanted.

As alluded to earlier, upon Bulloch's return from the Confederacy in March 1862, he too, like Commander North, had entered into contracts to build ironclads, though Bulloch's were constructed by Laird's. To make a long story short, both North's and Bulloch's ironclad projects came to naught due to the British government clamping down on the Foreign Enlistment Act. North's *No. 61* would be seized under Scottish law for the government and then sold to the Danish Navy. Bulloch managed, through complex legal and financial wrangling, to get the vessels transferred to French ownership, with Crown prosecutors dogging every step. He then had them sold, with the proceeds from the sale reverting to him. It was the proceeds from the sale of the ill-fated Laird ironclad 'rams' that paid for the purchase of the *Sea King*.

Coincidentally, Bulloch already knew about the *Sea King* before Mallory began to press him on the issue of obtaining a replacement for the *Alabama*. In the autumn of 1863, Bulloch was on the River Clyde inspecting the *Coquette*, a vessel he was intent on acquiring for a special mission. While there, he saw the *Sea King* before her epic first voyage out to the Far East. Thinking her an exceptionally fine-looking vessel, he marked her in his memory. When Mallory ordered Bulloch to obtain a new commerce-raider, Bulloch knew he didn't have time to build one from scratch, and in any event, the rigid enforcement of the Foreign Enlistment Act precluded it. He would buy a vessel that was currently afloat with characteristics closest to those that he would have designed into a purpose-built ship. Today's US

Navy, for example, would recognise this as the COTS, or 'Commercial off the Shelf' principle; it commonly specifies it in contracts, thus reducing cost. Bulloch, again, did it first.

By the first week of September 1864, the *Sea King*, the finest example yet of the work of Glasgow's Clyde shipbuilders, belonged to the Confederate States of America Navy, via the covert ownership of James Dunwoody Bulloch. The agent of destruction for the Union's merchant marine was Bulloch, and he had procured a new instrument of war that would be placed into the hands of a man who hated the Union, its navy and its money-worshipping merchants, Lt. James Iredell Waddell CSN. But where was Waddell?

4

What adventures shall we meet in her?

James and Anne Waddell had arrived in Liverpool in May of 1863, after a voyage from Halifax, Nova Scotia. They, along with other Confederate naval officers and other officials, had travelled as clandestinely as possible, but it is probable that the intelligence apparatus of the Union had tracked them and alerted the US consul in Liverpool, Thomas Dudley. Even if Union intelligence officials in North America had not alerted Dudley, the increasing furore over the 'Laird rams', the two ironclad warships being constructed covertly for Bulloch by Laird & Son in the nearby Birkenhead shipyards, would have made his local network of agents hyper-sensitive to the arrival of any new persons with Southern accents in the Liverpool area.

The Waddells' initial introduction to Liverpool was quick and quiet, as Bulloch believed in operational security, or, in the words of the modern saying, 'Loose lips sink ships!'. Bulloch had dispersed the incoming officers and ratings involved in his covert missions, along with any wives and children, throughout Liverpool and the surrounding villages, such as Waterloo and

Southport. This was his practice throughout his period of operations from Liverpool.

In May 1863, the fate of the Laird rams still hung in the balance as the British Government prevaricated over whether to seize the vessels, clearly at the instigation of the Union government of America. Bulloch, nervous over the large number of Confederate officers and ratings about Liverpool (particularly the new arrivals), dispatched Waddell and the others to Paris, where they would join the small Confederate naval enclave that centred on Commodore Barron CSN, the senior-ranking Confederate naval officer in Europe.

Following Bulloch's instructions, James and Anne Waddell left their lodgings in Liverpool for Paris not long after their May arrival. After consulting with Commodore Barron, and observing that the rest of the Confederate officers in Paris not attached to the Commodore's staff were essentially awaiting orders on meagre funds, the Waddells decided to embark on a mini-tour of Europe. For the next two months, they travelled throughout Europe, visiting France, Switzerland, Germany, Belgium, Scotland and Ireland. The Waddells returned to Liverpool from Ireland in mid July, but the Laird rams were still not finished and their building still in question, with the British government still undecided on their fate. For some reason, Anne Waddell now decided to return home to Annapolis, Maryland, and departed in August 1863. Maryland having not seceded from the Union, Anne was able to travel directly to America, most likely landing in New York, before proceeding southwards. Assuming it took several weeks to cross the Atlantic Ocean, plus the time involved in travelling to Annapolis, Anne Waddell may have been home for only a short time before a message arrived from James. The telegram, or message, from James, asked Anne to come back to Europe!

The British government had finally capitulated to the incessant demands of the Union government for the seizure of the Laird rams. On 8 September 1863, orders were issued from Lord Russell, the British Foreign Secretary, that Bulloch's precious ironclad rams must be seized from the Laird & Son shipyards. The South's dreams of a squadron of blue-water ironclads that would sweep the Union fleet away were being dashed.

Anne Waddell retraced her journey and arrived back in England. The Waddells, re-united once again, settled in for a long wait for events to unfold and for orders to be issued. They lived in Calais and Liverpool, but mostly Paris, near Commodore Barron's headquarters, keeping a low profile and associating with fellow Confederate expatriates. Life was tinged with the knowledge that at any moment orders could be received sending James off on a cruise that could end like the *Alabama*'s mission, while Anne would know nothing until after the fact.

Up until the middle of 1864, Waddell waited in frustration for orders, as news from North America of the Confederacy's declining military situation was reported by correspondents to both British and French newspapers. News usually arrived only two weeks after the fact, since mail packet boats from Halifax, Nova Scotia and Bermuda could make the transit readily, barring bad weather. In July 1864, one of the private owners of a blockade-runner in Liverpool offered James the command of one of his vessels and £1,000 sterling (£15,000 in today's money) per trip if he would take the position. Waddell first asked Commodore Barron for permission to take on the mission, who approved. But, after Waddell 'sleeping on the issue'

(Waddell's own words) and Anne pleas not to take the job,
Waddell turned it down.

Back in Paris in mid September 1864, Waddell was ruminating
to fellow officers that peace might not be too far in the future.
He would have had a much better idea of what was going on in
America, of course, because Anne had been back and forth
across the Atlantic with not only news, but personal insight into
the effects on the population; Maryland, while ostensibly pro-
Union, was largely Confederate in its sympathies. Again, the
death of his daughter Annie, and the seemingly hopeless prospect
of gaining a combat command, must have weighed heavily upon
Waddell's mind and morale, making him wonder if the conflict
was worth it, both personally and for the South. However, less
than a month later, the lines of history that been slowly and
inexorably winding towards an intersection in Waddell's life
were about to meet.

Bulloch received his official paper orders from Sec. Mallory of
the Confederate Navy on 30 August 1864, ordering him to
replace the *Alabama* with a new commerce-raider, by any means
necessary. Bulloch, of course, already had the *Sea King* under the
process of inspection and purchase, and before Mallory's orders
had time to yellow, the *Sea King* was in Bulloch's hands. By 5
September, Commodore Barron in Paris had held a confidential
conference with Waddell, appointing him to the rank of Lt.
Commanding and ordering him to report by 10 September to
Liverpool to take command of the *Sea King*. Waddell was
already in motion, for he was in Liverpool on 12 September.
Commodore Barron's written version of Waddell's orders (dated
only just before the *Sea King*'s departure) deserves a review here,
for its carefully worded content demonstrates the level and

nature of discussions that had already taken place about the projected cruise of the new commerce-raider.

Paris, France, 5 October 1864
No. 30 Rue Druot

Sir:

When the vessel under your command is ready for sea, you will sail on a cruise in a region of ocean already indicated to you in our personal interviews. The charts, which have already been sent you, are the best sailing directions which you can have.

Your position is an important one, not only with reference to the immediate results to the enemy's property, but from the fact that neutral rights may frequently arise under it; reliance, however, is placed in your judgement and discretion, for meeting and promptly discussing such questions.

It is now quite the custom of Federal *[i.e., Union]* owners of ships and cargoes to place them under British protection *[i.e., ownership]*, and this may at times cause you embarrassment. The strictest regard for the rights of neutrals cannot be too sedulously observed; nor should any opportunity be lost in cultivating friendly relations with their naval and merchant services, and of placing the true character of the conquest in which we are engaged, in its proper light. You will not hesitate to assume responsibility when the interest of your country may demand it, and should your judgement ever hesitate in seeking the solution of any difficulty, it may be added by the reflection that you are to do the enemy's property the greatest injury in the shortest time. Authority is vested in you to make acting appointments to fill any vacancies which may occur.

The maintenance of strict naval discipline will be essential to your success, and you will enjoin this upon your officers and endorse its rigid observance, always tempering justice with humane and kind treatment.

I am, Sir, very respectfully your obedient servant,

S. Barron

Flag Officer (Confederate States Navy)

(to:) Lt. Commanding James I. Waddell (Confederate States Navy)

This concise set of orders is the result of the original discussions held by Commanders John Mercer Brooke and Robert 'Bob' Carter with Secretary of the Navy Stephen Mallory. Both Brooke and Carter had served in the US Navy and, in particular, participated in a scientific expedition to the North Pacific and its whaling areas between 1853 and 1856. The commanders pointed out to Mallory the enormous size of the New England whaling fleet and that an assault on it would have a tremendous effect on the economy of the region, which had been the most ardent in its abolitionist and anti-Southern stance, while also sowing discord in the political arena at the national level. The economic destruction of the area regarded as the 'school of the seamen' by all US mariners would render a strong blow to the Union. Mallory liked the idea and instructed Commander Bob Carter to gather more information, and sent him across the Atlantic to Bulloch in Liverpool during September of 1864. Carter brought with him a cornucopia of intelligence and all the available charts for the whaling areas of the North Pacific that could be found – he also brought copies of Matthew Fontaine Maury's oceans and currents charts as well. Since Maury was himself a Confederate Naval officer, it is hard to imagine that he would not have been consulted on the operation.

Waddell was to have one of the most impressive intelligence collections assembled by either the Union or Confederate navies in support of any operation during the Civil War. With the additional help of a detailed briefing from Bulloch, Waddell, as he noted in his memoirs, had 'little else to do but follow the instructions given me'. Bulloch's detailed 'instructions' ran to hundreds of words.

As Bulloch quietly and efficiently directed the supply operations that would get the *Sea King* away on her mission, Waddell and his core of young officers, arriving from all parts of France, tried to make themselves as inconspicuous as possible. US Consul Dudley and his intelligence agents knew that something was afoot, but could as yet pin nothing on the wily Bulloch. In fact, several of the young officers, among them Midshipmen Browne and Mason, visited Bulloch at his office at 10 Rumford Place in Liverpool on 3 October 1864, where after promising them funds for uniforms and other personal supplies, he told them to avoid his office in future and to 'live as quietly as possible'.

Bulloch had already tried to throw Dudley and the rest of the Union intelligence operation off the scent by telling the men who languished about Liverpool awaiting orders for other ships to spread the word that they were 'going home', which in actuality, most would. Bulloch knew this was a last throw of the dice, and that for the lower-ranking men this would be their best opportunity for getting home before the war ended. He probably also knew that some of them, himself included, would never return to America.

Waddell meanwhile busied himself with making contact with his executive officer, Lt. William C. Whittle, and the other junior officers who would be crewing the *Sea King*. Bulloch evidently entrusted some funds to Waddell for dispersion to his men, for on 4 October 1864, the day following Browne's and Mason's visit to Bulloch, their new commanding officer visited them in their lodgings with the funds promised by Bulloch. Waddell and his executive officer, Whittle, told all the men they contacted to have their baggage ready to go by the week's end and that it would all be packed in wooden crates so that it could be loaded as cargo, thus ensuring secrecy.

Insofar as the enlisted men went, Bulloch and Waddell had talked to the surviving crew members of the *Alabama,* many of whom were still living around Liverpool, to see if anyone would sign on to the new commerce-raiding mission. They were able to find a little more than a dozen, but hoped that these men would help recruit more seamen – once they were under way, that is. The British Foreign Enlistment Act clearly prescribed the recruitment of British subjects on British soil. What Bulloch and Waddell were counting on were the persuasive arguments of the former crewmen of the *Alabama*. Just as with the *Alabama*, Bulloch was planning on the *Sea King* rendezvousing at sea with her crew and supplies, then completing her transformation from a ship of commerce to a commerce-raider. Since the unknowing members of the support vessel and those aboard the *Sea King* would not be on British soil, Waddell and his fellow Confederates could openly attempt to recruit a full complement for the vessel. Between the crews of both the *Sea King* and its support vessel it was thought that there would be no problem in gaining enough crewmen.

On the same day that Waddell was visiting his officers for the *Sea King,* on 4 October 1864, Bulloch was purchasing his support vessel, the *Laurel,* which would supply weapons and (hopefully) men to the *Sea King* for her conversion into a commerce-raider. Bulloch had already decided on a rendezvous point for the *Sea King* and *Laurel*: the Bay of Funchal off the coast of Madeira. Controlled by the Portuguese and lying not too far distant from the northwest shores of Africa, the island and its bay had been used by Bulloch for the *Fingal* and *Alabama* missions. It was a location that Waddell was familiar with as well, since he had visited the islands during his days aboard the USS *Germantown.*

Commodore Barron made a wise choice in selecting Waddell because he recognised that he had 20 years of experience with the US Navy in every ocean where the *Sea King* would have to operate, he was careful, and, most importantly, had a strong legal background, not only because of his family's tradition in law practice, but on account of his own studies. During Waddell's time aboard the *Germantown,* and later the fitting out of the *Saginaw,* he had spent every available extra hour reading law books. And it was this last fact that would help make the *Sea King* mission a success, and ultimately save his own life and the lives of his crew.

After purchasing the *Sea King* with the assistance of Richard Wright, Bulloch, knowing full well that both US Consul Thomas Dudley in Liverpool and US Minister Charles Adams in London were just steps behind his every move, had the ship moved about on short cargo runs. The Union intelligence net tried to figure out from where the *Sea King* would make her dash to sea. Bulloch audaciously had the *Sea King* put in at London, anchoring her beneath the very seat of British power, ostensibly taking on coal and cargo for a run to Bombay, India. In reality, she would be taking on the *Sea King*'s future Executive Officer, W.C. Whittle, who'd made a quick train trip south from Liverpool, along with Peter Corbett, the ship's master, to ensure that she made her journey out to the rendezvous with the *Laurel* off Madeira.

Meanwhile, the *Laurel* had been moved to a dock in Liverpool for loading with cannon, munitions, clothing, food and all the other supplies necessary for a cruise. Bulloch's cover plan for the *Laurel* was as masterful as the one he had constructed for the *Alabama*. He put it about that the *Laurel* was making a cruise to Havana, Cuba, via Matamoros, Mexico, and told the ship's agent, Henry Lafone, to sell tickets, which had already been 'pre-sold' to the Confederate officers and ratings, while pre-packing all the necessary materials and supplies into shipping crates (thus ensuring the ship could be balanced and weighted for transit, and to satisfy Her Majesty's Customs). Bulloch's ploy went so far as to issue actual tickets that would be given to the men. By 5 October 1864, both the *Sea King* and the *Laurel* were ready. All Bulloch needed was a telegram from London saying that the *Sea King* had sailed for the *Laurel* to be sent on her way, thus putting the operation into action.

On 7 October, Lt. William Whittle, operating under the *nom de guerre* of 'Mr Brown', met Richard Wright, the shipping agent responsible for the purchase of the *Sea King*, at Wood's Hotel in High Holborn, London. At precisely 11 a.m., Wright wandered into the hotel's dining room where he spotted 'Mr Brown' wearing, as arranged, a dining napkin tucked into his coat's buttonhole. Wright approached and asked, 'Is this Mr

Brown?' to which 'Mr Brown' responded, 'Yes'. They then left for Whittle's room, where Whittle produced a letter that showed his real name and rank in the Confederate Navy, and which also showed that he would be the Executive Officer of the ship. Wright and Whittle discussed particulars, then they left the hotel to meet Peter Corbett, Master of the *Sea King*, at a pub near where the vessel was docked. It was decided that Wright would board the ship immediately after the meeting, then disembark at the port of Deal on the English Channel. Whittle would slip aboard the vessel early in the morning, where he would respond to any challenge as 'George Brown', while Peter Corbett would ensure that the crew of the *Sea King* knew he was a passenger. With the last details tidied up, the men departed each other's company.

At 3 a.m. on 7 October 1864, Lt. Whittle checked out of his hotel and took a circuitous route through the streets of London to the River Thames. Looking over his shoulder and all around him, approximately an hour later he slipped over the rails of the *Sea King*. After less than an hour she slipped her mooring lines and began to drift with the tide and the current down the Thames. The greatest adventure of Waddell's life was about to begin.

In Liverpool, the early morning sun was beginning to break on the doorstep of James Dunwoody Bulloch's house when a telegram arrived alerting him that the *Sea King* had sailed. Bulloch immediately sent word to Master John F. Ramsay (actually an officer in Britain's Royal Navy Reserve) to prepare the *Laurel* for immediate sailing. Word was also sent at the same time to Waddell and the other officers and ratings to gather at Prince Albert Dock in Liverpool for transport to the *Laurel*.

At daybreak on Sunday, 9 October, the *Laurel* lifted anchor after clearing her papers for Matamoros via Havana.* She would never reach Matamoros, but she would deliver Waddell and his fellow Confederates to their destination, the *Sea King*. Waddell commented tersely in his memoirs: 'We left Liverpool in search of the cruiser in the Confederate supply vessel *Laurel*, on the morning of 9 October, 1864, for Funchal, Island of Madeira.'

Bulloch had carefully and quietly put his plan into action, and it remained to be seen how the Union would respond. He realised the Union intelligence agents were aware that something was afoot, but was unsure how much they knew. In all likelihood, if Bulloch had known the extent of the Union's intelligence about the *Sea King* mission, he might have cancelled it altogether. But strangely, the Union never got exactly the right information; the near mythical luck of James D. Bulloch covered him and his projects like a London fog.

Amazingly, as early as 11 April 1864, a letter to US Secretary of the Navy Gideon Welles in Washington, DC, from Captain Napoleon Collins of the USS *Wachusett*, then cruising in the Pacific, reported that the *Sea King* was going to be converted into a Confederate commerce-raider with her mission being to destroy the US Pacific whaling fleet. The information was collected from an English merchant located in Hobart, Van Diemen's Land (Tasmania), by the master of an American whaling ship. Besides the fact that the US Navy had been made

---

* Bulloch notes in his memoirs that he put out disinformation that the voyage was to Havana. Other sources, such as Whittle, noted the 'embellished' story that she would continue on to Mexico. Her secret orders were to return to Mexico.

aware of plans for the *Sea King* months before the actual event, it also shines an interesting light on the original reason for the ship's construction.

As previously noted, the *Sea King* was ostensibly built to be a fast cargo ship capable of getting the first season's tea to market in Britain, with a possible side use as a troop carrier for British troops bound for the Maori Wars in New Zealand. Yet the original request for the ship's construction came from a Mr Robertson of London. Bulloch's close business associate and assistant was Moses P. Robertson. Furthermore, the fact that this intelligence about the *Sea King*'s possible transformation into a Confederate cruiser popped to the surface in the same area of the world as the fast cargo ship's first voyage, and just after her departure from that region, seems more than coincidental. However, definitive proof of Confederate actions was hard to obtain, particularly as Bulloch played an astute legal game by sailing through loopholes in the British Foreign Enlistment Act. Bulloch made this possible by making sure that no one aboard the *Sea King* knew her true purpose. If the Union were to stop the *Sea King* before her rendezvous, only Master Peter Corbett and 'Mr George Brown' (Whittle) would know her destination and intended use – and they could dispose of what little incriminating paperwork they had quickly.

As it happened, on the morning of the *Sea King*'s escape down the Thames, the Union cruiser USS *Niagara* was patrolling off the mouth of the estuary, alerted to her possible sailing. But the *Niagara*'s lookout spotted a Spanish vessel, the *Cicerone*, and mistaking her for the description provided of the potential Confederate raider, raised the alarm. The *Niagara* gave chase for several hours, but the vessel slipped in and out of British national waters. Finally, she sailed out into open waters where the *Niagara* stopped her. For three days the Union vessel's crew tore apart the Spanish vessel, while the *Sea King* made good her escape. The Union Navy also had the USS *Sacramento* stationed in the English Channel on the lookout for the *Sea King*. She too failed to spot the *Sea King*. The legend of the raider had begun already, and before firing one cannon, or even raising her true colours as a Confederate ship of war.

The equally essential component of Bulloch's mission and Waddell's grand naval exploit, the *Laurel*, was in far greater jeopardy if she were stopped by Union ships. Loaded to the gunwales with war materiel and Confederates, the game would have ended immediately. And the Union had been alerted to her activities as well, though again too late. Once the *Sea King* had set free its first pardoned crew from a seized vessel, and they had reported to US authorities the identity of the commander of the Confederate raider, Welles would have known who Waddell was, for they had a history. Welles would have been catatonic with rage, while Waddell would have a grim satisfaction in finally beginning his very personal war of revenge. All this was to come; for at the moment, the *Sea King* and the *Laurel* sailed towards the Madeira Islands as Union warships helplessly flailed about the Atlantic in search of the Confederate 'ghost ships'.

On 14 October 1864, the *Laurel* sailed into Funchal, located on the south side of Madeira. Captain Ramsay on the *Laurel* fully expected that they would arrive before the *Sea King*, since she had a further distance to sail, so following Bulloch's orders he forbade his crew and the Confederates to go ashore in order to preserve secrecy about their mission. Waddell and his men had to wait it out aboard the *Laurel*, fretting that Portuguese officials would get suspicious about the ship, since most vessels immediately set liberty, or port call for their crew and passengers.

While Waddell gazed at the white-washed limestone buildings ashore, Captain Ramsay bent to his purpose and got the *Laurel* resupplied with coal almost the instant after she dropped anchor. When this operation was finished, and the coal boat pulled away, all fell quiet around the *Laurel*. After a couple more days of seeing the ship sitting in their harbour, with no apparent signs of leaving or bringing crew ashore, the Portuguese customs became suspicious and asked Ramsay why he did not leave. Prepared for anything, the wily Ramsay produced a couple of large broken gears and cogs for the official, saying he needed repairs. The Portuguese official suspected something was up, but appeared to have the attitude that he would get this strange ship away by any means, and took the broken machinery from Ramsay. He said he would get it repaired at the government repair shop, ensuring Captain Ramsay would have no excuse for not sailing. As the customs official drew away in his boat, Ramsay, Waddell and Whittle knew they had bought themselves a few more days; what they didn't know was that the US consul had already been at the Portuguese authorities to seize the ship.

The crow's nest of the *Laurel* was manned 24 hours a day, seeking signs of the *Sea King*. Late on the night of 17 October 1864, the lookout sighted a large, dark ship with only signal lights lit, slowly cruising outside the port of Funchal. The crew of the *Laurel* rushed onto the deck to see what they could make of the darkened ship sailing under the bright moonlight. Before any details could be ascertained, the dark ship pointed her bow south and steamed away. Minutes later she reappeared, steaming up from the same direction, then again turning and disappearing south for the remainder of the night. Some of the men whispered just beneath their breath, 'That's her!'. Waddell's and his men's nerves were taut with both excitement and anxiety for the risk of being discovered was at its greatest now.

At sunrise on the following day, the dark ship once again showed itself off the mouth of Funchal's port and gave the proper signal for Captain Ramsay to get under way and follow. The crew and passengers aboard the *Laurel* now knew this was the *Sea King*. Ramsay roused the crew to get steam up and be ready to raise anchor, while he signalled to the customs officials to bring out his ship's papers. Ironically, the customs officials who had been so interested in the *Laurel* before were now busy with other matters and could not make their way out to the *Laurel* until 9 a.m. The *Laurel* was cleared to leave port. As the *Sea King* hove into view once again, Portuguese fishermen, trying to hawk their fish to the crew of the *Laurel*, spotted the *Sea King* and began to shout, 'Otro *Alabama!*'. They knew that the *Alabama* had begun her famous career as a raider in the Azores, and now the Madeira archipelago would be the birth-place of yet another Confederate predator.

Once the *Laurel* had cleared away from Funchal and caught the *Sea King*, Waddell asked Ramsay if he would signal the *Sea King* to fall in behind the *Laurel* in order to lead her to the spot where the transfer of weapons, supplies and men would take place. Proceeding to a series of small islets known to sailors of the day as the 'Las Desertas', Waddell and Ramsay cruised for three hours along the shoreline of Deserta Grande before finding a suitable spot. Dropping anchor in a cove beneath a high cliff, the ships had 18 fathoms of water beneath their keels. Waddell then requested Ramsay to tie the *Laurel* to Corbett's *Sea King* in preparation for the transfer of supplies. As the two ships came together, Whittle slid across the rail of the *Sea King* onto the deck of the *Laurel*, seeking to give a quiet report to Waddell on the events that had transpired during the voyage out of London.

A frenzied effort soon broke out on both ships as all hands began the process of extracting the war materiel and other supplies from the *Laurel* and transferring them to the deck of the *Sea King*. Working non-stop for some 36 hours, the crews laboured to get the *Laurel* emptied of her incriminating cargo, for both ships were liable to discovery by any vessel wandering off course. As it happened, local Madeiran fishermen again found the two vessels and tried to barter or sell their goods. Waddell spotted an opportunity both to buy fresh food and to get extra labour, so he purchased all their stores and hired the fishermen to assist. Waddell also had a hidden agenda, as keeping the fishermen on board lessened the chance of them immediately gossiping about, or reporting what they had seen and heard aboard the strange vessels.

In the midst of all this, a ship's sails were spotted coming towards them. The *Laurel* dropped her ropes and sailed out to meet the suspicious vessel, which the lookouts thought might be a warship. Upon closing, Ramsay on the *Laurel* saw that she was British-flagged and turned about, re-lashing to the *Sea King,* then continuing the supply transfer. By early afternoon on 19 October 1864, the frenetic supply effort between the two vessels was complete. All that remained now was for Waddell to read his commissioning papers, and try to recruit as many seamen as possible from those aboard the *Sea King*.

Bulloch had instructed Captain Corbett on the *Sea King* to bring out as many single men as he could find who might be inclined to sail on a great adventure. Corbett had managed to find 45 men to sail out with him, thinking they were bound for Bombay, and not some God-forsaken, deserted island in the Atlantic Ocean. Now these men discovered they had been misled as to their true destination; and on top of that they were being recruited by a Confederate naval officer whom they had neither seen nor heard of before. Waddell was confronted by a grim-faced group of seamen. He needed to recruit 60 crewmen to the *Shenandoah*,* but he only managed to gain 22 recruits from both ships. The crew of the *Shenandoah* consisted of 24 officers and 22 seamen; even with the advantages of the Cunningham self-reefing sail system, they would have trouble with even the most basic of operations, such as raising anchor.

Waddell's Executive Officer, Lt. William Whittle, remembered the ignominious fate of the raider CSS *Rappahannock* when faced with the same situation. She had been brought out of Sheerness in November 1863 with only a token crew, then forced to port in Calais for repairs and a crew, and had never since sailed out of port. Whittle told Waddell: 'Call your young officers together and learn from their assurances what they can and will do.'

Holding a council of war with his own ship's staff, Waddell found that his young officers were more than ready to roll up their sleeves and work alongside the non-enlisted deck hands in order to get under way. They also pointed out that by now the US consul in Britain would have alerted both Spanish and Portuguese authorities to their probable whereabouts and that Union ships were probably racing towards the Madeira islands

---

* How and why the *Sea King* came to be known as the *Shenandoah* has never been established, though Bulloch begins to refer to her by that name in his memoirs.

at that moment, hoping to intercept them. Waddell, hesitant about embarking on the mission with such a young officer staff and an undermanned crew of deck hands, must have given thought to returning to a neutral port and abandoning the mission. But the enthusiasm of his young officer staff, and the realisation that for the first time in his naval career he would have a combat command – something he'd never achieved as US naval officer – would have over-ridden any self-doubt.

The *Laurel* and the *Shenandoah* cast off their mooring lines from each other around midday on 20 October 1864. Waddell gave the order to raise anchor shortly thereafter, but the deck crew, short-handed as they were, could not raise the anchor due to the long, heavy chain. Anchored over a spot some 18 fathoms in depth, it would take all hands; Waddell's energetic officers stripped down to working attire to lend a hand. Slowly the anchor was wound up into its well, but not before thoroughly exhausting all hands. It was 2 p.m. At 6 p.m. the *Laurel* turned about on her stern to sail away, her crew cheering the *Shenandoah*. The Confederate flag now replaced the Union Jack at the stern of the vessel, while Lt. Francis Chew, hanging over the stern rail, set about looking for a pot of black paint to cover the letters 'SEA KING' on the stern. Waddell and his young officer staff were now in full control of the Confederacy's last commerce-raider.

The young officers, who effectively held the same rank as Waddell and formed the core of his ship's staff, were a mixed-bag in terms of experience and age. Whittle's diary of the *Shenandoah*'s cruise around the world has recently been published, and one enigmatic passage in his manuscript would prove significant during the voyage. Whittle notes that before

leaving Liverpool, Anne Waddell had asked for a quiet word
with him. She begged Whittle not to get involved in any
arguments with her husband, as it affected him so, and made
Whittle promise he would not. His promise would be sorely
tested during the cruise.

So, as the *Shenandoah* moved off from her anchorage to the
southwest, Waddell surveyed a scene of chaos upon his upper
decks, with cannon, shot, coal, rope and every form of naval
supply scattered about and in need of stowing. Waddell noted,
'The deck was to be cleared of the stores thereon before the
battery could be mounted on the carriages, and gun ports were
to be cut, fighting bolts driven, and gun tackles prepared before
the guns could be used.' He concluded wryly that they could not,
at the moment, even defend themselves if spotted by a Union
cruiser.

For the next two days, all hands stowed gear and coal while
attempting to help the lone ship's carpenter rig up the ship's gun
batteries. Waddell was faced with several technical problems, the
first being that the *Shenandoah* was constructed to withstand the
stresses of cannons being fired from her deck, so the normal
manner of attaching the gun carriage recoil tackle would have to
be re-engineered. On top of that, the proper blocks and tackles
had not been shipped on the *Laurel*, so even if the cannons were
mounted, there was no tackle. Secondly, the storage of the
gunpowder was an issue; there was no secure, fireproof
storeroom as yet. For the time being, the powder was stored
directly beneath and alongside Waddell's cabin, in the lowest
part of the ship; the hope was that this would put it closer to the
waterline and lessen the chance of a lucky shot from an
adversary blowing the stern of the vessel off in a gun battle.

Waddell chuckled at the thought of his 'warm companion'.

By 23 October 1864, the *Shenandoah*'s crew had finally got her shipshape. Exhausted from their efforts – due to their lack of manpower – Waddell was faced with a dilemma. Bulloch had told him to wait a month before commencing operations in order to give Captain Corbett time to return to Britain to register the change in ownership of the *Sea King*. However, Waddell desperately needed more seamen, and the sooner he began to stop and search vessels, the sooner he was likely to recruit more sailors.

Just before 1 p.m. on the 23rd, the lookout on the *Shenandoah* spotted a sail on the horizon. Waddell gave orders for steam to be got up and to give chase after the vessel. By 4 p.m. the vessel had stopped and a boarding party led by the *Shenandoah*'s master, Irvine Bulloch, who was James D. Bulloch's half-brother, swung aboard the *Mogul*. Waddell and Whittle were suspicious that the vessel might be 'false-flagged', as her sail rigging and construction showed a clear Yankee heritage. Bulloch found her papers to be in order and that she had a legitimate registration with a London company, the *Mogul* being one of many Union merchant ships that had their ownership switched to British companies, or even sold outright. The *Alabama* and *Florida* had created more damage through fear, than any actual destruction. During the Civil War, more than three-quarters of a million tons of American shipping was transferred to foreign ownership, while the Confederate raiders would only destroy just over one hundred thousand tons.

Temporarily frustrated, Waddell released the *Mogul* to go on its way, while he set the course of the *Shenandoah* further west, hoping to spot vessels moving through an area where the normal transit routes of merchant ships intersected with the major ocean currents of the South Atlantic. Armed with copies of Matthew Fontaine Maury's oceanographic charts, and with his own experience of sailing in that region of the world, Waddell had a better chance than most at this game.

The next opportunity for the *Shenandoah*'s first capture came on 28 October. Just after midday the lookout shouted down that he could make out a sail in the distance. Setting a course that he hoped would allow the *Shenandoah* to intercept the vessel by twilight, Waddell ordered out all the sail possible. Fortunately the cutting-edge Cunningham self-reefing sails proved their worth again, for without them it is doubtful that the *Shenandoah*'s short-handed crew could have managed such a task. All through the day, and then into the night, the *Shenandoah* raced after her prey, still seeming never to get closer. At dawn on 29 October, the vessel appeared to be increasing the distance from the *Shenandoah*. Ship's Master Bulloch ordered the steam engines brought up to close the gap. Just before 3 p.m., the *Shenandoah* caught the fleeing ship, firing a blank cartridge and raising the Confederate national flag, known as the 'Stainless Banner', from her flagstaff.

The excited boarding party, again led by Master Bulloch, consisted of six men as well as Master's Mate Cornelius Hunt (who would write the first book about the *Shenandoah*'s cruise) and Midshipman John Mason. What Bulloch found was Waddell's ideal 'capture'. She was the *Alina*, whose homeport was Searspoint, Maine, and she was on a cargo run bound to Argentina from Wales, loaded with railroad iron. Her captain, Everett Staples, was the stereotypical Yankee sailor, stern and wily. Hustled aboard the *Shenandoah*, Staples' cargo manifest and ship's papers indicated that the railroad iron belonged to a British firm, who, so Staples said, were constructing a rail line in an unspecified South American country. Waddell studied the papers intensively, knowing that he needed a legal reason to declare the *Alina* as a legal prize, for he could then strip her of the gear the *Shenandoah* still needed, such as block, tackle and rope, but also food and fuel. His legal knowledge now aided his cause; Waddell cleverly noted that the papers had not been notarised. His officers agreed with his judgement and the *Alina* became the first prize of the *Shenandoah*.

The *Alina* was practically a new ship, and contained nearly everything that the crew of the *Shenandoah* might need to complete the fitting out of their cruiser. When the *Shenandoah* had been received by the Confederates from Captain Corbett, one of the first things they complained about was the sparseness of the accommodations. There was no furniture to speak of, no beds or hammocks, not even washbasins. The *Alina* was a virtual floating supply store for the *Shenandoah*. The *Alina*'s furniture, crockery, cabin doors, sails, ropes, blocks, tackles, and of course, food, were all removed to the *Shenandoah*. Once this was completed, the *Shenandoah*'s carpenter came aboard to put several holes in her bottom. He then scampered back up the ladderway and over the side rails. The *Alina* took only half an hour to sink. Waddell had appraised her at $95,000 in value for prize money – if they were able to collect it, that is.

One thing that Waddell and the *Shenandoah* were able to collect, though, was crew. Five men shipped on as seamen and one as a coal-passer. Arguably the coal-passer was the most important recruit in the very short-handed engineering department.

With the rest of the *Alina*'s crew secured in the forecastle, her officers on parole and at liberty to roam, Waddell had begun to turn the prow of the *Shenandoah* away from the scene of the *Alina*'s demise when a large ship was seen bearing towards them. The ship may have seen the *Shenandoah* and *Alina* alongside each other, and decided to change course itself to 'speak' to both, in other words to exchange news and newspapers. At any event, the moment Waddell ordered up steam on the *Shenandoah* to give chase to the unknown ship, she began to change course. The speed of the *Shenandoah* reeled in the large ship quickly, but upon closing a large Union Jack could be seen swaying from the jack staff. Waddell ordered steam dropped and the *Shenandoah* fell away from her chase and turned course southward.

As the *Shenandoah* moved south, Waddell had no idea how close they had come to being discovered and how right he had been in heeding the earnest pleas of his young officer staff to move out to sea. Captain Corbett had been arrested by the British consul in Tenerife for breaking the Foreign Enlistment Act on the same day that Waddell sank the *Alina*. The news from the Confederacy, if Waddell and his crew could have received it, was not much better; the Battle of Westport, Missouri, known as the 'Gettysburg of the West', resulted in a Confederate defeat and the Battle of Burgess' Mill, Virginia, though virtually a stalemate, bled Confederate forces of more vital manpower in the defence of Petersburg and Richmond. The crew of the *Shenandoah* sailed on in blissful ignorance.

From 1 November until the early morning hours of 6 November 1864, the *Shenandoah* moved south towards the equator. At twilight on 5 November, the lookout detected what he thought was a sail. Waddell, with nearly a week gone by since the last sighting of a ship, decided to take a calculated risk, and figured an intersecting course that he hoped would bring the *Shenandoah* into contact in the morning. At 5.55 a.m. the *Shenandoah*'s crew could make out the ship they had stalked through the night. A look through the captain's spyglass allowed him to breathe more easily as well – it wasn't a Union warship. Closing in, at 7.45 a.m. the *Shenandoah* lit off a round from one of her small signal guns; the vessel was only a small schooner, after all. When the round went off, a Union flag shot up the flagstaff. A satisfied smile crossed Waddell's face, as he knew another capture would not only get morale back up, but maybe provide some more manpower. As it happened, the little schooner, named the *Charter Oak*, gave the *Shenandoah* some unique 'prizes'.

The *Charter Oak*'s captain, a Mr Samuel Gilman, had his wife, his wife's sister and her young son on board. He only had a crew of two mates and three seamen, all of whom spoke Portuguese, and very little English. Examining her papers, and finding she was a true-blue Yankee-registered vessel, her fate was sealed. But, her cargo was precious to Waddell and the *Shenandoah* – it was furniture. So, the crew of the *Shenandoah* helped themselves to every conceivably useful piece of furniture they could find, along the way finding canned vegetables, mostly tomatoes, in the hold as well. Working feverishly throughout the day, the *Shenandoah*'s crew had the *Charter Oak* cleared of useful items by early afternoon; at 3 p.m. she was set afire. As winds were calm, she burned slowly, not disappearing beneath the waves until late in the evening with the *Shenandoah* standing off to ensure that no tell-tale debris was left behind.

The *Charter Oak* was the charm for Waddell and the

Shenandoah. After this, the captures came hard and fast. On 8 November the *D. Godfrey* out of Boston was set on fire and sent to the bottom. Six men from the *D. Godfrey* signed on as crew for the *Shenandoah*; their actions must have influenced the *Alina*'s crewmen still held prisoner, for they offered to sign on as well. The *Shenandoah* now had seven more crewmen. Executive Officer Whittle was breathing more easily with each capture now, for every time a vessel was taken, and crewmen volunteered, he was able to fill out the *Shenandoah*'s deck and engineering watches, thus lightening the workload for all concerned. Ironically, one of the men who signed on was an African-American, John Williams, who went into the galley as a cook.

By now the *Shenandoah* was becoming seriously overcrowded with prisoners, paroled ship's officers, and of course, two women and a six-year-old child. Waddell knew he needed to relieve the pressure on the cruiser's resources and spaces, but he also knew that if he released his prisoners onto a passing ship, confirmation of the *Shenandoah*'s activities and location would instantly be communicated to Union authorities. He had no choice. In the early morning of 9 November 1864, the *Shenandoah* lowered her propeller and made steam towards a sail located with the first flash of the coming dawn. Thought initially to be a Yankee vessel due to the rigging of her sails, she proved to be the Danish vessel, *Anna Jane*. Waddell hailed the ship's captain, and after some careful negotiation the captain of the ship agreed to take aboard eight of the *Shenandoah*'s prisoners; Waddell was provident and got rid of his most troublesome captives. The Danish captain got a ship's chronometer, a barrel of ship's biscuit and a barrel of beef for his trouble. The chronometer would make a handsome sale if the

Anna Jane did not need it, earning a tidy sum for the captain.

Almost exactly 24 hours later, at 5.30 a.m. on 10 November, the *Shenandoah,* mainsail set, came upon the strangest vessel it would see during its cruise, the 'hermaphrodite' brig *Susan.* The term hermaphrodite refers to the fact that the *Susan* had a contraption mounted on one side of her hull that drove a shaft connected to a pump, which in turn continuously pumped the leaky vessel out. It was obvious that she was slow, for Waddell noted that barnacles grew on her bottom; he didn't think the benighted crew had much chance of making their destination port of Rio Grande du Sol in Brazil. Apparently, Captain Hanson and the crew of the *Susan* thought the same and all volunteered to join the *Shenandoah.* Waddell was forced to decline Hanson's offer to volunteer as he was Jewish. While Waddell had no problems with his religion, he reckoned his younger and more class-conscious Southern gentlemen officers might object.

Taking what coal they might need, as Cardiff 'smokeless' coal was her cargo, the crew of the *Shenandoah* quickly scuttled the barely functional vessel and moved on, pressing ever further southward towards the equator, searching for her next Yankee prize. Running with her topsails out, at 5 p.m. on 11 November, a lookout spied another ship on the weather beam. By 7 p.m. Lt. Whittle was ordering the screw (propeller) to be lowered, topsails in, and preparing to give chase. From 8 p.m. until midnight, the *Shenandoah* steamed after her quarry. They could tell she was a large ship, as she had six topsail yards. Finally, a few minutes after midnight on 12 November, the *Shenandoah*, having closed the chase, fired off a blank round from her gun. The vessel began to pull up and drop sails.

She was the *Kate Prince*, registered in Portsmouth, but her home port was in New Jersey and she was outward bound with a load of Cardiff coal. Waddell knew he had a valuable capture, for a full-rigged clipper ship could be worth an enormous sum to the entire crew in prize court after the war. When Whittle made his way aboard the clipper he found a crew ready to abandon the ship wholesale for the *Shenandoah*, and, astonishingly, the captain's wife, who was along for the voyage, wanted her husband's own vessel burned. Apparently her husband was a Yankee Captain Bligh in the making and the crew and his wife were keen to be rid of him and his ship. Whittle, amazed at this turn of events, returned to the *Shenandoah* with this startling news and the *Kate Prince*'s papers in hand.

Waddell, listening to his Executive Officer's story as he pored over the *Kate Prince*'s paperwork, must have laughed more than once at what he heard. Unfortunately for the Confederate commander the humour went flat once he'd perused the ship's cargo and registry. The cargo was owned by a British company and had all the correct paperwork. This time, all the letters had been properly stamped and witnessed. Waddell would have to release the *Kate Prince*, much to the consternation of the captain's wife and crew – and his own crewmen, who were eager for prize money. The only benefit for the *Shenandoah* would be in the *Kate Prince* taking away more prisoners, including the women and small boy still aboard from the *Charter Oak*. The captain agreed to this, under bond. Just before the two vessels parted, the captain of the *Kate Prince* sent a present to the grumbling crew of the Confederate cruiser. For their trouble, they got two barrels of potatoes.

Almost the instant the *Kate Prince* disappeared out of sight, another ship came into view of the *Shenandoah*'s forward lookouts. This time it was a bark named the *Adelaide*, flying Argentinian colours. Her captain, a man named Williams, was brought aboard for interrogation and for a look at his ship's papers. Waddell and his staff, after cross-examining the captain, declared the vessel condemned for destruction. The boarding party of the *Shenandoah* was literally pouring oil and breaking out doors to fire the ship when, at the last moment, one of the boarding party's officers came upon a cache of private letters that proved that the *Adelaide* and her cargo actually belonged to a strong Confederate sympathiser named Pendergast. Waddell would have sent the *Adelaide* to the bottom based on the captain's apparent attempts at prevarication. Williams was bundled back aboard the *Adelaide* with admonishments from Waddell about telling the truth in the future, and a letter of apology to Mr Pendergast stuffed into his pocket. The *Adelaide* continued westward as the *Shenandoah* moved off in a generally southward direction again.

The *Shenandoah* caught sight of her next victim in mid morning on 13 November 1864. Waddell soon realised this vessel was a fast sailer and once again ordered up steam, lowered his screw, and began a full-on chase. By 3.30 p.m. on the same day, the Confederate cruiser was racing alongside the *Lizzie M. Stacey*, a fast schooner from Boston, Massachusetts, the heart of the empire that James Waddell and upper-class young officers such as Lt. Grimball hated so much. After a cannon shot the wave-skimming schooner dropped her sails, stopping as if an anchor had been dropped to arrest her motion. Her captain, William Archer, was an irascible old seaman who rounded on members of Waddell's boarding party after they commented that they were amazed that the *Lizzie* was being sailed in such open sea. Archer proudly informed them that only the day before he had been raced by a British man-of-war, whose crew cheered them as they rushed by. Waddell approvingly eyed-up the fast little schooner with the idea of converting it to an auxiliary raider, but decided not to due to his still low crew numbers. This was even after three men from the *Lizzie M. Stacey* signed onto the *Shenandoah* as crew. Again, one of the three was African-American and went to the galley as a cook. By the time the crewmen from the *Lizzie M. Stacey* had signed onto the *Shenandoah*'s crew, the death warrant for their former vessel had been signed by Waddell. At 4.30 p.m., the *Shenandoah* began hauling fires and hoisting her screw. Finishing the transfer of any essential supplies they could find, the boarding party fired the *Lizzie M. Stacey* at just after 6 p.m. on 13 November 1864.

At the moment that Waddell was burning a small Yankee schooner in the South Atlantic, General Sherman and his Union divisions were beginning the wholesale destruction of Atlanta, Georgia. Sherman had warned Confederate Gen. Hood of his intentions beforehand. Hood replied, 'This unprecedented measure transcends in studied and ingenious cruelty all acts ever before brought to my attention in the dark history of war.'

The *Shenandoah* crossed the equator for the first time on 15 November 1864. As is traditional, 'King Neptune' and his 'court' appeared to receive his new 'subjects', that is, those among the crew of the *Shenandoah* who had never crossed the equator. It was a sign of just how little blue-water experience Waddell's young officer staff had, for only Lt. Lee had crossed the equator before. Waddell, of course, had crossed several times. For the new subjects of 'King Neptune' it was an evening of ribbing and fun as the new acolytes were 'interviewed' and given their 'rewards', usually a bath of seawater, grease and soap, mixed together of course, or maybe even a shave using molasses. All of the crew took it in good fun except the sail-maker, Alcott, who proclaimed loudly that he had been across the equator, but still got 'rewarded' by 'King Neptune' anyway. This respite from the normal routine of shipboard duty was a good release from stress for the crew, and Waddell knew it. While much has been written about the tensions aboard the *Shenandoah*, largely based on the edited shipboard diary of Lt. Whittle, the *Shenandoah*'s cruise was remarkable for its good discipline, even by the standards of today's navies.

While Whittle carried out his role as executive officer with a firm hand, Waddell settled into his job as captain and commander, for though he was ranked under the policies of the Confederate Navy as 'Lt. Commanding', by naval tradition he was referred to as 'Captain'. Keen to instil pride in his polyglot crew, Waddell issued an order that all officers were to wear their Confederate grey officer coats and either black or blue trousers (there was a shortage of grey material). This provoked the usual grumbles and gripes, but Waddell was intent on presenting a professional appearance to both friend and foe.

November wound to its end with the *Shenandoah* still moving south and eastwards, the crew complaining about the lack of captures, not knowing that Waddell's orders mandated that he 'turn the corner' of Africa and be racing towards Australia by 1 January 1865. If the *Shenandoah* ran into a potential prize, so be it, but James Waddell, as ever, would stick strictly to his orders. On 4 December 1864, just that happened when not one ship, but several, crossed the path of the *Shenandoah*. Early that morning the *Shenandoah* sighted the Sardinian ship *Dea del Mare*. On chasing her down and boarding her, it was discovered that her papers were in order; she was merely on a run from Genoa to Rangoon. Having released the ship, the *Shenandoah* spotted two more sails in the distance along its course and again began to give chase, but abandoned this shortly afterwards. By 11 a.m., the crew could make out the island of Tristan da Cunha. By the afternoon, lookouts had another sail in their view, and this one would prove to be a prize for the *Shenandoah*.

First seen at 4.30 p.m., by 5.40 p.m. the *Shenandoah* was alongside her, hoisting the English colours. The unlucky vessel, the *Edward*, replied by breaking out the Union flag, thus sealing her fate. Waddell ordered the English colours replaced by the Confederate flag. The crew of the *Edward*, a whaler, were so busy cutting up a whale that they had hardly even noticed the arrival of the *Shenandoah*. Only when a boarding party arrived aboard the *Edward* and hustled Captain Charles Worth away to the *Shenandoah* did the whalers realise their probable fate. Waddell and Whittle examined the *Edward*'s papers, and deciding that she was legally a prize, promptly claimed her as such. After all, she was a whaler from New Bedford, Massachusetts, and that was all Waddell needed to know. Knowing the vessel would be thoroughly supplied with a vast amount of material that the *Shenandoah* could use, and that nightfall was approaching, Waddell ordered off the crew of the *Edward* and held them in the forecastle of the *Shenandoah*, while sending Ship's Master Bulloch and Master's Mate Minor to the *Edward* to secure the whaler for the night.

On 5 December 1864 the crew of the *Shenandoah* enjoyed an early Christmas. The *Edward* was so full of provisions and other necessities of nautical life that all hands were engaged in an all-day effort to empty her. Hundreds of barrels of beef, pork, and sea biscuit, as well as quantities of those 'creature comforts' beloved of all seamen – tobacco and coffee – were carried over to the *Shenandoah*. Flour, clothing, sugar, rope, blocks, tackle, sails; the list seemed to be never-ending. The long boats of the *Shenandoah* shuttled back and forth as the Confederate cruiser slowly circled the *Edward*, keeping a wary eye out for other vessels that might wander upon the scene. The following day was spent stowing the tremendous amount of stores and other booty from the *Edward* aboard the *Shenandoah*, which must have nearly been bursting at the seams of her storerooms. Once the *Edward*'s stores had been picked over, she was set afire late in the afternoon; the *Shenandoah* drifted away at half-speed towards Tristan da Cunha, like a lion satiated by its kill.

Just before 8 a.m. on 7 December 1864, the *Shenandoah* came abreast of the main settlement on Tristan da Cunha and hoisted the Confederate flag to alert the islanders. Waddell peered through the foggy gloom at a settlement of grass-roofed houses located on Falmouth Bay (now obliterated by a lava flow that occurred in 1961) to see if any pilot boat would come out as the *Shenandoah* idled down her engines, stopping far enough off shore so that he could escape if a Union warship were to appear. As Waddell ordered the longboats out and all the prisoners and their meagre belongings into them, a solitary boat pulled away from the shore towards the Confederate cruiser. By the time the men of the *Edward* had been piled into what, until recently, had been their own longboats, the Tristan islander had pulled alongside the *Shenandoah*. To the amusement and chagrin of Waddell and his crew, they discovered that the Tristan islander was a

Yankee who had settled on the island years before and become its 'pilot' and chief 'trader'. The wily Tristan Yankee immediately tried to sell Waddell fresh fruits and vegetables, whereas Waddell had wished to land his prisoners and trade for fresh food. In the end, Waddell sold the islanders flour at a cheap price, and bought their meat and fowl at a high one. The Tristan Yankee had come out on top of the Confederates, even if he didn't know about the Civil War. Waddell, ever the gentleman sailor, also sent ashore rations specifically for the now marooned captain and crew of the *Edward*. A letter was also sent to the captain of the *Edward* noting that the food was for their use so that they would not have to depend upon the islanders' meagre supply of food.

At 3 p.m. that afternoon, the *Shenandoah* turned her bow in a direction that would make the watching islanders of Tristan da Cunha assume that they were heading to Cape Town, South Africa. For that matter, most of the crew of the *Shenandoah* probably thought the same as well, for had not Rafael Semmes and the *Alabama* enjoyed leave ashore at Cape Town? But Waddell, again sticking to his orders, and knowing that enough time had passed for news about his raiding to have made it to the ears of any US Navy ship patrolling the South Atlantic, was laying a false trail. After a few hours, and having made sure the *Shenandoah* was out of sight of Tristan da Cunha, Waddell had the helmsman change course; they were sailing south and east on a heading that would take them far south of Cape Town and the Cape of Good Hope. The Confederate cruiser was also entering into the wildest seas in the world, an area known as the 'Roaring Forties'.

Waddell was taking both an extraordinary chance and a

unique opportunity. He was still trying to get around the Cape of Good Hope ahead of his orders and to Australia as rapidly as possible. The Roaring Forties, named after the latitudes that they covered, offered a high-speed conveyor belt of wind, unrestricted by any land mass, that could propel them at near yacht-racing speed to Australia. However, these same unstoppable winds also create super-waves, big enough to sink a vessel without any trace. If the *Shenandoah*'s crew made a mistake, there would be no one to help and likely no trace of them ever to be found. It would be as if they had disappeared off the face of the world's oceans. Waddell pushed the *Shenandoah* towards one of her greatest challenges of the cruise.

As the *Shenandoah* ploughed through ever wilder seas towards the Roaring Forties, Waddell's guess that the Union Navy was aware of his activities was correct. Since leaving England, four Union warships had either tried to intercept or pursue the *Shenandoah*: the USS *Niagara, Sacremento, Onward,* and *Iroquois*. None had yet even caught sight of her. Before any of his Union captains' reports had reached Washington, the petulant Union Secretary of the Navy Gideon Welles knew who the captain of the *Shenandoah* was: James Iredell Waddell, the upstart who dared to demand his back pay and then dared to go over Welles' head and send a letter directly to the President, Abraham Lincoln. Welles knew full well that for Waddell, a man driven by honour, this was a personal war between them. Welles knew he could not get at Waddell physically, but he knew that news could spread around the world faster than even the mighty US government could manage. At some point, the decision was made to arrest Anne Sellman Waddell.

It is probable that it was Welles who put the idea before Union

Secretary of State William Seward, who was already infamous for his hard-nosed attitudes towards Northerners who supported the Confederate cause. Seward issued the orders, with the knowledge of Lincoln, and Anne Sellman Waddell was arrested and imprisoned by the US Army Provost Marshall responsible for Maryland. Exactly what charges she was arrested under may never be known. A meticulous search through the US National Archives revealed no trace of the arrest documents, though they may exist, uncatalogued, in a state archive. The only document from the period that alludes to the affair is a request for probation made after the war's conclusion to Provost Marshall.

If James Waddell, now entering the Indian Ocean, had known that his wife had been arrested by Union authorities with the complicity of Welles, Seward and Lincoln, it is almost possible to imagine his personal code of honour being so affected that he would have resorted to unrestricted warfare against all Union ships, or worse. And what Welles was counting on was that somewhere, somehow, the global grapevine of ship gossip would pass along the information that Mrs Waddell was a Union prisoner. Welles couldn't get at the *Shenandoah*, but he could damn well get at Waddell.

The *Shenandoah* was still racing under sail towards the treacherous and mountainous seas of the Roaring Forties. Having brought up the propeller of the *Shenandoah* on 8 December 1864, Waddell, having heard what he thought were strange noises coming from the prop and prop shaft the night before, wanted it thoroughly inspected. However, due to the propeller well being located directly beneath the pilot's house, it had to be removed first in order for it to be fully inspected. For two days the ship's carpenter and his assistants laboured to remove the pilot's house and then hoist out the propeller and its mechanism. O'Brien, the engineering chief, looked over the propeller-bearing case and found a crack. The *Shenandoah* was still capable of steaming, but at reduced power, O'Brien told Waddell. The Confederate commander knew that Cape Town could repair the vessel, but he was tied to orders and the fact that he knew in his gut that Union warships were stalking him. Waddell was a product of the 'old' US Navy and knew how to sail a ship. He would sail to Melbourne, Australia, some 6,000 miles away, and get the *Shenandoah* repaired, re-coaled and the crew rested, there in the balmy Pacific. But first the *Shenandoah* had to survive the transit.

On 11 December 1864, the *Shenandoah* sailed past the invisible line that marked the Greenwich Meridian, and on 13 December passed into the Roaring Forties. By 16 December she had passed round the Cape of Good Hope, though far to the south, and was beginning to feel the wintry fury of the bottom of the world. The crew, mainly the officers, suffered from the violently malevolent seas through which they sailed. The enlisted ranks, sleeping below decks in hammocks, merely swayed as they slept. The officers, on the other hand, suffered being tossed, turned and literally thrown from their bunks as the vessel dropped, wallowed and leaped through the walls and cliffs of water. On 17 December, a 'ship-killing' wave of such size descended upon the *Shenandoah* that the entire deck of the vessel went under water. It was only through the quick thinking of Lt. Whittle, who happened to be serving as the office of the watch at the time, that the raider was saved. Ordering all hands to seize axes and break out the ports, they were just able to get the tons of sea water to drain off the *Shenandoah*.

The speed at which they travelled seems almost impossible to imagine. On one day she covered just over 240 miles. By 19 December 1864, the foul weather had eased somewhat and thoughts were beginning to turn to how they would celebrate Christmas. Realising that the weather was so atrocious that trying to sail against it on his intended course was madness, Waddell ordered the main topsail to be close-reefed, and then turned the *Shenandoah* to run with the waves. A round of rum was ordered on for the crew after this, a welcome extra bit of warmth in the frigid seas and winds. Now running before the winds and waves, the crew counted the hours until Christmas dinner. The Officers' Mess would partake of the results of cook Hopkins' efforts with his Tristan Island geese and pig. Along with these centre-piece courses, Hopkins served up fresh potatoes, corned beef and mince pies, as well as seasonal desserts and cakes. While the side dishes won approbation from all, at least when they weren't sliding off the table and crashing to the deck in the tossing mess, the goose and pig were apparently a bit long in the teeth.

The weather dropped sufficiently over the next few days for the storm-battered crew to get some rest and for storm damage to be repaired on the *Shenandoah*. A lesser gale struck on 28 December 1864, but the by now well-seasoned crew shrugged this one off as a mild irritation. A more serious irritation, however, had arrived at Tristan da Cunha on the same day. Captain Rodgers and the USS *Iroquois* reached the island on 28 December 1864, where he found the *Shenandoah*'s landed prisoners from the *Edward* and the *Lizzie M. Stacey*. Carefully interrogating the Tristan Yankee pilot, Rodgers got the ex-prisoners aboard rapidly, then steamed away north for Cape

Town at full speed, or at least the best speed that his dilapidated boilers could make. Waddell had laid his false trail carefully, and the USS *Iroquois* fell for it.

While the USS *Iroquois* headed north to Africa through the wintry seas, the CSS *Shenandoah* continued to plough rapidly westwards towards Australia. The first prize capture since the beginning of the month came on 29 December when the *Delphine*, out of Bangor, Maine, was spotted. The weather was not good, the *Shenandoah* did not have her boilers up, and the *Delphine* had the advantage of having the wind with her. Luck played her hand in the Confederate raider's favour again, for the *Delphine* was just as surprised to find a vessel in that empty part of the seas as the *Shenandoah* was. The *Delphine* actually made for the *Shenandoah* on an intersecting course, hoping to get the latest news and gossip. Waddell smiled with satisfaction as the *Delphine* hauled up on the *Shenandoah*, who was wearing an English pennant. Ordering the helmsman of the *Shenandoah* to turn her into the wind to drop her speed rapidly, the *Delphine* passed behind the *Shenandoah*, giving the Confederate vessel the wind advantage.

At the same moment as the *Delphine* got ready to hail the *Shenandoah*, Waddell ordered the English banner hauled down, and the 'Stainless Banner' hoisted. The *Delphine*'s helmsman spun her wheel, throwing the smaller and more nimble bark about, to race away. The *Shenandoah* fired a blank cartridge from her signal gun, but the *Delphine* continued to race further away; Waddell ordered the crew of the Whitworth gun into action. As the gun crew sprinted out to load and aim the piece, the sails of the *Delphine* began to drop. Whether the captain of the *Delphine* had a spyglass trained on the deck of the

Shenandoah is unknown, but if he had pressed his advantage in speed, it is likely that he and his ship would have got away. As it was, Waddell was delighted with his luck.

The captain of the *Delphine*, William G. Nichols, was in a right uproar when he came aboard. He was even more put out with himself when he saw the jury-rigged gun carriage tackle of the *Shenandoah* and realised that he probably could have made good an escape. As it happened, he was carrying a cargo of agricultural machinery, bound for Burma, having left London some time before. Nichols had several problems with Waddell seizing his ship. First, his wife, Lillias P. Nichols, was aboard, and second, his wife's middle initial stood for Pendleton, the name of her father, who owned two-thirds of the *Delphine*. Nichols himself owned one-third. So, he faced not only losing the ship, but his entire fortune as well as most of his father-in-law's. His final problem was his wife. And soon she would become Waddell's and the *Shenandoah*'s, problem.

When the *Shenandoah* had thrown up the Confederate flag, it was not Captain Nichols who shouted at the crew of the *Delphine* to break away and try to flee the raider – it was his wife Lillias, screaming at the top of her lungs. Only when the *Shenandoah* fired its first signal gun did Nichols begin to believe that the cannonballs from the Confederates might be more injurious to his health than his wife's anger. Dragging his sea-heels all the way to the *Shenandoah* to face Waddell's inquiries about his behaviour, and to have his papers examined, Nichols concocted a story that he hoped would save his ship, and him, from the Confederates – and his wife. Captain Nichols immediately began blubbering away before Waddell that his wife had been made thoroughly sick from the cannon fire and that he feared for her health and life. Waddell, a man whose chivalry exceeded that of even the wildest romantic's vision of a Southern gentleman, courteously ordered the *Shenandoah*'s surgeon over to the *Delphine* to have a look at Mrs Lillias P. Nichols. He was suspicious, but his Southern manners came to the fore, as always.

Upon arriving on the *Delphine* and being escorted to Mrs Nichol's cabin, Surgeon Lining found himself face to face with a Yankee panther in full possession of both her faculties and her health. Lining escaped over the side of the Yankee bark back to the safety of the *Shenandoah* and reported to Waddell that the whole story was a lie, and tossed this hot Yankee potato back into his commander's lap; and he probably raided the surgeon's cabinet for some 'medicinal' refreshment before returning topside to see the forthcoming fireworks. Waddell was not going to let some Maine Yankee get the better of him and certainly not let a Yankee woman find his manners lacking. One of the *Shenandoah*'s boats was hoisted over the side and brought alongside the *Delphine* where, after some deft rigging of a bosun's chair, Mrs Lillias P. Nichols was lowered, in high dudgeon, from the Yankee bark into the Confederate boat. Her arrival on the deck of the *Shenandoah* was at once a revelation and a cause of apprehension to the Confederates. As Waddelll remarked, 'I was surprised to see a tall, finely proportioned woman of 26, in robust health standing before me, evidently possessing a will of her own, and it soon became palpable she would be the one for me to manage, and not the husband.' Mrs Nichols had already stage-managed the transfer of her six-year-old son over from the *Delphine*, ordering the deck crew of the *Shenandoah* about, to their amusement, then confronting James Waddell in stern tones as to what he intended on doing with the

Nichols and the crew of the *Delphine*. The crew of the *Shenandoah* had wild seas to ride all the way to Australia, and now they had a wildcat on board. It would be a most interesting cruise to Melbourne.

Leaving the *Delphine* burning at around 11.30 p.m. on 29 December 1864, the *Shenandoah* continued her race to the west, and the year 1865. The further from the South the *Shenandoah* sailed, the worse the situation became for the Confederacy. The nascent republic was beginning its death throes.

The *Shenandoah* had gained another six men from the crew of the *Delphine*, including a couple of what Waddell would have called 'real Yankee seamen'. Why they would have volunteered for Confederate service he didn't know, but they were good, professional sailors, and he was happy to sign them on.

Mrs Lillias P. Nichols, her son, and her hen-pecked husband were settling into the cabin directly across from Captain Waddell's stateroom. Waddell, ever the gentleman, took the social offensive by holding 'evenings' with the Nichols, in order to develop a good rapport with Lillias. He also invited his officers to join in, which introduced some light entertainment to break up the normally humdrum evenings aboard the ship. Lillias and Waddell knew what each other was about, she playing the younger officers for all she was worth for special attentions, while Waddell, the older, wiser gentleman, matched her every attempt to obtain some special bit of courtesy or attention, with firm, but polite, refusals.

New Year's Day 1865 passed with the *Shenandoah* still rushing westwards towards Australia, with the weather slightly the worse. The health of the crew matched the weather, with maladies ranging from toothache to conjunctivitis arriving at

Surgeon Lining's door. James Waddell's health suffered as well, and he recorded in his memoirs that he felt very down. A recurrent bout of headaches had returned, probably brought on by the continuous stress of monitoring his young officer staff – something that his excellent executive officer, Lt. Whittle, constantly admonished him about – as well as the normal pangs of loneliness brought on by being in command. The reminder of home life that was constantly before his eyes, the Nichols family, would have induced a subtle homesickness that affected him as well.

On the morning of 2 January 1865, the *Shenandoah* arrived off the islands of Amsterdam and St Paul. Waddell knew the islands were a regular stop for Yankee whaling ships and hoped to catch some in port. Stopping far offshore, Lt. Grimball led a group of officers ashore in a whaleboat, hoping to find some Yankee ships or supplies that they could capture. No Yankees were to be found, but they were able to bring some fresh food and meat back on board, including a rather hapless penguin that became a sort of mascot for the Confederates. Waddell, frustrated at not finding any whaling ships, ordered the *Shenandoah* away from St Paul the same day, taking leave of the island in the late afternoon. Still keeping his own counsel as to where the *Shenandoah* was headed, Waddell was faced with two choices. Should he try to sweep up around the west of Australia and gather in any Union vessels he found there, with the potential for one escaping and alerting the rest of the Pacific, or should he head directly for Melbourne for re-supply and shore leave?

Waddell knew there was residual fear amongst the Union merchant navy since the *Alabama*'s cruise, which had got as far east as Singapore, but he didn't know that his own ship's reputation had already spread so far and fast that the '*Alabama* effect' was compounding itself – the more successful he was against shipping in the normal shipping lanes, the more shipping insurance rose, and the more the owners transferred or sold their vessels to owners in foreign countries. Also, and this has not been confirmed due to the manner in which James Dunwoody Bulloch maintained his secrecy, but it is likely that in conversations with James Waddell, Bulloch expressed a more forthright opinion of what he thought the chances of the Confederacy were in surviving the war, much less winning it. This argument stands on fairly strong legs when one reads Bulloch's lengthy and detailed instructions to Waddell before the cruise. It may even be possible that Bulloch intended to send a message, or messenger, by some means to Melbourne to inform Waddell of changes to his original instructions. And this idea becomes more interesting in light of the fact that Waddell began to reveal to his officers that he had decided to make for Melbourne as rapidly as possible, 'in order to catch the mail boat'. James Dunwoody Bulloch's papers, missing for over 140 years, might shed light on this subject, were they ever to reappear.

The *Shenandoah* continued her flight west. For the next two weeks she ploughed on as if the entire Union Navy were on her heels. In reality, Gideon Welles had ordered another warship, the USS *Suwannee,* to pursue the *Shenandoah* with authorisation to pursue her into any ocean in the world and to 'destroy or capture her'. Pausing to repair the propeller mechanism once again, with Engineer O'Brien becoming more concerned about its condition and stressing that it should not be used, Waddell did not cease the *Shenandoah*'s relentless flight towards Australia until 17 January 1865, when the Confederates came across the *Nimrod*. The *Nimrod* was an American-built, but British-owned ship, carrying cargo from Plymouth, England, to Adelaide, Australia. Waddell and his staff pored over her papers, decided everything was in order and the *Shenandoah* parted company with her. The *Shenandoah* continued towards Australia, with Waddell trying to get every bit of speed he could out of here. He was dead keen to catch the mail ship.

On 22 January, the *Shenandoah*'s lookout caught sight of another ship sailing in a parallel course and direction to their own. Waddell was not interested in any seizures now that he was closing in on Australia. He wanted more speed, and against the advice of Engineer O'Brien, asked for more steam. O'Brien feared the stress would tear the propeller mechanism and the stern out of the ship, but Waddell would not be dissuaded.

The morning watch on 25 January caught the first sight of Cape Otway, Australia. By nearly mid afternoon, the *Shenandoah* was steaming into Port Phillip's Bay, having stopped to pick up a pilot at its mouth. The tired Confederate raider then proceeded into Hobson's Bay, where she was boarded and inspected by an Australian health officer who, having cleared the vessel, scurried quickly away to shore to telegraph the authorities in Melbourne that a Confederate ship-of-war was inbound.

At 6.45 p.m. the CSS *Shenandoah* dropped anchor off Sandridge, the main port area of Melbourne. The *Shenandoah* had been at sea some 90 days since her commissioning off the Madeira Islands and she was in need of repair and re-fit. The crew were in need of rest and relaxation as well. But Lt.

Commanding James Iredell Waddell wanted to get his reports onto the mail ship bound for Europe so that Commodore Barron and Commander Bulloch knew what his condition and position were, while getting arrangements made for essential repairs for the ship. The crew would get shore leave, but only for as long as it took to get the *Shenandoah* back to sea. It wasn't just the chance of the Union Navy catching up with him while in anchorage, or the fact that the British colonial authorities might allow their neutrality rules to be bent in favour of the local US consul's diplomatic complaints. No, James Waddell knew that his arrival in Australian waters was finally the beginning of the audacious operation that Confederate Secretary of the Navy Mallory and Commander James Dunwoody Bulloch had conceived: the destruction of the American Pacific Whaling Fleet.

5

I have the honour to announce

The arrival of the CSS *Shenandoah* in Melbourne's harbour on 25 January 1865 was tumultuous. From the moment the vessel was boarded by the harbour pilot, the news that a genuine Confederate raider had arrived at the very doorstep of the capital of Her Britannic Majesty's Colony of Australia had been electrifying. Australians piled into steam boats, tugboats, yachts, tenders and every kind of craft that could sail to go out and meet the now famous successor to the *Alabama*.

The overwhelming enthusiasm of the reception by the Australians mitigated, somewhat, the disappointing news contained within the journals and newspapers that the harbour pilot, Mr Johnson, had brought aboard at Hobson's Bay. The Confederacy continued to suffer a staggering series of defeats, shrinking ever more beneath the blows of the Union army and navy. Waddell and his officers knew that the most serious loss to the Confederacy was the seizure of Wilmington, North Carolina. The Union Navy had now succeeded in cutting off the Confederacy from the rest of the world. The other bad news was the capture of the css *Florida*. They were the last Confederate commerce-raider now, and any hope of ever sailing the *Shenandoah* into a Confederate port was gone. But the Confederacy still fought, and while it survived, they still had their orders to carry out.

The first official action by James Waddell was to send Lt. Grimball ashore with an official letter to Sir Charles Darling, the Governor-in-Chief and Vice-Admiral of Australia. The letter requested permission to take on coal, effect repairs, and to parole and land his prisoners, including the indomitable Mrs Lillias P. Nichols. What followed was a classic case of bureaucratic hair-splitting and waffling around an issue. Sir Charles, after holding an emergency session of his advisors, responded that the *Shenandoah* would have permission to refuel and land her prisoners, as well as re-provision. He then passed the issue of ship repairs over to James G. Francis, the commissioner responsible for customs and trade matters. Francis' orders from Sir Charles were to get a detailed list of the supplies and repairs that Waddell required, while the request to transfer prisoners was relayed to the US consul, William Blanchard. Sir Charles also implied that Commissioner Francis might also gently inquire as to when Lt. Commanding Waddell might be departing Melbourne.

In his report back to Commodore Barron, Waddell recounted the difficulties experienced at the beginning of the cruise, largely relating to the lack of manpower, the successes in captured prizes, and the condition of the *Shenandoah*. Waddell closed his report with a hopeful statement that wished for an 'honourable settlement' to the Civil War. All Waddell could do was continue to follow his last standing orders, as no message, or new orders, were waiting for him in Melbourne.

Just after Paymaster Smith delivered the *Shenandoah*'s outgoing post ashore for transfer to the outgoing mail ship, Commissioner Francis' first letter to James Waddell arrived aboard the *Shenandoah*. It was early afternoon on 26 January 1865. Francis stated that Sir Charles had granted permission for the *Shenandoah* to stay in Australia and effect repairs. Francis then asked for specifics about what the *Shenandoah* needed for re-supply and repair, as well as details of her prisoners. Waddell dashed a curt response back that he had already contacted Langlands Brothers & Co., a famous ship repair firm with home offices and yards in Britain, to survey the *Shenandoah*'s propeller mechanism for repairs. (In fact, Waddell had already hired a gang of ship's caulkers to start work on the ship that afternoon). Waddell's letter was ferried ashore to Commissioner Francis' office. Francis shot back an equally short response that inquired about a list of prisoners that the *Shenandoah* had on board. Away went his letter to the *Shenandoah*.

Waddell, ripping open his second communiqué from Commissioner Francis, responded by asking for alcoholic refreshments such as brandy, beer and champagne, among others, and tropical weight cloth material, so that the men could make tropical uniforms. As an afterthought, Waddell noted that the prisoners that he had intended to land at the Sandridge anchorage had left of their own accord aboard boats that had been ordered out from shore. Waddell posted back his latest response to Commissioner Francis. Again, the *Shenandoah*'s shore boat ploughed towards shore.

Waddell had not allowed any of the *Shenandoah*'s boats to be used to transport prisoners ashore when the vessel first arrived because official permission for the Confederate raider to anchor and remain in Australian waters had not been granted by Sir Charles. The formidable Mrs Lillias P. Nichols, with her son and husband in tow, had been dispatched ashore at the first possible moment, largely due to Mrs Nichols' own indignant and haranguing requests. Executive Officer William C. Whittle was only too happy to see the back of them. Mrs Nichols responded by saying she hoped to see the *Shenandoah* burn.

Whatever Mrs Nichols' sentiments might be, the *Shenandoah* had become an overnight sensation in Australia. The Australian newspapers had first heard of her exploits about a month beforehand, believing that Rafael Semmes was in command of a new raider. When the *Shenandoah* arrived without Semmes, the newspapermen could hardly believe that he was not aboard, in hiding, or that he had been surreptitiously dropped ashore. But when they finally came around to the fact that James Iredell Waddell was in fact the commander of the *Shenandoah*, the newspapers who were 'Southern' in attitude painted him as a fine example of a Southern gentlemen, youngish-looking and with a quietly confident demeanour. The 'Yankee' papers simply called him and his crew pirates, and ranted at the duplicity of their government in allowing the *Shenandoah* even to enter Australian waters, though if Her Majesty's government had wanted to keep the Confederates out, there was little they could have done. Melbourne simply had no defences, no coastguard, and certainly no navy.

Waddell, eager to garner all the good press and support he could, opened the *Shenandoah* to public visitations. The response was overwhelming. On 29 January 1865 so many people were trying to get to Melbourne harbour to take one of the many boats ferrying tourists out to the ship that Executive

Officer Whittle had to order steamers and boats to stand off because there were so many people topside. He feared for their safety and for his crew's personal gear, as Confederate uniforms, and the buttons from them in particular, were very popular.

The 'letter' war between Waddell and Commissioner Francis had finally abated. Waddell testily submitted a list of prisoners, pointing out that he had given a list to a Mr McFarlin of Customs on 25 or 26 January. It was a moot point for both sides, for by now Mrs Lillias P. Nichols and family had already thundered into the offices of US Consul William Blanchard, where she fulminated in some detail about the *Shenandoah*. She did mention that the commander, James Waddell had been quite a gentleman, however.

With relations between the Confederate raider and the Australian authorities operating in the clear now, serious repair work could begin on the *Shenandoah*. On 30 January, Waddell received a letter from Langlands Brothers & Co. that their survey of the *Shenandoah*'s propeller mechanism had revealed far more serious problems. The entire outer sternback was shot, and needed to be replaced, in addition to the recasting of the parts for the propeller mechanism. Langlands said the *Shenandoah* would have to be brought out of the water, onto what was called the 'government slip' (built by Her Majesty's government, but leased to private firms), but this could not be accomplished for three more days. For Waddell, as far as he knew, every day in port was another day that could bring a Union warship into Melbourne harbour, but there was nothing he, or his crew, could do but await repairs. Meanwhile the *Shenandoah*'s crew, and Waddell, enjoyed their celebrity status in Melbourne, being famous, or infamous, depending on view of the curious Australian onlookers.

On 4 February 1865, the *Shenandoah* was finally towed to Williamstown where her stores could be offloaded, making her ready to go on the slip. Even this took time, and it was not until 9 February that the *Shenandoah*, ex-*Sea King*, was on the slip. She found herself out of her native element and under the care of shipbuilders again for the first time since her construction in 1863 at A.H. Stephens' shipyard on the River Clyde. But the shipbuilders and engineers of Langlands had little time to consider such things, being under pressure from Waddell and the Australian government to get repairs completed. They were to work around the clock until the job was done.

While Waddell fumed, Whittle fretted, and the rest of the *Shenandoah*'s crew prowled the streets of Melbourne on shore leave, US Consul William Blanchard had been trying every diplomatic and legal device he could to have the *Shenandoah* seized. Constantly gathering intelligence and notarised statements from other former prisoners like the Nichols family, Blanchard was trying to build a case that Waddell and the *Shenandoah* had violated the British Neutrality Act on several points, and hoping to stimulate the Australian courts into action.

Blanchard had met his match in Waddell, however. Aware that Blanchard had been circulating information that he would pay a bounty to any crewman from the *Shenandoah* who would desert and give evidence about the Confederate raider's activities, as well as anonymous threats to sabotage the ship, Waddell took action. He fired off a letter to the commissioner of police about Blanchard's activities in trying to encourage desertion from the *Shenandoah*'s crew and requested the assistance of the police in apprehending the deserters and returning them to the ship. It is not known what legal advice

Commissioner Standish may have received on the matter, but the fact that the Confederacy was regarded as a 'recognised belligerent' by Her Majesty's government created a legal grey area. The commissioner declined Waddell's request, but Waddell had exposed the Union's tactics, via Consul Blanchard's actions, and gained a subtle bargaining chip for later.

On 31 January, Waddell wrote a letter to Captain Thomas Lyttleton, head of the water police for Melbourne harbour, requesting 'police protection for the Confederate steamer *Shenandoah*'. Waddell was taking the rumours of attempts to sabotage, or seize, the *Shenandoah* seriously, but also creating a trail of legal paperwork that could be used in the future. Lyttleton, not receiving Waddell's letter until the morning of 4 February, did not reply to Waddell's request until 8 February, by which time the *Shenandoah* had been emptied of her stores and was due to be hauled out of the water at Williamstown the next day. Lyttleton apologised generously to Waddell for the late receipt of his request for police guards, and put the Williamstown water police on alert. However, Lyttleton's slowness in replying suggests that there were some back-room discussions about how to honour this request. Whatever the reason, Waddell had again added to his paper trail, and gained another valuable card that might be used in the future.

All this had taken place in the background as the *Shenandoah* was getting hauled out of the water for her most serious repairs, the reconstruction of the stern and the propeller mechanism. Even as the vessel was being pulled up onto the slip, Commissioner Francis had begun harassing Waddell again with letters, the first on 7 February 1865. This time he wanted to know when the Confederates were leaving. An exasperated

Waddell, tired of the official harassment and with having to explain commonsense naval matters to someone who was clearly a landlubber, replied laconically that a tremendous gale had precluded the *Shenandoah*'s hauling out; he hoped she would be out of the water by nightfall.

Delays of one sort or another meant that the *Shenandoah* still wasn't on the slip until 9 February, by which time Francis was demanding an exact date of departure for the raider. Francis was probably aware that US Consul Blanchard had been piling numerous statements and letters in front of Sir Charles, demanding the Australians take action against Waddell and the *Shenandoah* for violations of the Foreign Enlistment Act. Blanchard had particular information that several Australians had been recruited for the *Shenandoah*, including one who was on board at present serving as a cook. Looking over the stack of incriminating information laid before him, Sir Charles did what any self-respecting politician would do, and promptly handed it to the police. The police department detectives investigated the matter thoroughly and came to the same conclusion as Blanchard. The Australian men had broken the Foreign Neutrality Act. The Queen's Neutrality Proclamation, issued by Queen Victoria in the spring of 1861, also applied to the men as well. Warrants were issued and Lyttleton, the same police chief who had already had dealings with James Waddell, was charged with carrying out the arrest of the Australians aboard the *Shenandoah*.

Captain Lyttleton and several constables arrived at the Williamstown slip on 13 February to serve warrants on the Australian men. Lt. Commanding James Waddell was ashore, as evidently was Executive Officer William C. Whittle, leaving Lt. Grimball as the Officer of the Day. Lyttleton attempted to board the vessel and as Waddell recorded in his memoirs, 'Lt. Grimball refused to allow the search.' The next day Lyttleton returned with his constables to the *Shenandoah*. This time Lt. Commanding Waddell was aboard. Waddell adamantly refused their request to search the ship but offered to have his master-at-arms and several petty officers search the raider for the men. As a last riposte to the Australians, Waddell then grimly commented that 'the *Shenandoah* would be defended at every risk of life'. Lyttleton, who obviously had specific details of the men's appearance and duties, refused Waddell's offer of a new search, and with the North Carolinian's stern threat of military action singing his ears, marched off in a huff to report to his superiors.

Lyttleton's report soared upwards through the normally clogged bureaucratic channels of officialdom like paper atop a chimney fire. Sir Charles roared at Commissioner Francis to rescind permission for the *Shenandoah* to remain in port and that all repairs and supplies being carried out by any British subject be halted. Perhaps trying to outdo his own superior's fury, Commissioner Francis ordered the police at Williamstown to surround the ship and to secure all the equipment within it. Francis, thunderstruck by Waddell's threat of military action if the Australians tried to board and search the *Shenandoah,* also called in 50 fully-armed British soldiers. The *Shenandoah* would not be permitted to sail until it allowed the ship to be searched by British police. US Consul Blanchard may have celebrated upon hearing this news, thinking the Confederates were about to commit an act of war against what they had perceived to be their greatest friend, the British Empire. But if Blanchard was celebrating, he was doing so too soon. He had not reckoned on the legal skills of James Iredell Waddell. All the years of Waddell's off-duty study of international and maritime law were about to pay of in spades, with a little bit of poker-face bluffing thrown into the game.

At sundown on 14 January, Sir Charles sent a letter to James Waddell on the *Shenandoah*. The letter stipulated the reasons for the securing of the vessel and the repair slip, and the suspension of workers from performing their repairs. Darling told Waddell that the *Shenandoah* was going nowhere until it had been searched. Waddell called a conference between himself, Executive Officer William C. Whittle, Lt. Grimball and Lt. Lee. All agreed that their refusal to allow British police on board was proper and in accordance with long-standing principles of international law regarding the sovereignty of a nation's ships. The junior officers suggested a new search of the ship be carried out, and that the results of the search be noted in the official reply to Sir Charles.

Waddell's reply to Sir Charles was essentially an exploitation of the legal weaknesses of Britain's Foreign Enlistment Act and Queen Victoria's Proclamation of Neutrality. Britain had tried to play it both ways for too long, and Waddell was about to give turnabout fair play. The letter pointed out to Sir Charles that (a) international legal precedent was that the deck of a ship was considered to be representative of a particular nation, (b) that the said ship was unencumbered from all alleged crimes committed afloat, and liable only for those committed ashore, and (c) that if such crime occurred ashore, then police ashore should present the necessary warrants to the master-at-arms of the said ship for the application and arrest of the warranted persons. Waddell sent the letter over the side, and told the crew to prepare to repel boarders.

As Waddell's messenger scrambled his way towards Sir Charles' offices, the repairs on the *Shenandoah* were being finished. She was nearly ready to re-enter her native element, the sea. As night closed in, with the situation still unresolved, a doubled watch of Confederate naval officers and enlisted ratings anxiously peered over the rails at equally pensive Australian policemen and British soldiers. Waddell knew he was in an exposed position; the *Shenandoah* could easily be damaged in an attack, rendering her useless for sea again. He decided to pull another legal argument out of his bag of tricks and called for the tug *Black Eagle* to come and stand by to pull the *Shenandoah* off the slip. The captain of the *Black Eagle* replied that he could not do so because he would be violating the order of the government. With this reply in hand, Waddell composed his master-stroke letter, in which he inquired of Sir Charles if the 'refusal to permit the launch of the ship amounted to her seizure, and I respectfully begged to be informed if such was known to his Excellency the Governor and met with his approval'. Waddell handed this letter to Lt. Grimball, instructing him to put it directly into Sir Charles' hand and to await his reply.

Sir Charles didn't know the Confederacy was dying by the hour now. Nor did Darling know that Prime Minister Palmerston and his Foreign Secretary, Lord Russell, had come to see the real military and political fate of the Confederate republic, and were now trying to make all amends possible to the Union, who ostensibly had the most powerful army and navy in the world at that moment. All Sir Charles knew was that Britain had recognised the Confederacy as a lawful belligerent, that Waddell had stringently adhered to the conditions of Queen Victoria's Proclamation of Neutrality, and that in the case of possible violations of the Foreign Enlistment Act, if they had occurred, as Waddell earnestly argued, they had occurred ashore, and not on his vessel, which was, according to the prevailing tenets of international law, a ship carrying the flag of a nation. Had not Britain herself recognised the pseudo-republic by granting the Confederacy belligerent nation status? Sir Charles realised he had been legally out-manoeuvred. He penned his reply and sent Lt. Grimball away to the *Shenandoah*.

Darling's reply to Waddell was simple, 'The suspension of the permission given to Her Majesty's subjects to aid in the necessary repairs and supplies of the ship *Shenandoah*, dated the 14th instant, is relieved, in so far as launching the said vessel is concerned, which may be proceeded with accordingly.' Darling tried to save face by implying that he might try to re-force the outstanding issue, that of the illegal Australian recruits, but he was by now trying in any way possible to get the Confederates out to sea and away from his jurisdiction. US Consul Blanchard would have been stunned when the news reached him.

At 5.30 p.m. on 15 January 1865, with Sir Charles' letter recorded aboard the *Shenandoah*, it having been shown to the relevant authorities in the Williamstown ship yard, the *Black Eagle* pulled the *Shenandoah* back into the sea. She made her own way to anchorage, dropping only one anchor and keeping her boilers up in case she should need to escape an attempt at sabotage, or worse yet, the surprise arrival of a Union warship.

Waddell, still smouldering with rage at the behaviour of the Australians, lobbed one parting shot at Commissioner Francis in his original, unedited memoirs, saying that he was 'a business partner of the American Consul [Blanchard], and also a member of Gov. Darling's ministry, [and he] bore a conspicuous and ungenerous hostility to the *Shenandoah*'s mission'. With this, Waddell turned his mind towards more important work, clearing off from Melbourne.

All during 16 and 17 February, skiffs, barges and other supply vessels re-shipped the *Shenandoah*'s stores, while other small steamers and boats brought fresh provisions. Interestingly, when the *Shenandoah* issued a call for more coal to top up her bunkers, the vessel that came alongside was the *John Fraser*, out of Liverpool, and owned by Fraser, Trenholm & Co. The vessel had only recently arrived with a load of Cardiff coal, which when burned produced little or no smoke, and was prized by raider and blockade-running captains alike. If Bulloch had wanted to send out any new secret messages, men, or supplies, this would have been the moment they would have been delivered. Waddell noted in his memoirs, written years after the fact, that the suspicion about the *John Fraser* lingered. All Waddell would say was that her appearance in Melbourne harbour was a coincidence.

Early on the morning of 18 February, the *Shenandoah* raised her anchor to leave Melbourne harbour. By 7 a.m., ship time, she was heading towards the head of Port Phillip, at her helm the same harbour pilot – Mr Johnson – as when she came in. Johnson had encountered professional difficulties since he and Waddell had last met, running a vessel aground. But Waddell had responded in kindness to a plea by his brother to let him take the *Shenandoah* out again so as to regain his reputation. Johnson repaid this kindness by informing Waddell that the harbour-master, a Captain Ferguson, had asked Johnson to inform him of any 'irregularity' amongst the *Shenandoah*'s operations, or if Waddell should stop to take on men from ashore. This only confirmed Waddell's opinion of the Australian government.

Having reached the limit of Johnson's responsibility as harbour pilot, the *Shenandoah* paused long enough for him to be dropped off for shore. The Confederates were keen to be on their way, realising that any incoming vessels would inform the authorities as to their direction. As with their departure from Tristan da Cunha, Waddell began to leave a false trail. He merrily sailed the *Shenandoah* in the same direction until nightfall, then checking carefully that no vessels' lights could be sighted, turned the *Shenandoah*'s bow towards Round Island in the Bass Strait. Hopefully no trail had been left for the Union warships he knew had to be following the *Shenandoah*. Not only was the USS *Iroquois* hunting the *Shenandoah*, but four other ships had been ordered specifically to hunt her down: the USS *Santee, Suwannee, Wachusett* and *Wyoming*. Since the Atlantic, Mediterranean and Pacific naval units had also been informed of her operations, and were on the lookout for the *Shenandoah*, to all intents and purposes the entire US Navy was looking for Waddell now.

The *Shenandoah* enjoyed good sailing weather on her way towards the Bass Strait, which was good for some 'unknown' guests aboard, who soon made their appearance. The forward deck crewmen were astonished to hear noises coming from the iron bowsprit, which was hollow. The access hatch fell open and men soon began crawling and pulling themselves out. Other inaccessible areas of the ship soon began to come alive with the voices of men too as they extracted themselves. Before long, a bemused James Waddell was presented with the sight of 42 men who had stowed away aboard the *Shenandoah* with the desire to

Left. James Iredell Waddell
(All images courtesy of US Naval Historical Center)

Above. Anne Sellman Waddell, daughter of an Annapolis merchant and wife of James Waddell.

Below. CSS *Shenandoah*, James Waddell's only combat command.

Gideon Welles, US Secretary of the Navy during the Civil War.

Stephen Mallory, Secretary of the Confederate States Navy.

James Dunwoody Bulloch (left) and his half-brother Irvine Bulloch (right). James D. Bulloch, who would become the uncle of Theodore Roosevelt, greatly affected future naval strategies of not only the US, but other naval powers through his adept use of commerce cruisers.

President Abraham Lincoln. He agreed that Anne Waddell should be imprisoned or place under house arrest. Lincoln also infamously suspended *habeas corpus* during the American Civil War.

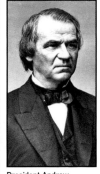

Secretary of War, Edwin Stanton. He aggressively arrested anyone with Confederate sympathies, bringing the Union dangerously close to becoming a police state.

Lord Palmerston. A cautious political pragmatist with Southern leanings, he would not recognise the Confederacy unless an overwhelming military victory was won by them.

Lord Russell, charged with carrying out Queen Victoria's Neutrality Act. Russell's adversary was the aggressive US Minister Charles Adams.

President Andrew Johnson. Originally he believed in severe punishment for all former Confederates, but political reality and the extreme loss of life and devastation of the Civil War brought him to the belief that reconciliation was the way forward for America. His series of general amnesties and pardons made it safe for James Waddell to come home in 1867.

Drewry's Bluff, James River, Virginia. The site of James Waddell's naval gun battery duel with a Union naval squadron in 1862.

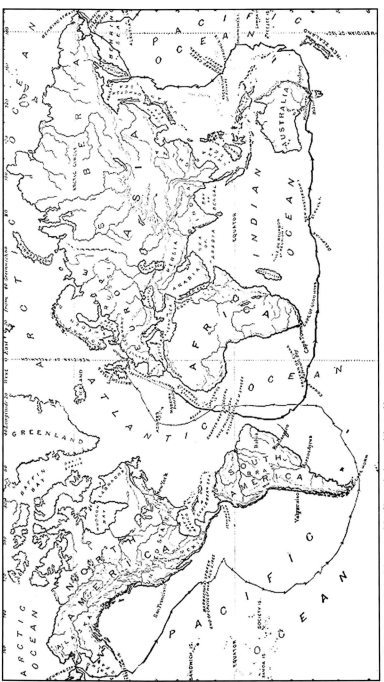

James Waddell's own chart of the route of the *Shenandoah* around the world.

Left. Queen Victoria. She ordered the British Government to be firmly neutral during the American Civil War.

Above. Commodore Barron. The senior Confederate naval officer in Europe, and based in Paris, he presided over a community of Confederates abroad.

Below. css *Florida.* James Bulloch's first contract-built commerce raider, constructed in Liverpool.

css *Alabama,* the most famous and most successful Confederate raider, also built in Liverpool.

Rafael Semmes, raised to the rank of Rear Admiral in the Confederate Navy after his brilliant campaign in the *Alabama*, he would be imprisoned on Gideon Welles' orders at the end of the Civil War.

Charles Manigault Morris, commander of the css *Florida*, the first of the three most successful Confederate commerce raiders.

Left. Ulysses S. Grant. Papers found in the US Grant archives indicate the political liabilities of James Iredell Waddell were removed in 1883, just three years before Waddell's death in 1886.

Below. The commissioning paper for the midshipman A. H. Waring, with whom Wadell duelled early in his naval career.

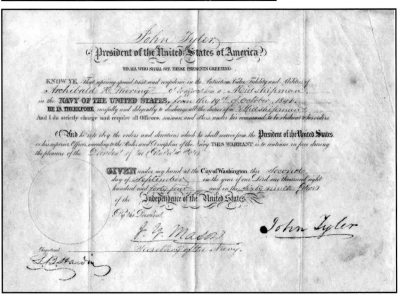

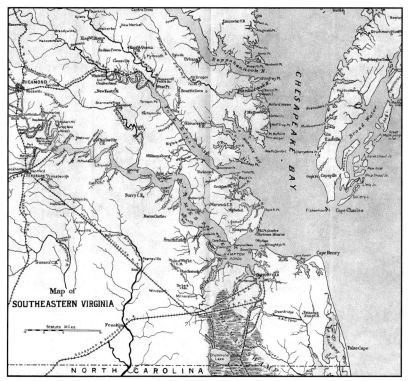

A view of the Chesapeake Bay area separating Virginia from Maryland, the waters across which Waddell escaped south to join the Confederate Navy. The winding course of the James River leading to Richmond shows Drewry's Bluff, the Confederacy's 'Gibraltar', where Waddell fought his naval gun battle against an attempt by the Union Navy to capture Richmond.

474,3   174,6 = 489,14   309,23   11,13   239,21
Saunders. Lieuts. Chapman and Evans arrived here a few days
679,31   353,12   523:16 = 657,6   465,16   453,19   163,21   32,27
since   from   Nassau too   late   to   join   Captain Semmes,
     737,21   633,24   496,15   668,13 523,8 537,10
so that they have reported to me as the senior naval officer. I
               737,21   144,24   427,21
am sorry to say that they are both indisposed, but I believe not
670,15
seriously so.

A typical secret message used by the Confederate Navy during the Civil War, this one generated by Commander North, the agent who spent much of his time in Scotland attempting to get ironclads and other vessels built covertly, though never successfully. This message was seized and used as evidence by the US government after the war.

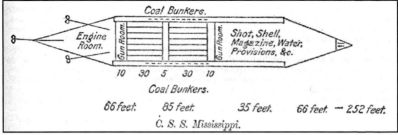

The css *Mississippi*. A crude drawing of the ironclad that Waddell would have served on had it not been scuttled, or blown up, at the Battle of New Orleans, when the Union fleet, led by David Farragut, managed to seize the seaport before the Confederates could complete the *Mississippi* and her sister ship, the *Louisiana*.

The css *Pampero,* the 'lost' Confederate commerce raider. Built covertly by Lt George Sinclair with the assistance of Commander James Dunwoody Bulloch, located in Liverpool, the *Pampero* was financed by monetary sleight of hand, that being bonds issued for the value of 25 bales of cotton. The Union government pressured the British government into securing the vessel after its launch, but Sinclair and Bulloch's secret methods were strong enough to withstand a full court investigation into her true ownership. At the end of the Civil War, the British government still had no full idea of her origin.

A period drawing of the css *Shenandoah*.

The css *Shenandoah* destroying the Union whaling fleet in the Arctic in 1865.

One of the more well-known images of the css *Shenandoah* navigating through ice-floes in the Arctic.

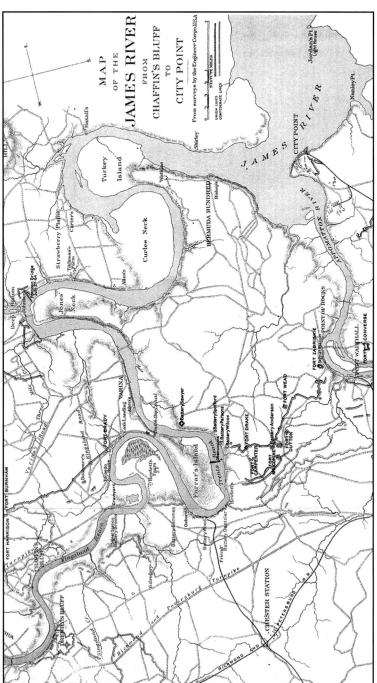

The area around Richmond, Virginia showing Drewry's Bluff, from the official US government report on the American Civil War compiled by the War Department, today's US Department of Defense.

John P. Bankhead, commander of the Union warship *Wyoming*, one of many Union vessels that chased the elusive Waddell and the *Shenandoah*.

James Iredell Waddell after the Civil War. A widely copied image that portrays Waddell in a suitably stern and unsubdued pose.

President James K. Polk, the American president who promulgated the 'Manifest Destiny' policy best and whom relied on the US Navy to project his vision outside American shores.

Secretary of State William H. Steward. With an almost racial hatred of Southerners, he constantly goaded other members of Lincoln's administration to be more severe on any suspected Southern sympathizers in the north. His policies were partially responsible for the arrest of Anne Waddell.

President John Tyler. Under his administration America completed a treaty with Britain (1845) that brought the present-day state of Washington into being and settled the boundary dispute and then annexed the Republic of Texas as the State of Texas after its war of independence from Mexico. Almost forgotten is the fact that he 'went south' at the beginning of the Civil War and served as a representative in the Confederate House of Representatives.

Officers of the css *Shenandoah*. Those seen in this image include former Assistant Surgeon Edwin G. Booth (seated), and (standing, left to right): former Acting Master Irvine S. Bulloch former Passed Assistant Surgeon Bennett W. Green; former First Lieutenant William H. Murdaugh; and former Passed Assistant Surgeon Charles E. Lining. (Information courtesy of the US Naval Historical Centre)

Above. The famous yacht *America*, which became the css *Camilla* in the Civil War and served as a fast, but very uncomfortable, blockade runner for several important missions.

Left. US Secretary of the Navy, George Badger, the civilian head of the US Navy who signed Waddell's original commissioning papers as a midshipman.

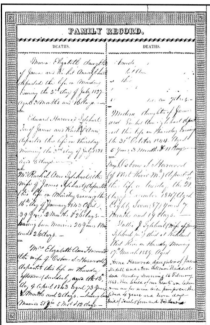

Left. The US Navy 'Dismissed officer's list', the list kept by Gideon Welles of former US naval officers who 'went south'. Waddell was one of the last to do so, and probably before being arrested.

Below left. This sad page that puts paid to the oft repeated mis-truth that the Waddells never had any children: 'the child of our heart was taken from us . . . died of scarlet fever and diphtheria'. The Waddells would never be far from each other for the rest of their lives, except during his epic Civil War circumnavigation.

Below right. Rear Admiral William B. Shubrick, one of the admirals involved in the Mexican–American War, operating in both the Pacific and the Gulf of Mexico.

sign on to the raider's crew. Merely commenting in his memoirs about what few men he had lost to US Consul Blanchard's activities, Waddell smugly noted that most of these men were fine 'young American seamen'. Waddell had them signed on, and his delighted executive officer, Whittle, began assigning them to their various departments and watches. For the first time in the whole cruise, Whittle had a complement of men who could virtually fill all the required duties, thus lightening the load on all.

As the new men settled into their duties, Waddell directed the *Shenandoah* towards the north. They were entering the first week of March 1865. For the next week they sailed on, up through Farn and Conway islands, then past Fiji and the Ellice Islands. A tremendous northeast gale then set upon the Confederates, of such ferocity that even Waddell noted that it was the worst he had seen in 23 years afloat. It lasted four days. Executive Officer Whittle was forced to lead an emergency repair party to secure one of the raider's cannons when it tore loose from its gun tackle. Had they failed in their effort, the tremendous weight of the cannon and carriage could have caused it to tear through the ship's side and sink the ship.

On 10 March the *Shenandoah* was passing by the Howe and Norfolk Islands. The northerly winds had frustrated the forward progress of the vessel since leaving Melbourne and this was growing tiresome to Waddell, who wrote that, 'failing to pick up the trade wind, and being wearied from excessive heat and a deluge of rain, I ordered steam and steered in search of the trades, sighted Drummond Island, and ran sufficiently near to communicate with natives who came out in canoes'. Waddell and his crew were disappointed to learn that no vessels had stopped at the island, but the Confederates, even those who had already sailed in the Pacific, were still intrigued by their first contact with native islanders. The extraordinary voyage of James Waddell and the CSS *Shenandoah* was about to transcend itself, becoming more than just a military operation, but an unknowing and rudimentary anthropological and historical record of the Pacific islanders they would meet.

Waddell noted that, 'the native islanders are of copper colour, short in stature, athletic in form, intelligent and docile', and 'were without a rag of clothing'. This temporary intercourse with the Pacific islanders was a welcome break from the tedious on-board routine, foul weather and lack of passing ships that the Confederates had endured since leaving Australia. For Waddell, it may have been the thing that broke him out of a deep melancholy that had been affecting him for several weeks, according to the diary of Executive Officer William C. Whittle.

Whittle's log shows him to be increasingly concerned over Waddell's seeming depression and lack of communication, not only with him, but with the rest of the officers. What Whittle, and every historian since who has mulled over Waddell's behaviour, did not realise was that the anniversary of the death of his beloved daughter, Annie, had taken place on 16 February, right at the height of the near-hostilities with the Australian colonial authorities. The mental stresses must have been considerable, for Waddell had confided in no one about this, not even Whittle, who appears from his diary to have considered himself a friend of not only James, but also of his wife, Anne.

Leaving Drummond Island behind on 24 March, the *Shenandoah* made a northwest course and on the following day they re-crossed the equator, this time heading north. While Waddell's melancholy had subsided, the crew's morale was ebbing away due to the lack of sighted sails. They had hoped to surprise a large number of whalers at anchor off Drummond Island, as it was well known to be used by whalers for getting supplies of fresh food and water. There had been no whaling ships, however. Several more days of rain-filled squalls marked the progress of the *Shenandoah*. On 29 March, the skies had stopped pouring out their woes upon the Confederates who, late in the afternoon, finally spotted a distant sail. Their last sighting and seizure had been on 29 December 1864, in the Indian Ocean.

Chasing until near sundown, the *Shenandoah* closed the distance and fired off a blank cartridge from the signal gun once more. The unknown vessel popped out the Hawaiian flag, Hawaii still being an independent country at the time, and dropped sails to come to a halt. Ship's Master Bulloch led a boarding party to the vessel, where they found a nonchalant but cautious, Captain Hammond at the command of the *Pelin*, an island trader who bought and sold tortoise shell, among other things. Waddell, not wanting to spread any information that the *Shenandoah* was operating in the area, had maintained the guise of a Union warship. Hammond, a reticent Dutchman, was unsure and coyly deflected any questions about whether he knew where any whale ships were located. Either Hammond, or one of his subordinates, did finally let slip that they had seen whalers at Ponape Island, then known as Ascension.

Almost before Bulloch's boat was back aboard the *Shenandoah*, Waddell had the raider underway. Not trusting the Dutchman, Waddell had the *Shenandoah* pass by Kosare Island, known then as Strong's Island, before heading to Ponape. Circling the main anchorage and seeing no sign of vessels, the Confederates sailed on towards Ponape. Passing some 12 miles off Pingelap Island (then McAskill Island), on the morning of 31 March 1865, Waddell didn't deign to change course to investigate the tiny speck of an island. He was making for Ponape. Twelve hours later, with night upon them, Waddell ordered all sails close-hauled for the evening. He wanted to creep up on any unsuspecting Union whalers in the morning.

At 9.30 a.m. on 1 April, the *Shenandoah* got her first sighting of Ponape. At 10.30 a.m. Waddell ordered up steam. Shortly thereafter an exultant lookout shouted that he had spotted four ships. Waddell noted later on in his memoirs that, upon hearing the lookout's call, he thought that 'if they were not whale ships it would be a very good April Fool's'. Coming around to Lea Harbour, the Confederates spotted a whaleboat on its way out towards them. As Waddell thought the whalers might be British, he decided to bring the *Shenandoah* to a halt to speak with the oncoming whaleboat in order to see what information he could find out about the situation. Waddell and his Confederates had got their luck back. The man who had been frantically rowing out towards them was Thomas Harrocke, sometime harbour pilot, self-appointed emissary to Ponape, and all-around jack-of-all-trades. He was British as well, which in Waddell's mind meant he could probably be telling the truth about what he knew.

Executive Officer Whittle hurried Harrocke into Waddell's cabin, where the two Confederates told him they were a Union warship and wished to be taken into the anchorage. Harrocke had lived for so long amongst the native islanders that his English had almost left him, and they had considerable difficulty in making themselves understood. Waddell and Whittle told him they would pay him to take the *Shenandoah* into the anchorage where the whalers were, but if he ran them aground, he would be punished. Looking at the stern countenance of Waddell and the revolver strapped to Whittle's side, Harrocke understood what punishment would be meted out to him and in any language. With Waddell at his side the whole time, the terrified Harrocke brought the *Shenandoah* carefully into Lea harbour. The anchor lines were let out and after getting the ship held fast, Waddell ordered off four boats, each containing a boarding party headed for each of the anchored ships. Lieutenants Grimball, Chew, Lee, and Scales each led one of the parties.

Waddell had issued specific instructions to the lieutenants that the most important thing they should search for were nautical maps that showed where the whale fleets were currently operating. Waddell said in his memoirs that, 'with such charts in my possession, I not only held a key to the navigation of all the Pacific Islands, the Okhotsk and Bering Seas, and the Arctic Ocean, but the most probable localities for finding the great Arctic whaling fleet of New England, without a tiresome search'. As the boarding parties pulled away smartly from the *Shenandoah*, the 'Stainless Banner' of the Confederacy snapped up the jack staff again, while the signal gun barked out its challenge. Harrocke, befuddled by what was going on, asked in broken English what was occurring. The answer from the Confederate officers was that they were going to seize the ships, check their papers to make sure they were American, and if so, burn them. Harrocke was stunned.

Soon, Waddell received back signals from all the boarding parties that all four ships were indeed Union whalers, and more importantly, they all had the maps that Waddell desperately desired. Looking back now, the intelligence windfall that Waddell gathered could arguably be compared with the British Royal Navy's capture of a Nazi Enigma machine in World War II for the destruction that Waddell would wreak with this information would ultimately cause America's merchant marine to lose its global pre-eminence until World War II, at a nearly incalculable cost to the economy.

The boarding parties soon returned to the *Shenandoah* with maps, ship's papers and other documents, but no captains. Waddell's lieutenants discovered to their amazement that all the whalers' captains had gone ashore to visit a missionary on a social call! As the afternoon came on, Waddell ordered the boarding parties to begin seizing any useful items for the *Shenandoah*, while keeping an eye out for the returning captains. Sure enough, as dusk fell a small boat could be seen setting off from the shore towards the whaling ships with a group of what appeared to be very merry men, the social call to the island's missionary apparently having been toasted liberally. The shore boat got most of the way towards the quartet of whale ships before they noticed the 'Stainless Banner' on the *Shenandoah*. The rowing slowed and they made to turn about for shore, but Waddell had a longboat with men and weapons waiting to go. The Confederates were upon the whaling captains before they could escape, and before they could say 'Nantucket' they were aboard the *Shenandoah*, facing a very abrupt and unpleasant end to a day of 'socialising'.

Waddell and Whittle interrogated the captains and pored over their papers one by one. The *Edward Cary* was out of San Francisco and the *Hector* was out of New Bedford,

Massachusetts; they were both large, fully rigged ships. Waddell pronounced them condemned. The *Pearl* was a smaller vessel, a bark, and hailed from New London, Connecticut. She was condemned. The last vessel, the *Harvest*, was more problematic, for she flew the flag of the nation of Hawaii, her captain and crew swearing that she had been bought, and was owned, by a Hawaiian. What Waddell saw was a collection of papers that specified an American provenance, and no current bill of sale to a Hawaiian. The *Harvest*, too, was condemned. Moving swiftly to consolidate the whaling ships and their recalcitrant captains and crew, Waddell had the captains and most of the seamen imprisoned. One captain was so venomous in his conduct towards Waddell and his officers that he had him put in 'double irons'. Waddell accepted only seven men who wished to sign on to the *Shenandoah*, and only two of them were 'Yankees'.

Knowing that the transfer of articles from the whalers would take some time, and that Ponape would be a good anchorage to rest the crew and replenish the *Shenandoah*, Waddell decided to find out what he could about Ponape and its inhabitants. At 10 a.m. on 2 April, a formal boarding party consisting of six men with weapons, led by Master's Mate Cornelius Hunt, with the Englishman Harrocke as translator, departed for Ponape's shore to visit the chief king. Only an hour later, Hunt's gig returned, accompanied by 'seventy war canoes, each decorated with old faded bunting or coloured cotton', as Waddell remembered. The chief king sat in the *Shenandoah*'s boat, surrounded by his four sub-kings, 'each with a wreath of flowers upon his head, and an apron of sea grass falling from the hips half-way to the knee'. Their appearance exceeded any description that Robert Louis Stevenson had ever written about Pacific islanders. The

Confederates were at once agog and amused.

With the dignified chief king aboard, Waddell was temporarily at a loss due to Harrocke still being over the side in the boat, but once he had gained the *Shenandoah*'s deck, Waddell began to introduce himself. The chief king replied through Harrocke that he was King Ish-y-paw. As the rest of the king's party and escort climbed up onto the deck of the *Shenandoah*, the Confederates were astonished that the women amongst them were as naked as the men, wearing only a token piece of cloth as decoration. Trying to keep the tone of the visit as formal, yet friendly, as possible, Waddell ushered King Ish-y-paw and his personal escorts into his cabin for drinks and a discussion. The North Carolinian began a slow, but careful, talk with the king, halting when Harrocke had trouble getting his translation across to the dignified Polynesian. Waddell explained that the whale ships were from a country that was at war with his country, pointing out that the country of the whale ships had committed atrocities against women and children, as well as burning homes. King Ish-y-paw nodded his head in acknowledgment that he understood. Reaching his ultimate point, Waddell said that President Jefferson Davis, the 'king' of his country, had ordered Waddell and his men to capture the ships of the North wherever they could and then destroy them. Applying his legal knowledge at a more basic level, Waddell said that he would respect the laws of the king and that he would give all the useful cargo and materials to the king and his people. To round out the deal, Waddell asked King Ish-y-paw if he would supply warriors to guard the anchor cables and mooring lines that the *Shenandoah* had run ashore in order to secure her in Lea harbour; the king would also be given a sizable number of muskets.

King Ish-ya-paw was so overwhelmed by the respect given him and the size of the 'gifts' that were offered to him, that the king wanted Waddell to take one of his daughters as his wife. Noting that the king's daughter was rather rotund, and certainly not attractive by any standard, Waddell pointed out to the king that in his country a man could only have one wife, and he was already married. The king was downcast for the moment, but brightened at the tremendous treasures he was about to receive.

The next day King Ish-y-paw's subjects began their pillage of the Yankee whaling ships. By that afternoon the *Pearl* was on fire, having been stripped to her bones by the Ponapeans. The *Edward Cary* and *Hector* were burnt the following day. The pillage paused now, as the *Harvest* had vital stores that the *Shenandoah* could use, and Waddell wanted to give his crew some shore leave. He declared a general liberty for the next five days. If not on watch, the officers and men could do as they pleased. It was as close to a vacation in paradise as any of them would ever experience. While some of the men took the opportunity to go inland and explore the islands, others took boat trips, while Waddell paid a reciprocal visit to King Ish-y-paw at his home. An exchange of gifts took place after a discussion about politics, such as the king could understand, and Waddell gave the earnest king a silk scarf. King Ish-y-paw reciprocated by giving Waddell a remarkable shoulder sash, or belt, that had been woven from coconut fibres and wool. For once, the superiority that James Waddell felt his civilisation had over the Polynesians fell away. He wrote, 'The belt is peculiar, exhibiting skill in the art of weaving and taste in blending colours.' He continued, with some emotion: 'It is preserved as a memento of the only sovereign who was fearless enough to extend hospitality to a struggling people and to sympathise with a just cause. His nature was not corrupted by politics.' King Ish-y-paw of Ponape had done what Queen Victoria of Britain, Napoleon III of France, and Isabella II of Spain had feared to do: to recognise and treat with the Confederate States of America. (This is something the Polynesians were still proud of over a hundred years later, when Micronesia released a postage stamp featuring the CSS *Shenandoah*.)

On 10 August 1865, Waddell had the emptied *Harvest* towed out towards a bank of shoals, where it was set on fire. Meanwhile in the Confederacy, or what was left of it, General Ulysses S. Grant of the Union Army was sitting in one of the small rooms of the Appomattox County Courthouse in Virginia, talking with an old colleague he had not seen face to face in several years, separated as they were by the Civil War. His friend was General Robert E. Lee, and he had just surrendered the most significant body of troops in the Confederacy, the Army of Virginia, to General Grant. President Jefferson Davis and his cabinet were on the run, and the Confederacy was in its final days. In the Pacific Ocean, Waddell and his officers were paroling the captains' crews, sending them ashore with some supplies, weapons and a small boat. They were oblivious to the irony that as they were paroling Union merchantmen, in Virginia, General US Grant was granting liberal amnesty and parole to Confederate army officers and enlisted men. They could go home. The men on the *Shenandoah* were still headed away from home and away from a nation that no longer existed.

After a few days' sorting out final details, the *Shenandoah* weighed anchor and exited Lea harbour with the English pilot Harrocke at the helm again. Pausing just outside the harbour mouth, Waddell made a gift of one of the whaleboats to Harrocke, who was paid as well. Sending the delighted 'ambassador' of Ponape over the side, the *Shenandoah* turned her prow to the northwest.

Another day of good cruising weather began on 14 April, though by afternoon the winds began to build in intensity. In Washington, DC, at the same time, President Abraham Lincoln was about to be shot by John Wilkes Booth at Ford's Theatre. The nation had been coming to its senses after four long years of blood-letting, and now the Northerners would be in a vengeful mood. James Waddell had no way of knowing that every action that he and his men took from now on would be viewed through the prism of piracy, a word used in the mid nineteenth century that carried the same meaning as terrorism does today.

For the next three days, the *Shenandoah* sailed on north by north-eastwards, until on 17 April 1865, she reached a position that would allow her to patrol for clipper ships and other cargo vessels bound to and from China. Slow-cruising between the islands of Saipan and Wake, the Confederates constantly scanned the horizon for ships, spending nearly a week in this activity. With his usual careful eye on the crew's morale and the ship's physical appearance, Executive Officer Whittle took advantage of the slow patrolling to run the crew through drills and perform some of the never-ending essential maintenance chores that were required to keep a warship 'ship-shape'. By the end of the week the crew were grumbling from boredom and the drills. A new diversion was needed; that is, a ship to capture.

Waddell, in his memoirs, casts little light on his thoughts about failing to see a single ship, but he did comment that Lt. Whittle 'had time to get things in good condition'. However at some point Waddell had decided it was time to move on northwards, though he was trying not to get into the Arctic before May arrived, as he knew the weather and ice could be problematic. Early on the morning of 28 April, the order was given to raise the telescopic smokestack, raise the fires on the boilers, and make way under steam. They were headed north across the 45th parallel. Searching for prey continued as they made their way across seas that seemed increasingly to fight their forward progress. On 13 May, the ship's barometer plummeted in just a few minutes as the stunned crew watched a low black cloud hurtle towards the *Shenandoah* from the northeast. Before the crew had time to batten down her hatches completely, she was staggered by a blast of wind that seemed to emanate from Poseidon's very mouth. The *Shenandoah* was nearly rolled over, her list to port so extreme that the ends of the sails on the lower mast went beneath water. Sails were blown out, blown up, and blown completely away. Waddell and Whittle struggled to regain control of the ship, their commands being almost inaudible in the screaming winds and fierce thunder. Waddell said in his memoirs that, 'it looked impossible to get the *Shenandoah* across the 45th parallel'. The gale departed as rapidly as it came, leaving the shocked crew to replace their sails and look after the minor injuries inflicted on the crew from being tossed about. But, it was a lesson well-learned about the vagaries of the weather as they went further into the North Pacific.

On 20 May, the *Shenandoah*'s lookouts could make out the snow-covered peaks on the Kuril Islands, the enormous archipelago of islands that stretch 1,300 kilometres from Hokkaido, Japan, to the Kamchatka Peninsula of Russia. With a strong northeast current flowing, by the following day the

Shenandoah was passing between islands known today as Onekotan and Paramushir into the Sea of Okhotsk, searching for whaling ships. For the next three days, Waddell had the *Shenandoah* steam close in along the western side of the Kamchatka Peninsula, knowing from the information that he had obtained from the captured whaling captains' maps at Ponape, and from Lt. Matthew Fontaine Maury, as well as ex-whaling men aboard the raider, that the coastal area was frequented by whalers. Unfortunately, through no fault of Waddell's, he had arrived early in the area, not wishing to venture there until the first week of June. He knew the cold fogs that frequented the sea often hid ice, which could trap a ship, or worse, send it to its death. A tight watch was maintained with Waddell constantly monitoring his young officers, often to the consternation of his executive officer, Lt. Whittle. But Waddell was adamant that the ship and mission were his responsibility, and he would not allow a momentary lapse in attention to run them aground, particularly in one of the world's least hospitable places. Fortunately, the *Shenandoah*'s luck still held and the weather remained quiet.

On the afternoon of 27 May, six days after entering the Sea of Okhotsk, the Confederates spotted a sail in the distance. Nearly eight months after the *Shenandoah* had departed London's docks as the *Sea King*, she was finally about to embark on the mission that the Confederate Navy had envisioned. That same day – actually 26 May 1865 in the western hemisphere – Lt. General Simon B. Buckner surrendered the Confederate troops of the Trans-Mississippi Department in New Orleans, where Lt. Commanding James Iredell Waddell had fought in his first battle for the Confederate Navy. It was also the third anniversary of his commission from the Department of the Confederate Navy in Richmond, Virginia, which, along with the rest of the government of the Confederate States of America, now did not officially exist.

For Waddell and the men of the *Shenandoah,* the Confederate nation still existed, as they were far beyond the reach of any form of communication. And until substantiated information was received by them that the war was over, or orders were received from their superiors, they would fight on. The vessel that crossed their path that afternoon was the *Abigail*, a whaler out of New Bedford, Massachusetts. They were the enemy and they were where the next fight was. The lookouts on the *Shenandoah* had spied the *Abigail* through a large and jumbled ice pack, with some of the ice piled so high that they seemed almost like miniature icebergs. The *Shenandoah* had to work her way around the ice pack before she could proceed directly towards her next victim. Waddell had the Russian pennant run up the jack staff of the *Shenandoah*, so when the *Abigail,* captained by Ebenezer Nye, spotted the Confederate ship, he promptly had the Union 'Stars and Bars' run up, and made all sail towards her, thinking her to be a Russian warship patrolling the Sea of Okhotsk.

The *Shenandoah* and *Abigail* bore down upon each other at such a rate of speed, that the Confederates were almost on top of the Yankee whaler when the 'Stainless Banner' of the Confederacy popped out, accompanied by the cold echo of a shot from the raider's signal gun. Caught dead to rights by Waddell, Nye on the *Abigail* dropped all sail and hove to for a boarding party. Lt. Scales led the boarding party onto the whaler, the laconic Yankee captain waiting patiently for them to clamber aboard. Nye, musing upon the situation, commented that he reckoned he had been caught fair and square, and that he had heard the Confederates were up to some new tricks. The earnest Yankee was speaking from personal experience, as he had been the captain of a previous vessel that had been stopped and sunk by Rafael Semmes and the *Alabama*. Thus, though Nye would have been hard pressed to celebrate his historical notoriety, he became the only Union merchant captain to have had two vessels sunk by two different Confederate raiders, the *Alabama* and the *Shenandoah*. Even Waddell, though he had no love for the New England Yankees, must have felt a bit of sympathy for Nye. However, Nye's own crew had nothing but harsh words for their Jonah-like captain. They reckoned the only thing he could find was Confederate raiders, and swore never to sail with him again. As a final personal indignity to Nye, the *Abigail* had been named for his wife, hoping she would bring him good luck.

The Confederates began to rummage through the *Abigail*'s holds, looking for useful cargo, when the boarding party came upon every naval officer's worst nightmare after being at sea for a long spell – a hold, not just full, but overflowing, with alcohol. Nye had shipped kegs, barrels, and bottles of poteen, gin, rum, whisky, and every other form of alcoholic beverage that was consumable by man. It was a quantity of such magnitude that the drink-starved sailors were absolutely agog. The first boarding 'party' was well under way, powered by drink, by the time the officers, led by Whittle, got wind of the situation. With Whittle scurrying about with the *Shenandoah*'s Master-at-Arms trying to secure the inebriated seamen, more men from the *Shenandoah*, sent to help get the situation under control, joined the 'Tennessee tea party'. An exasperated Whittle ordered away another party, consisting of marines, to get the first boarding parties under control – and they promptly joined the celebrations as well. Waddell, who had expressed some doubts about Lt. Scales' abilities from the start, was not amused by this breakdown in discipline. By the time Lt. Whittle got the celebrations under control, there were more sober prisoners aboard than Confederate sailors – and fortunately they were in irons.

All through the night of 27 May and into 28 May, Waddell struggled to get order restored aboard the *Shenandoah* and to get useful stores and supplies transferred from the *Abigail*, no mean feat when most of the Confederate deck crew was 'full-rigged' and 'flying before the wind'. Waddell had exploded, and to be fair, he had a right to be livid. He paid his volunteer seamen better than any 'real' navy they might serve in and he had a liberal policy when it came to the daily grog ration, even doling out extra rations when the occasion, or weather, called for it. Moreover, it had come to his attention that pilfering had taken place aboard the *Abigail*, not only by the seamen, but by some of the officers. Waddell came down on his misbehaving crew. He hauled Lt. Scales over the coals when a bottle of whisky was found in his quarters. He also demoted his clerk, Blacker, a man who had been a captain of his own ship when he sneaked aboard the *Shenandoah* in Melbourne, after Waddell suspected he had helped to secretly stow a case of whisky in with the cook (who, of course was in hot water as well). His Olympian anger began to subside only when he had written a general ship's order concerning the pilfering of goods from captured ships, reminding all that any goods must be surrendered to, and accounted for by the *Shenandoah*'s executive officer and paymaster.

The *Abigail* was left behind and set on fire around midday on 28 May. With the general order of the ship coming back under control, the *Shenandoah* steamed on a course north by northwest, generally following the shoreline of Kamchatka. By 1 June, the *Shenandoah* was patrolling a bay just off the peninsula's northernmost point, Zelev Shelekhova, and enjoying fine sailing weather. Waddell had come to this location both on the recommendation of Master's Mate John F. Minor, who had served aboard whalers in the past and his interrogation of the crew of the *Abigail*.

By 3 June, the weather had begun to change, quite literally, overnight. By noon that day heavy rain began to strike the *Shenandoah*, quickly adhering to the exposed surfaces of the ship's rigging and freezing. Executive Officer Whittle sent men up into the rigging to try to break away the ice, but it re-formed as quickly as they could break it away. For once, the Cunningham self-reefing sails were a hindrance, as traditional block and tackle sail rigging allowed easier removal of ice. The more enclosed Cunningham mechanisms were difficult, if not impossible, to free. Waddell, also on deck directing a similar de-icing effort, heard a lookout aloft sound the alert for pack ice, being pushed in their direction by a steadily increasing east wind. Waddell's worst fears were being realised. He was losing steerage as a solid pack of ice was bearing down on the *Shenandoah*. They would be wrecked, and if not all drowned, then cast ashore in one of the world's most remote and inhospitable areas. The entire crew understood that their very survival was now at stake. They did not need any further admonishments about what they had to do, which was to get the rigging de-iced and get the frozen sails down. Once that was accomplished the helm would answer and steerage would be regained.

As the freezing deck-hands clung to the masts and yardarms fearfully chipping ice with axes and belaying pins, Waddell saw that they would not clear the ship's rigging in time to save the *Shenandoah* from the ice pack. The lookouts in the rigging were told to spot any opening in the ice pack and immediately report it below. Anxious hours passed before a nearly frozen top lookout shouted down that a passage had appeared. Waddell considered his options, and decided that an attempt at saving their lives was better than hesitating. The bow of the *Shenandoah* was turned into the ice-free passage. The *Shenandoah* now set a record that no other Civil War combatant, not even the more famous *Alabama*, could claim. She was the first and only warship, either Union or Confederate, to be surrounded by, then locked in ice.

The ship soon took on the appearance of a vessel on an Arctic expedition, with tremendous ice formations hanging from every protuberance. By dawn, the gale had dropped and the sun cast itself upon a scene that delighted even the most exhausted members of the crew. After the morning mess, an effort was begun to move the *Shenandoah*. As the helmsman carefully nudged this way and that way with the bow, trying to push the ice out of the way, the rest of the deck crew were involved in chopping down the ice from the rigging. Waddell, seeing a chance to get free fresh water without having to run his fresh water condenser, had all the ice possible saved in casks, barrels, buckets and anything that could hold water.

By 1 a.m. on 5 June, the *Shenandoah* was free of the ice. Waddell decided to take one more very careful look for whalers by trying to make it to the island of Ostrov Svyatovy Iony, then known in English as St Jonas' Island. After a few hours' efforts to the north, the *Shenandoah* found herself once more imprisoned by ice. After working her free yet again, much more easily this time, Waddell called an officers' meeting to discuss their current predicament and to sound out a course of action. While Lt. Grimball and Master's Mate Minor thought they should still try for Ostrov Svyatovy Iony, Minor admitted that they still had some 200 miles of ice to get through. While the officers noted that most of the whaling was done in the shallow coastal waters, such as the bays, to attack whaling ships in those waters would be a violation of the international legal precedent. The chance of being discovered by a Russian man-of-war, while remote, also had to be considered; the Tsar of Russia, Alexander II, was an open supporter of the Union, having sent a Russian squadron to America early in the Civil War, so the possibility of waking the Russian bear was not a good idea. Waddell agreed to the legal points Whittle, Chew and the others had put forth, but still wondered aloud if he should not still put an effort in to get to Ostrov Svyatovy Iony. In the end, a vote was taken and the majority position was to go no further into the ice with the *Shenandoah*.

Waddell and the *Shenandoah* nudged gently northward until land was spotted early in the morning of 6 June. The course was changed to head towards what was determined to be Cape Alewin in order to begin a parallel course that would bring the raider along the coast of Kamchatka as she began her turn south to exit the Sea of Okhotsk. The following days were fine, clear and calm, extraordinary conditions for the Sea of Okhotsk during the springtime. Whales and dolphins were spotted leaping in the placid seas, enjoying their own respite from the normally unpredictable weather. On the *Shenandoah*, however, the usual malaise had returned to the crew when too long had elapsed between ship sightings and captures. Strangely though, this had no dampening effect on the captured whalers from the *Abigail*, as 12 men signed on to the *Shenandoah* as crewmen, landsmen, or marines. They had no idea that the Confederacy no longer existed, and that they were joining a ship with dubious legal standing.

On 13 June, the *Shenandoah* exited the Sea of Okhotsk, passing Onekotan Island once again. Her course was now north and her destination was the final stated objective of the cruiser's mission, the Bering Sea and the Pacific whaling fleet. Having left the Sea of Okhotsk and several days of exceptional weather behind, Waddell's course towards the Bering Sea presented several problems, including unknown currents, winds, and of course, fog. He intended to pass between the two main Komandorski Islands, noting in his memoirs that 'currents about islands are irregular in direction as well as force'. However, within just a few hours of passing by Onekotan Island, fog, brought in by an increasing easterly wind, descended. Waddell, unable to get a navigational fix either by sun or stars, decided to make his course more north-easterly, hoping to compensate for this influence. If he reckoned wrong, they would run aground on Komondorski Island. A nervous 24 hours passed, but Waddell felt reasonably sure in his navigation, writing, 'I knew from the dead reckoning the ship must be near the passage.'

Waddell was right. At midday on 16 June, the forward lookout on the *Shenandoah* gave the shout of 'Land, ho!', as recorded by Waddell. The fog had cleared just in time, and long enough for Waddell to establish that this was Copper Island, the more westerly of the two Komandorski Islands, and that he had cut his luck close. He reckoned that they were 37 miles off their course, as determined by dead reckoning, and gave the helmsman an order for an immediate change to port tack. Just in time, the *Shenandoah* was able to skirt around the island and between its sister island, Bering. As the *Shenandoah* made to enter the Bering Sea, Waddell, still nervous about unknown reefs and currents, gave the order for steam to be brought up and the sails to be brought in. Waddell and the *Shenandoah* had finally reached their intended operational area, eight months after leaving the docks of London. Not a single Confederate crewman nor a single Union prisoner had been lost so far.

The first fog-free day that they had seen since entering the Sea of Okhotsk came on 18 June. Waddell noted that the sailing in the Bering Sea was 'not of the most delightful character; changes of weather were more sudden, and although fogs did not last so long as in the Sea of Okhotsk, they were more frequent'. Waddell made sure solar navigational checks were performed at every available opportunity; if the thought of shipwreck in the Sea of Okhotsk brought a shiver to the spine, such an occurrence in the Bering Sea was an even more horrible prospect. For three more days the *Shenandoah* sailed northwards, until shortly after noon on 21 June, a lookout spotted Cape Navarin, Russia, off to the northwest. Another lookout thought he saw a ship's sail to the west, and the cruiser turned about to give chase. Unfortunately, upon closing, the disappointed Confederates found themselves trying to seize a huge rocky crag that soared up out of the seabed. Course was returned to the northeast once more and they continued to sail through the rest of the longest day of the year.

The following day was when Waddell's and the *Shenandoah*'s luck returned. It also marked the beginning of a short but intense campaign of destruction that would do more to damage the economy of the United States of America in the long-term than any other action the now defunct Confederate States of America could have ever imagined. As the *Shenandoah* nudged ever closer to crossing 180° longitude, better known as the International Dateline, the lookouts and deck crew began to spot large chunks of whale blubber and other parts of the great sea mammals floating in the slush ice. They knew whalers were nearby.

At 9 a.m., lookouts spotted two sails. Waddell ordered up steam and the *Shenandoah* gave chase. By 11 a.m. she had come up on the *William Thompson*, a whaling ship out of New Bedford, Massachusetts. Lt. Grimball and a group of enlisted men formed the boarding party, who had orders to secure the ship and then make way behind the *Shenandoah* towards the second sail sighted by the lookouts. As soon as Grimball signalled the *Shenandoah* that he had control, Waddell ordered up full steam and gave chase once again to the next ship. A few minutes after midday, the *Shenandoah* was alongside the whaler *Euphrates*, also from New Bedford. This time it was Lt. Sidney Smith Lee who led the boarding party onto the whaler. Lee quickly got the men of the *Euphrates* into the whaleboats and over to the *Shenandoah*, while finding some useful stores, three chronometers and one sextant. The moment Lee got his prize booty onto his longboat, fires were set and the *Euphrates* was blazing by the time he and his boarding party regained the ladder of the *Shenandoah*. By this time, the *William Thompson* had caught up with the *Shenandoah* and Lt. Grimball began the process of transferring useful stores, including thousands of gallons of fresh water, to the Confederate raider. Before this procedure could be finished, however, the aloft lookout spotted another ship. Waddell broke off the cargo transfer, ordered up steam again, and began to pursue the newly sighted ship.

Close to 7 p.m. the *Shenandoah*, flying her Russian pennant, came upon the *Robert Towns*, herself flying a British flag. Waddell, always suspicious of vessels that might false-flag like himself, had the captain hauled aboard, along with his papers. A cursory examination of the registration papers and a talk with the skipper established that she was an Australian ship. Waddell packed the nervous captain back over the side, and the *Shenandoah* moved off to return to the *William Thompson*, where Lt. Grimball and his boarding crew were continuing their dissection of the doomed whaler.

Surgeon Lining had joined the boarding party for the *William Thompson*, keen to restock his medical cabinet, and perhaps find some new reading material in the form of more current newspapers and journals. What he found dismayed him, as he found the newspapers, though many weeks old, reporting the end of Sherman's march up through the Carolinas, the surrender of General Robert E. Lee and his Army of Virginia, as well as the abandonment of Richmond, the capital of the Confederacy. A sombre and thoughtful Lining brought his grim booty of reading back aboard the *Shenandoah* for the officer's wardroom to digest.

The *William Thompson* was set on fire at 3.30 a.m. on 22 June (ship's log time, as the *Shenandoah* was moving back and forth across the International Dateline). Twenty minutes later, the *Shenandoah* steamed away, only to find herself almost immediately smothered by a fast-building fog. All engines went to stop and the *Shenandoah* lay to for the night. Conditions improved at noon, for a gentle puff of breeze carried away the fog to reveal a flat, clear sea and sky. Immediately the lookouts above shouted down that they had spotted more ships. The lookouts kept shouting ships, until the incredulous crew below realised there were nine in total. A virtual squadron of Yankee whaling ships was about to be swept from the sea by the *Shenandoah*.

As the Confederate raider picked her way through the ice towards the nearest two, Waddell and his men could see foreign flags flying from their jack staffs. Deciding not to approach them, for if they dropped search parties over the side of the ship, their unusual behaviour would be observed by the other whalers, Waddell directed the helmsman to move on towards the next closest ship. She was the *Milo*, another member of the steadily diminishing whaling fleet from New Bedford, and she was in the middle of helping one of her whaleboats bring in what would prove to be her last whale. Waddell had the *Shenandoah* brought right up upon the *Milo*'s stern so that he could shout across to the captain, Jonathan Hawes, to come aboard the raider with his papers. Hawes came aboard all right. He stormed onto the quarterdeck of the *Shenandoah*, thundering imprecations and shouting that the Civil War was over. Waddell, amused, but intent on establishing whether the Civil War really was over, gave Hawes a good grilling, but the old Yankee was a stern customer. Indeed Waddell was quite literally facing him eye to eye, as for once he had met someone his own size (a bit over 2 metres).

With Waddell pursuing his usual lawyerly manner of questioning, Hawes grudgingly admitted that he had no documentary evidence for saying, as Waddell quoted in his memoirs, that he 'believed the war was over'. Waddell, implacable as ever, replied, 'that was not satisfactory'. Hawes then went on to comment on the *Shenandoah*'s appearance and of her flying the Russian flag, saying that he had 'taken the steamer to be a telegraph vessel, which they had been expecting to lay a cable between Russian America [Alaska was then still a Russian territory] and Eastern Siberia'. By now, Waddell had begun to warm to the curmudgeonly old Yankee and offered him and his ship a deal that would also benefit the *Shenandoah* and her crew.

The Confederates now had the captains and crews of the *Abigail*, the *Euphrates* and the *William Thompson*. If they took on the crew of the *Milo* as well, they would rapidly diminish the *Shenandoah*'s supplies, cause a security problem, or worse yet, if the Confederate cruiser hit an iceberg, suffer an unprecedented disaster. On a personal level, Waddell had noted that Captain Hawes had his wife and daughter on board the *Milo* too, and Waddell always had a soft spot for the ladies and children. So Waddell proposed to bond the *Milo* if Hawes would promise to take on board all the prisoners and sail directly to San Francisco. All Hawes had to do was sign a bond in the amount of $40,000 US, due to the Confederacy upon the war's end.

The lookouts were eying the next two closest whaling ships as Hawes went over the side back to the *Milo*. Accompanied by another Confederate boarding party, so as to make sure that the *Milo* didn't depart too soon, they were barely under way when Waddell got word from the lookouts that the two whaling ships had made full sail and were heading to what they hoped was safety, an ice field. Waddell put the *Shenandoah* about, and what must have been the strangest event in the naval history of the

American Civil War began, as the Yankee whalers were trying to widen the distance between them and the stalking raider, while the *Shenandoah*, unable to find a passage through the ice, resorted to cannon fire with her big guns. The crew of the 32-pound Whitworth rifled cannon put a round in front of the bow of the furthest fleeing Yankee whaler. The whaler hesitated on her course. Another round from the *Shenandoah*'s Whitworth battery put a hole in the whaler's sail. The whaler, in Waddell's words, 'hove to, and her master received it as an order to come out of the ice floe and submit to the fate which awaited him'.

She was the *Sophia Thornton*, formerly a member of the New Bedford whaling fleet, now about to join the squadron of doomed New Bedford ships at the bottom of the sea. Lt. Scales led out the boarding party with orders from Waddell to bring her about and fall in with the *Milo,* as soon as her officers were aboard the *Shenandoah*. The *Milo* was still trailing the *Shenandoah* like a Roman slave as Waddell ordered full steam and maximum revolutions on the propellers. His new prey was a fast bark, and it would be a challenge even for the fast-sailing *Shenandoah*. For the next two hours the bark flew ahead of the chasing black raider. At the extreme of the range of the Whitworth guns, another round was loosed off. Fortunately for the fleeing bark, the round landed a scant few yards from her stern. But her captain knew that if one of the rifled shots hit her, it would tear her apart, as she was not as strongly built as a ship-rigged whaler. The captain of the *Jireh Swift,* Williams, gave the order to drop sail and stand by for the Confederate raider's approach. Lt. Smith-Lee led out a boarding party which, to their amazement, found a 'captain and crew with their personal effects packed and ready to leave for the *Shenandoah*, and the

Jireh Swift was in flames 20 minutes thereafter', according to Waddell's memoirs.

An enormous amount of activity occurred all at once now. The order was given to the prisoners to take anything from the *Sophia Thornton* they felt they might need for a voyage to San Francisco. While a riotous looting spree was carried out by former crewmen of all the captured whalers, Waddell interrogated Captain Williams of the *Jireh Swift* as to what news he had had of the Civil War. Williams replied that 'he did not think the war was over', according to Waddell's memoirs, but went on to add that he 'felt certain the South would yield eventually'. Waddell still did not have information that he felt he could depend on.

That night, the *Shenandoah* lay alongside the *Milo* and *Sophia Thornton*. Waddell had made the crew of the *Sophia Thornton* swear that they would burn their own vessel before boarding the *Milo* to sail south to San Francisco on the following day. Since he was concerned about the possibility of the sheer numbers of Yankee whaler men being in their favour should they try to re-seize the *Sophia Thornton*, Waddell gave the order for the whalers to cut down her masts and warned that the Confederates were watching them and that the eight-inch cannons were loaded and ready to fire if they failed to comply. Thus, the grumbling whalers were forced to perform one last desecration of their own ship before night fell on the Arctic.

By 23 June, all the captured whalemen and their officers were aboard the *Milo*. In the never-ending daylight of early morning, the *Shenandoah*'s lookouts caught sight of yet two more ships to the south and west at 6.30 a.m. The raider roused herself to give chase once more in what had become an ongoing naval massacre of merchant vessels.

Within 30 minutes of the *Shenandoah*'s leave-taking of the *Milo* and *Sophia Thornton*, the whalers had kept their promise, setting the *Sophia Thornton* on fire and quickly packing themselves aboard the crowded *Milo* for the journey south to San Francisco. The suddenness of the firing of the *Sophia Thornton* suggests the whalers may have been trying to use her death blaze as a warning to the other whalers in the area. If so, the *Susan Abigail*'s captain had been inattentive. At 8.10 a.m. on 23 June, the *Shenandoah* came up on the *Susan Abigail*, a whaler out of San Francisco. As usual, the boarding party brought back a recalcitrant captain – this one named R.R. Redfield – ship's registry and other papers. But this time the *Susan Abigail* had other items the Confederates had not seen in some time, such as tobacco, needles, twine and even articles as unusual as calico; Redfield had a sideline in trading with the Eskimo who lived along the borders of the Bering Sea. The boarding party also found a cache of even more recent newspapers to bring back aboard the *Shenandoah* to Waddell and the crew.

Waddell took only a cursory look over the *Susan Abigail*'s papers before condemning her. She was obviously Yankee. What held his attention much longer, and elicited a lengthy discussion with her captain were the newspapers. According to Waddell's memoirs, the newspapers carried articles that said, 'Southern government had been removed to Danville (Virginia)', and that 'at Danville a proclamation was issued by President Davis, announcing that the war would be carried on with renewed vigour, and exhorting the people of the South to bear up under their calamities'. Between these two quotes, Waddell also commented that the newspaper reported – erroneously, it turned out –that a large portion General Lee's Army of Virginia had gone south into North Carolina to join General Johnston's forces to stop General William T. Sherman's continuing pillage through the South. On reading that, the only way that Waddell would have stopped his combat operations would have been through direct order by naval superiors, who now no longer existed, or completely verifiable intelligence from a trusted source outside the United States of America that the Civil War was truly over.

Ironically, on that same day the very last Confederate army unit surrendered. Brigadier General Stand Watie, a chief of the Cherokee Nation, surrendered his Confederate Indian unit at Doaksville in the Indian Territory of what is now the state of Oklahoma. The CSS *Shenandoah* was now the last surviving Confederate military unit. Any future operations would leave Waddell doubly suspect in the eyes of the world, for though communications were not rapid, he had an endless stream of information that strongly implied the war was over. Illegitimate operations would be treated as piracy, and he knew it. Waddell had listened to Redfield's pleas and he had read the newspapers, but nothing definitively proved the war was over. The *Susan Abigail* was ordered to be burned after all her useful stores were shipped to the *Shenandoah*. Waddell retired to his cabin that night with much to think about.

The following day saw the *Shenandoah* began a course that would take her to St Lawrence Island, but progress was hampered by an intermittent sea fog. With visibility often dropping to zero, they were forced to stop because of the ice floes. Putting a hole into the *Shenandoah* after sailing half-way around the world and dying a hideous death in Arctic waters was not a prospect that Waddell would entertain. On 25 June, Waddell decided that the winds were not sufficient to manoeuvre in waters that contained an ever-growing amount of ice. From this moment until the *Shenandoah* left the Bering Sea, she sailed under steam power. In mid morning the lookouts saw two ships nearby. Beginning their chase at 10 a.m., by 11 a.m. they had closed the distance enough to see that one was a Hawaiian bark, and the other a French-flagged ship; Waddell ordered the *Shenandoah* back onto her original course of north by east.

Though Waddell did not know it, the French vessel, the *Gustav*, was commanded by Captain Vaulpré, who had almost had his vessel sunk by a Russian warship during the Crimean War. He had been saved by an American vessel warning him of the marauding Russian. Vaulpré felt that he had to return the favour to the American whalers and spread the word about the *Shenandoah*'s degradations. He turned the *Gustav* north to do just that.

By that afternoon, the *Shenandoah*'s lookouts had laid eyes on her next victim, the *General Williams*. A chase began at 3 p.m. and a little over two hours later the *Shenandoah* had her cornered, and a boarding party was dispatched to bring off her captain, crew and papers. It was a quick process, even though her captain, William Benjamin, protested vehemently. Waddell did not like the look of him, calling him 'a dirty old dog'. Noting that 'he was the second of his kind that we had met', Waddell believed him to be Jewish, like the captain of the *Susan*, which the Confederates had destroyed months ago. The *General Williams* was ordered burnt, but not before three chronometers, one sextant and $405 dollars had been taken from her.

While the usual cargo transfers and other dealings were taking place between the *Shenandoah* and the *General Williams*, a small group of Eskimos had arrived off the Confederate raider's side from the island of St Lawrence. Once again, the Confederates came face to face with a culture as different from their own as the Polynesians of Ponape. Lieutenants Chew and Scales traded for Eskimo clothing, consisting of a parka, pair of boots and gloves each, while others wanted the Eskimos' walrus ivory. They were bundled back over the side, however, once the destruction of the *General Williams* began.

The *Shenandoah* had barely finished with the *General Williams* when the lookouts roared out 'Sails!', once again. A slow but careful chase was undertaken through the ice floes in the first hours after midnight, now the morning of 26 June. As the Arctic twilight began to strengthen into proper daylight, the sun shone upon another clear, dazzling day. For the Yankee whaling fleet, it was to be another very bad day. The *Shenandoah* came upon the *Nimrod* first. Captained by William Clark, he became the second Yankee whaling captain to have commanded two ships sunk by two different Confederate raiders. His previous vessel, the *Ocean Raider*, had been seized by the *Alabama* in early October 1862. When he was brought aboard the *Shenandoah* he was astonished to see Ship's Master Irvine Bulloch, who had served upon the *Alabama*. It was an amusing reunion for Bulloch, but presumably not for Captain Clark.

Quickly getting the *Nimrod*'s crew and navigational gear aboard, Waddell had the *Shenandoah* turn onto the *William C. Nye* and the *Catherine*. By 4 a.m., all their crews were aboard an increasingly crowded *Shenandoah,* with Waddell pondering how to deal with the surfeit of prisoners he had on board, over two hundred at least. The possibility of an uprising by the large number of outraged whalers was undoubtedly in the forefront of his mind. Coming to a decision that he knew would not be popular, Waddell ordered 12 whaleboats that had been taken from the three captured whaling ships into the water alongside the *Shenandoah*. The whaling men were ordered into the boats, which had been roped together, and given warm clothing, food and water; the entire flotilla was then tied to the stern of the *Shenandoah* with an armed marine standing watch over the tow rope, just in case an escape attempt was made.

Almost at the same moment as the *Shenandoah* got its strange flotilla into the water, and she got under way herself, the topside lookouts cried out again, 'More ships!' Five ships had been spotted, and when the *Shenandoah* had closed upon the first one, Waddell recognised it as the *Benjamin Cummings*, a vessel he had been warned about, presumably by one of the captured whaling captains, as having had smallpox aboard. Turning away, they still had four whaling ships trapped, their sterns up against a wall of ice with nowhere to go. The *General Pike,* captured first, had no captain, and the leading mate, a man named Crowell, was now in charge of her. Crowell told Waddell, as recounted later in his memoirs, that 'If you ransom the *Pike,* her owner will think me so fortunate in saving her that it will give me a claim on them for the command'. Waddell kept this in the back of his mind as the *Shenandoah* swept up the *Isabella* and the *Gypsy* and brought their officers and crews aboard. Only the *Isabella* had any cargo of use to the *Shenandoah,* that being water, and after she had been brought alongside and emptied of this always precious substance she too was burned, just like the *Gypsy* before her.

Waddell had the leading mate of the *General Pike* brought before him and told him that he would bond the *Pike* and parole all the whaling men. The bond would be for $30,000, payable to the Confederate government upon cessation of hostilities. Crowell probably smiled inwardly, as he knew the war was over and the Confederacy no longer existed. Still, since he had signed a bond with Waddell, he would now be responsible for getting 250 men aboard his small ship back to San Francisco safely, after all.

At noon on 26 June, the *Shenandoah* was at 64° 21' N by 172° 20' W. Still seeing more sails to the north, Waddell endeavoured to pursue them as well, but now he found that a northerly headwind was blowing. Normally, that would not be a problem, but as they were operating under steam his approach would be given away, for although Cardiff 'smokeless' coal worked a treat at lower latitudes, in the Arctic the heat from his funnel produced a tell-tale plume of smoke. He would go back to sails for a while, hoping he could navigate the ice floes under wind power.

On the following morning, the *Shenandoah* cruised carefully north-eastwards towards Diomede Island. Waddell reports in his memoirs that he saw 11 sails and tried to keep a slow but gentle chase on, hoping not to reveal himself. Throughout the night this game carried on and then into the morning of the 28th, when a calm descended and the pursued ships came to a halt in East Cape Bay, known today as Cape Dezhnev. The *Shenandoah* languorously approached wearing an American pennant on her jack staff. Her greatest day of destruction, and what would be her last day of combat operations under the Confederate flag, was about to begin.

Noting that the wind was too light for the ships in East Cape Bay to move off, Waddell had kept his eyes on a ship that was still labouring to get up to the cape and decided to capture it first. The *Shenandoah* fell upon the *Waverly* at 11 a.m. after a chase of some three hours. Waddell quickly brought the 33 men aboard, along with their possessions, and had her put to the torch. The *Shenandoah* spun about on her stern and steamed north for Diomede Island and the other whaling ships. At 1.30 p.m. the *Shenandoah* came upon an extraordinary sight. Nine whaling ships were surrounding another whaling ship, which was flying the US flag upside down from her jack staff, an international signal of distress. The whaling ship flying her emergency pennant was the *New Brunswick*, commanded by Captain Alden Potter. The day before she had struck ice severely, putting a hole in her hull, and was slowly sinking. As the whalers traditionally did in such situations, Potter had sold off as much of the ship and its cargo as he could to the other whaling ships that came to assist. This was an attempt to reduce the financial impact on the owner's purse, though the ships tended to be insured. Potter's biggest concern was how to save his crew, and himself.

The *Shenandoah* entered East Cape Bay and came upon the beleaguered *New Brunswick* and the nine other powerless-to-help whaling ships at 1.30 p.m. The men on the *New Brunswick* believed that the black-hulled vessel was part of the Western Union Telegraphic Expedition's fleet of cable survey ships. The fact that Waddell had the US flag lightly flapping from his jack staff also helped create that false assumption. Captain Potter sent over a boat to ask Waddell for help, saying that 'the *Brunswick* had struck a piece of ice a few hours before, which left a hole in her starboard bow twenty inches below the waterline, and asked for assistance'. Waddell replied, 'we are busy now, but in a little while we will attend to you'. The wily North Carolinian then inquired as to which of the whalers was the *James Maury*, to which the man in the boat responded with an outstretched arm and said, 'That one!' Waddell did not know it, but the man in the boat was Jeremiah Ludlow, captain of the *Isaac Howland*, one of the whaling ships he was about to burn. He had been sent over by Captain Potter to ask for help. What Ludlow must have thought about Waddell's rather bizarre answer to his request for help is not known, but surely it must have spooked him somewhat.

As Ludlow's boat pulled away back to the stricken *New Brunswick*, Waddell ordered up every available boat, of which there were five, and had every man armed. Obviously, because there were ten vessels in all to capture, speed and surprise were of the essence. The captains and leading petty officers, ship's papers and registry books must be brought back to the *Shenandoah* for interrogation and adjudication of their ship's status as prizes.

The five boarding parties made off through the bone-chilling waters, avoiding the odd ice floe, as they wound their way towards their respective targets. Once they were almost upon them, Lt. Grimball aboard the *Shenandoah* loosed off a round from one of the guns, while the US flag was quickly hauled down to be speedily replaced by the 'Stainless Banner' of the Confederacy. The stunned whaling fleet, knowing they were cornered and without defences, immediately dropped their American flags. All they could do now was wait and see what their fate would be. The whalers *New Brunswick*, *James Maury*,

Isaac Howland, *Nassau*, *Congress*, *Hillman*, *Covington*, *Martha* and *Nile* were captured in short order. But one ship displayed Yankee pluck: the *Favorite*, out of Fairhaven, Massachusetts. Captain Thomas G. Young was made of stern stuff, and had also fortified himself that afternoon with whisky against the cold and the Confederates. Young crawled atop his stern cabin armed with rifles, pistols and muzzle-loaded harpoon guns. When the boarding party led by Lt. Scales arrived off the side of the *Favorite*, Young, wildly drunk by now, roared at the Confederates to 'Stand Off!' Waddell, watching with his spyglass, ordered the helmsman to bring the *Shenandoah* about as a parallel order was given to the main battery to fire. More precisely, the gun battery was ordered to fire directly into the *Favorite* if she did not surrender. Waddell had come from the far side of the world without losing any crewmen or harming any Union civilians and he would be damned if he would lose good men to a fool Yankee whaler.

The officers and men of the *Favorite* knew it was a lost cause, and argued with Young that it was of no use to strike up a defence against the armed raider. The Confederate boarding party continued to stand off as the *Shenandoah* closed until she was directly alongside the *Favorite*. Young was now face to face with the devil incarnate, as far as he was concerned, Waddell. Waddell, who considered his own conduct so far to be remarkably restrained, did not even deign to speak to the maniacal drunk and told Executive Officer Whittle to take charge. Whittle ordered Young to drop his colours. Young reportedly said he'd see Whittle dead first. Whittle ordered the main gun batteries loaded and aimed. The men of the *Favorite*, who until now had assumed a menacing watch on the deck with muskets and pistols, began to blanch at the sight of the rifled artillery aimed directly at them. They headed for the boats. Waddell, who had no real intention of firing into the whaler, tried to keep a straight face as Whittle ordered Sgt. Canning and three of his marines to go over in a boat and storm the *Favorite*. The Confederate marines were confronted by a resolute Young, who warned that he would shoot if they did not stop. As Canning and his men made to climb onto the bark, Young pulled the trigger on one of his whaling muskets. There was a click. Nothing happened. His crew, knowing he would get them all killed with his drunken behaviour, had secretly removed all the fuses and striking pins from his arsenal. The fearsome Yankee meekly surrendered to the Confederate marines and was led away onto the away boat, headed for the *Shenandoah*. Upon arrival, Waddell looked him over and slapped him in irons in the forecastle to sleep off his liquor.

While the boarding parties looted the other whaling ships, literally working double-time to get them all cleared of supplies, men and papers, Waddell was intent on one vessel in particular, the *James Maury*. The captain of the *James Maury* had died during her whaling cruise, leaving his widow and three children, who were aboard, without means. Waddell had heard from one of the whaling captains captured at Ponape that Slumon Gray had died of appendicitis off Guam. He'd also heard that Gray's body had been 'preserved' by putting it into a cask of whisky. Waddell assured Mrs Gray that the 'men of the South did not make war on women and children', and that, 'though an example to the contrary had been set them by their Northern enemy, we preferred the nobler instincts of humanity'. And with that, the *James Maury* was bonded and ordered to serve as a transport for all the captured whalers. The *Nile* was also spared a fiery grave in the cold Arctic waters. She and the *James Maury* would see San Francisco.

Nine vessels were destroyed on 28 June 1865, with two more bonded. A total of 336 men had been captured. Nine men signed onto the *Shenandoah* as crewmen. Moreover, since leaving Las Desertas in the Madeira Islands of the Atlantic, Waddell had commanded the *Shenandoah* through the destruction of 32 vessels and the capture of an estimated 1,100 captains, officers, seamen and civilians. And not one fatality had occurred. It was an extraordinary and unsurpassed achievement in the annals of naval warfare. Though Waddell did not know it yet, the combat career of the *Shenandoah* had ended. It did not matter, for James Iredell Waddell had become the 'Sea King'.

The last remains of the burning whale ships were sinking beneath the frigid Bering Sea just before midnight on 28 June, when the *Shenandoah* etched another unique record in the history of the American Civil War, becoming the only combatant to operate north of the Arctic Circle. Waddell ventured only a short distance, marking 66° 40' N as the *Shenandoah*'s 'furthest north' before turning about. As he noted in his original, unedited memoirs, 'in consequence of her great length, the immensity of ice and floes, the danger of being shut up in the Arctic Ocean for several months, I was obliged to turn her prow southward and reached East Cape just in time to slip by the Diomedes [islands] when a vast field of floe ice was closing the strait'.

The young officers of the *Shenandoah* may have thought the 'Old Man' was playing it too safe once again, but Waddell was being prudent on several counts. First, as he noted, such a long vessel is at a disadvantage for Arctic operations, making it easier to be caught in the ice at one end, while at the opposite end a water current or an opposing ice floe could twist her hull until she split apart and sank. The next, and fairly common-sense reason, was that the *Shenandoah* was constructed for speed, and not strength, even with her novel iron framework beneath her teak sides. Finally, from a military point of view, the bonded whalers had a head start towards San Francisco where, once information about the *Shenandoah*'s operations had been relayed to government officials, the US Navy would, for all they knew, swarm after her like angry wasps.

The *Shenandoah* crept south, with a careful eye out for ships and an even more watchful eye out for ice. At 1.30 a.m. on 1 July, the gods of the Arctic tried to lay their hands upon Waddell and his ship.

The *Shenandoah* had been making six knots when she ploughed into an ice pack and the impact threw the vessel backwards. Whittle, racing back up the ladder believed the rudder was torn from its chains, while Waddell clambered up from the captain's cabin to survey the damage. As Waddell noted in his memoirs, the *Shenandoah* was 'blocked in on all sides by ice 20 to 30 feet in thickness'. Luckily though, the only damage appeared to be a broken tiller chain and some badly scraped copper, but they were still in serious trouble. Waddell recorded that 'warps and grapnels were run out as on a previous occasion, and she was swung in the right direction and with strong rope mats over her bow (which extended on either side to the fore channels) to protect her from bruises; steam was gently applied and with a large block of ice resting against her cutwater she pushed it along to open a passage, and in this way we worked the *Shenandoah* for hours until she gained open water'. This is a calm and cool recounting of an absolutely terrifying event that almost sank the 'lucky' raider. The tiller chain was repaired, but the crew's confidence had been shaken by the near-miss and Waddell decided it was time to play it safe and run for open waters.

As the *Shenandoah* licked her wounds from her close encounter with the Arctic and crept slowly south through a maze of ice, she caught sight of two ships. The first one, the *Robert Towns*, was French-flagged with the paperwork to match, and released. Later the Confederates stopped the *Kohola* and checked her cargo and papers. This ship proved to belong to the Kingdom of Hawaii, so Waddell released her as well. But her captain told Waddell and his crew that General Lee had surrendered and that President Abraham Lincoln had been assassinated by a Southern radical, John Wilkes Booth. As the Hawaiians continued their voyage north into the Arctic Sea, the Confederates, though they had heard the same news before, still could not bring themselves to believe that any Southern gentleman would assassinate President Lincoln, no matter how much he was hated.

The Arctic tried to take the *Shenandoah* for her own one last time as she made for the Amutka Pass in the Aleutian Islands, the gateway to the Pacific Ocean. A 'black fog closed upon us', Waddell noted, 'and shut out from our view the heavens and all things terrestrial'. Once again, Waddell and his officers were navigating by dead-reckoning in some of the world's deadliest waters. The was the pivotal moment in Waddell's entire career, insofar as his navigational skills were concerned. If he was wrong, they would run aground on the Aleutians and tear the bottom out of the *Shenandoah*, condemning the survivors to a slow death, if they made it ashore. For three days and two nights,

Waddell worked the navigation calculations constantly, staying on watch. Finally, on 4 July, the *Shenandoah* cleared the Amutka Pass, exactly where Waddell had calculated it would appear. They were in the Pacific, headed south, but where?

In his memoirs, Waddell says that he decided after a few days heading south that he would try to plan a surprise attack against the city of San Francisco. He noted,

'the newspapers which were captured gave intelligence of the disposition of American naval vessels and I was not unfamiliar with their commanding officers or their sagacity. In the harbour of San Francisco was an ironclad commanded by Charles McDougal [*sic*], an old and familiar shipmate of mine; we had been together on the *Saginaw* and McDougal was fond of his ease. I did not feel that he would be in our way, any officer of the *Shenandoah* was more than a match for McDougal in activity and will; there was no other vessel of war there, as I concluded from San Francisco newspaper reports, and to enter the port after night and collide with the iron ram was easy enough, and with our force thrown upon the ironclad's deck and in possession of her hatches, no life need have been lost. McDougal could have been with the officer secured, and e'er daylight came, both batteries could have been sprung on the city and my demands enforced. Prudence indicated communicating with a vessel recently before attempting the enterprise.

Many armchair admiral's have belittled Waddell's possible 'enterprise' against San Francisco, mostly based on the fact that the other officers made no comment in their diaries or logs, with the exception of Midshipman John Thomson Mason, who surmised the North Carolinian might have a go at the California Yankees. Several facts support the argument that Waddell did

seriously consider undertaking the operation. The argument that
the *Shenandoah* could not have 'matched wits' with the ironclad
stationed in San Francisco harbour does not hold water either.
The USS *Camanche*, an early bastardised monitor ironclad, had
been built in pieces, shipped aboard another ship, the USS *Aquila*,
to San Francisco to be put together there. Unfortunately, the USS
Aquila sank at her anchorage, leaving the Union Navy to mount
a salvage effort to raise the pieces of the ill-gotten warship. So
Waddell faced an ironclad that had already been sunk once,
commanded by an officer, McDougall, who had none of the
warlike characteristics of his Scottish ancestors, who numbered
amongst the legendary naval forces of the Lords of the Isles.

Waddell's cruise down the North American coast, in the last
few weeks of July 1865, was an effort to reach the trans-Pacific
shipping lanes where he knew the *Shenandoah* would cross paths
with a vessel outbound from San Francisco. Any ship they
stopped, hopefully another Yankee, would have the latest
information on who was in port in San Francisco and would also
be carrying the latest newspapers. Waddell thought they were
'more than a match for any thing we might meet under canvas',
and the *Shenandoah* and her crew probably were prepared for
anything. Anything, that is, except bad news.

6

The Sea King:
A brilliant and dashing cruise

The *Shenandoah* fled the cold waters of the North Pacific Ocean, following a course that James Waddell knew would soon intersect with the main shipping route between San Francisco and ports in the Far East. Roughly paralleling the coast of the North American continent, the Confederates enjoyed a respite from the foul weather and sea conditions of the Arctic and Bering Seas, finding endless days of sunshine and ever increasing warmth throughout July 1865.

Waddell had still not confided in any of his officers about his possible raid on San Francisco, though one of his most junior officers, Midshipman John Thomson Mason mentioned in his diary on 17 July 1865 that, 'We are avoiding the California coast where we might take our chances of capturing one of the mail steamers. The skipper of course must know best, but I think we might make the attempt. My humble opinion is that we will go home as hard as we can stave it & any more prizes we may capture will come our way.' Mason's thoughts would seem prescient in the light of events that unfolded in a few short weeks.

Waddell, though, was still entertaining thoughts of San Francisco. Two days later, Waddell sprang a surprise: an all-hands drill, exercising the gun crews to their fullest extent, something they had been unable to do due to the terrible weather conditions in the North Pacific and because of the dearth of crewmen throughout the voyage. Waddell's memoirs are silent on the performance of the gun crews, but Lt. Francis Chew noted in his diary that Waddell hoped that he would 'see that order [and] quickness [which are] attained on a man-of-war after long practice, forgetting that he has never ordered this exercise before, and that we have to labour under great disadvantage in working our guns. The guns' crew have been drilled very little; for months after getting to sea we had no men to put at the guns, and of late, dispensing of captured vessels has occupied all our attentions and time.'

However Waddell was disappointed with the gun crews' performance. Executive Officer Whittle reflected in his diary that the men had done well 'for the first exercise'. What Whittle did not realise was that Waddell had been a gunnery instructor at the Naval Academy years before. And like all officers who have served in training commands, the difference between practice, perfection and the reality was coming as a shock to Waddell, who always expected professional performance.

By 24 July, the speed of the *Shenandoah* had carried the last Confederates to a position parallel with the border of California and Mexico. They had traversed the length of the 'American' Pacific coast, and had not spotted a single sail. At this point, it is hard to know if Waddell had given up on the idea of raiding San Francisco, or if he hoped to turn closer to Mexico in order to capture a mail steamer bound from California to Panama.

Waddell's time in Panama years earlier would have made him acutely aware of the amount of shipping along the 'mail run', as well as the potential value in picking off a shipment from the gold fields of California.

In fact, unbeknownst to Waddell, about the same time as he considered attacking San Francisco the vessel *Golden City* had departed San Francisco for England, via New York, with $1.46 million in gold bullion aboard her. The US Mint in San Francisco itself had trumpeted in the local papers that it had minted $19 million in silver and gold currency for that year. If Waddell had known this, the fate of San Francisco would have probably been sealed. As it was, wind and luck saved the city.

Another week went by with Waddell still steering the *Shenandoah* southward. Finally, on 2 August, just after the midday bell had been rung, the lookout shouted that sail had been spotted off to the northwest. They were at 16° 20' N by 121° 11' W, and nearly a thousand miles west of the Mexican coastline. Waddell was keen to get information quickly, so steam was ordered up for the first time in many days, and the chase was on. At 4.15 p.m. the order to stop engines was given; the *Shenandoah* had come upon the last vessel she would ever halt, a small bark named the *Barracouta*. The boarding party was led out by Ship's Master Irvine Bulloch, the half-brother of the man who had organised the Confederate Navy's overseas commerce-raiding programme, Commander James Bulloch. Irvine Bulloch had as much 'ship sense' as his brother, and realised as soon as he swung over the side of the *Barracouta* that the English pennant she flew matched the build and rigging of the sails that she wore. The captain of the *Barracouta*, who appeared sympathetic to the Confederate cause, delivered the harshest news to Bulloch and his boarding party. The war was well and truly over. The newspapers the *Barracouta* carried told a sad and continuous tale of Southern defeat and despair. The surrender of General Robert E. Lee, the capture of President Jefferson Davis and Vice-President Alexander Stephens, as well as the barely believable assassination of Union President Abraham Lincoln, were told in stark terms that were as awful as any words uttered by Homer. The Union had triumphed and the United States of America was once again the sole sovereign government of all the land between Canada and Mexico, from the Atlantic Ocean to the Pacific.

When Bulloch's boarding party came near the *Shenandoah*, the glum and despairing looks upon their faces told a story no words could convey. As they regained the deck of the last Confederate naval vessel, the words spilled out: the war was over. The entire crew was stunned as the word was passed, none more so than Waddell.

At the moment of actually receiving the dire news of the Confederacy's collapse, however, all Waddell was able to do was order Lt. Whittle to 'de-militarise' the *Shenandoah*. Lt. Dabney Scales, Watch Officer at that critical moment, recorded the following in the ship's log: 'Having received by the British bark *Barracouta* the sad intelligence of the overthrow of the Confederate Government, all attempts to destroy the shipping or property of the United States will cease from this date, in accordance with which First Lieutenant William C. Whittle Jr. received an [order] from the Commander to strike below the battery and disarm the ship and crew.'

For the men aboard the *Shenandoah* who were actually commissioned by, or enlisted into, the Confederate Navy, the news was not just emotionally devastating, but terrifying, as they knew that their combat operations had carried on months after the war was acknowledged to be over by every major power in the world. The newspapers from the *Barracouta* labelled the *Shenandoah* and her men pirates. In an age where the term 'piracy' was equivalent to 'terrorism' in today's world, the words of Waddell's young executive officer detail a 'situation desperate to a degree to which history furnishes no parallel. Piracy is a crime not against one nation *but against all* [author's emphasis added]. A pirate is an enemy of mankind, and as such amenable to trial and punishment against the laws of nations, by the courts of any country into whose hands he may fall.' What Lt. Whittle had enunciated so clearly, Waddell knew well, as not only had he studied international law pertaining to maritime matters, referring constantly to his library of legal books, but he had adhered strictly to international conventions during his combat operations against Union vessels. From Waddell's perspective, the Union had been the one constantly breaking the accepted international laws of nations. The stopping of the British vessel *Trent* by a Union warship in 1861 to seize the Confederate commissioners, Slidell and Mason, on their way to Britain, nearly caused Britain to declare war on the US, openly purchasing war munitions and shipping them to the US; and then in 1864, there was the illegal seizure of the CSS *Florida* from inside a Brazilian port, causing Brazilian forces to pursue and open fire, to no avail, but prompting a major diplomatic brouhaha. This last event would come back to haunt the United States of America in a few years, and help Waddell.

But on 2 August 1865, Waddell was first going to have to help himself, his men and his ship. They were alone and being hunted

on every ocean of the world by the world's two most powerful
navies, the United States Navy and Her Majesty's Royal Navy.
The Royal Navy had come into the hunt after Britain's Prime
Minister, Lord Palmerston, in a politically pragmatic move,
declared the Union rejoined, and removed the belligerent nation
status from the Confederate States of America, since it in effect
no longer existed. Removing that status made the CSS
Shenandoah a pirate ship and her commander, James Waddell,
the chief pirate. The Royal Navy was ordered to stop her and
seize her wherever she might be found on the world's oceans.

In America, outrage about the Confederate raiders had been
simmering since the end of the war. The news that the
Shenandoah had not sunk, as had been rumoured widely, and
had stalked and destroyed the main body of the US whaling fleet,
sent British and American relations to a new low. Loud calls for
war against Britain were now being made in Congress and the
nation's newspapers. Prime Minister Palmerston, a master of
realpolitik, recognised soberly that the newly re-united States of
America, though they might be war-weary, had the world's
largest, most advanced, and most combat-ready military. Meanwhile the Prussians, led by Otto von Bismarck, had been victorious in the Second War of Schleswig against the Danes, and were
rising to power on the British Empire's east. Palmerston faced a
very real possibility of two significant military threats
confronting the British Empire at once. With
this in mind, Palmerston had a government edict prepared to
send throughout the entire British Empire, ordering that the
Shenandoah be seized if she entered into any British port.
Furthermore, he ordered authorities to 'detain the vessel by force
if necessary' and then instructed Royal Navy warships to capture

her 'upon the high seas', if need be. Palmerston hoped this would begin to placate the furious Yankees in Washington, DC, while he kept a watch on events transpiring between Austria and Prussia. He would withhold issuing the document for the moment, while he pondered the political landscape, but he knew it would have to go out soon. Ironically, the commerce-raiding activities of both Waddell and the now legendary Rafael Semmes of the *Alabama,* inspired the officers of the nascent navy of Prussia, and its descendants, the Imperial German Navy and Kriegsmarine, to study their tactics.

Months before, in Liverpool, James Dunwoody Bulloch had heard the news of the Confederacy being carved up into pieces like a dying snake. As Sherman's marauding divisions decimated the Deep South, US Grant's army was battering the Confederacy's head at Richmond. Bulloch knew the end was near and was dispatching, as best he could, the remaining Confederate personnel home from across Europe. But the *Shenandoah* was uppermost in his mind. Back on 23 June 1865, the same day that the Confederate Cherokees of Brig. Gen. Stand Watie surrendered in the Oklahoma Territory, Commander Bulloch wrote out an order to Waddell in the form of a letter, informing him of the demise of the Confederacy. Bulloch expanded on his earlier advice to Waddell as to what to do, but as Bulloch noted, 'the present condition of the *Shenandoah* and of the point at which this letter may reach you renders it impossible to give specific instructions to the disposal of the ship'. Bulloch, not knowing what else to say, simply told Waddell to do his best.

The last act of the Confederate government was then carried out, not in North America, but in Britain. Bulloch forwarded the

letter to Confederate Commissioner Mason, who placed it before
Earl Russell, Britain's Foreign Secretary, asking if he would send
copies of the letter to the major ports of the Pacific where the
Shenandoah might be expected to dock. In the end, the document was sent to British consuls around the world. With that,
and a gentlemanly word, Commissioner Mason accepted the best
wishes of Earl Russell, and the Confederate States of America
passed into history. All this had transpired without Waddell's
knowledge, due to the slowness of communications in those
days. Strangely enough, Bulloch's adherence to duty and
responsibility in sending out the last Confederate naval order,
would, like the *Florida* affair and the incident in Brazil, come to
Waddell and his men's aid in the future. For because Great
Britain transmitted the order *cum* letter through her foreign
service, and still regarded the Confederacy (on that day) as a
lawful belligerent (Britain being a major foreign power and
signatory to the Treaty of Washington), an established trail of
legal paperwork had been created. The slowness and lack of
communications would provide a solid defence for Waddell and
the *Shenandoah*.

For Waddell and his young officers, there was still
considerable cause for concern. Although the crew had written a
petition to Waddell, stating that they would loyally follow his
command and go to any port he chose, the commissioned
officers were in a different situation. They had been dubbed
pirates, and thus were more legally liable if captured by any
major power, and more likely to face hanging for piracy. It was
that simple. They had to make a dash for a port where they
could de-mob and disappear for a while until they could figure
out what to do. The young officers were so concerned that they

presented Waddell with a petition, inquiring in the most tactful of language what their destination might now be.

On 4 August, as recorded by Ship's Surgeon Lining and Midshipman John Mason, Waddell, no longer Lt. Commanding Confederate States Navy, had the ship's crew assemble on the man deck for a 'captain's call'. Waddell began his speech by confirming that the war had ended and then thanked them all for their service. He then touched on the issue that concerned him and every other commissioned officer on the *Shenandoah*: that they must be careful not to be captured and that they must make port in a suitably neutral country. Otherwise they risked being charged with piracy, the full consequences of which were well known. Finishing his speech, Waddell made note of the petition from his officers that inquired as to their possible destination. Mason and Lining recorded that their former commander said, 'I shall take the ship into the nearest English port and all I ask of you men, is to stand by me to the last.' Waddell then alluded to what history would remember of the *Shenandoah,* and the feat they were about to attempt, when he said, 'As for our cruise, it is a record which stands for itself and all you have to do is be proud of it.' Waddell's men cheered the speech, with more than a few officers and deck hands doing so as tears flowed down their cheeks.

By 5 August, the deck guns and Whitworth rifles had been de-commissioned, but due to their size and weight, they were shifted below deck immediately. Waddell had them covered with tarpaulins and well-roped. He had still given no inkling of his destination, though the diary/log of Executive Officer Whittle notes a course shaped 'S by E _ E' on both 4 and 5 August, or as he said in layman's terms, 'It is deemed proper that we should cross the Equator to the Eastward of 115 W in order to clear with the SE trades the Tahita group of islands.' This same general direction was followed until 12 August.

There has been a spate of books that have mined the diaries of Waddell's subordinate officers (it was Waddell's order that they all keep one), trying to build a picture of him as an incompetent, indecisive and incapable commander, calling his memoir a typical romantic 'Lost Cause' manuscript, which tried falsely to embellish his lacklustre career. This is blatantly incorrect on several counts. In the first place Waddell never intended to publish his memoir. It was provided to Major Gen. Marcus J. Wright, a Confederate general hired by the US government to acquire official and unofficial Confederate documents, by Waddell's wife, Anne Sellman Waddell, after his death. Only one document pertaining to the *Shenandoah* was published in his lifetime, and that was a private letter printed in a newspaper, allegedly without his permission. Secondly, Waddell, like Bulloch, was operating more by legal precedent than by military principle in this operation. Waddell alone was charged with carrying out the *Shenandoah*'s mission, adhering strictly to Bulloch's orders when required, operating under his own initiative when necessary. The North Carolinian understood that every time a ship was seized, the legality of the action must be as clear as possible, for if the South won, it stood to garner the financial rewards of the bonded vessels. If the South lost, it had to show that the still-born nation had operated as a lawful belligerent under the accepted norms of international maritime treaties (such as the Treaty of Washington) and protect its military personnel from undue prosecution or persecution. Futhermore, the success of the *Shenandoah*'s cruise showed that if Waddell were as incompetent as he has been made out to be by 'armchair admirals', then the operation would have been a disaster. But Waddell would end the cruise of the last Confederate cruiser in a fashion that would be acknowledged by the observers of the day, and the historians of the future, as an extraordinary feat of navigation and sailing. Finally, in the confidential conversations between Bulloch and Waddell in Liverpool, Bulloch would have reiterated to Waddell that returning to Europe after completing the mission would have been the best option, due to the Confederacy's network of covert financing. The Confederate Navy – at least Bulloch's part of it in Europe – had been run on a shoestring, and even at the end of the war had some financial resources and contacts to assist a returning cruiser crew.

On 17 August, Waddell had shaped his course for the *Shenandoah* more towards the south-southwest as they crossed the equator into the southern hemisphere. The crew believed they would be headed to Australia, expecting a warm and sympathetic welcome there. Waddell still refused to reveal his hand as to the 'nearest English port'. Meanwhile, the fact that the *Shenandoah* was now a de-militarised ship began to affect discipline and morale. When Lt. Scales failed to appear on time for quarters, Waddell had him called to his wardroom for an explanation. Waddell knew that the normal military rules of behaviour aboard a warship no longer applied, so decided to apply 'civilian' justice by telling Scales that he was relieved of duties aboard the ship until the end of the cruise and to consider himself as a passenger. Waddell then ordered his clerk, the former Australian ship's captain, John Blacker, to take Scales' watches. Master's Mate Hunt then refused duty under Ship's

Master Bulloch, and got the same sentence from Waddell as Scales. Waddell decided he would stand the watches, which threw even more coal upon the fire. Surgeon Lining noted in his diary that the fractious situation eventually resolved itself, but not before morale dropped further on the ship.

The *Shenandoah* was bearing down on Cape Horn on 1 September 1865, with winds from the northwest until a desultory calm set in at midnight. For the several days before, the winds had been light and variable, so as the ex-raider set up to transit below the great cape of South America, all aboard kept a weather eye on the barometer, waiting for one of the tremendous gales that regularly roared out across the 'Forties'. Waddell and his lost command were exiting the South Pacific at just the right time, and not just where weather was concerned. While he could not know that the Royal Navy was looking for him, he knew the US Navy would be. In fact, the USS *Saranac* was chasing the *Shenandoah* as she sailed south, while two more warships were patrolling the main east-west trade routes from Hawaii to California. Meanwhile the USS *Iroquois* had reached Cape of Good Hope on 8 August 1865, where she joined the USS *Wyoming*. If that wasn't a daunting enough challenge for Waddell, the USS *Wateree* and USS *Saint Mary's* were operating off the coast of South America. And yet, all the pressure from his young officers to take the *Shenandoah* into the 'nearest' British port, Waddell's experiences in the US Navy – and in precisely the same areas in which the US Navy warships were now looking for him – meant that he knew where not to go.

On 6 September, the *Shenandoah* was blasted by a following gale. Travelling at speeds that still allowed her to make speeds of 15 knots per hour – even though her copper-bottomed hull was fouled with marine growth – she was breaking her own personal distance records almost every day. On 9 September, Waddell was informed by Executive Officer Lt. William C. Whittle that the *Shenandoah* had logged an incredible 262 miles in 24 hours.

A few days later, the lookouts spotted their first sail in several weeks. The vessel, an English ship named the *West Australian,* spotted the masquerading *Shenandoah* and made signals for the Confederates to close and 'speak'. But Waddell instructed that no ship would be responded to, nor any flag raised, since the ship was in legal limbo (though Waddell likely realised that the victorious Union would claim all former Confederate property as property of the Union government). Whittle noted that same day in his log that three more vessels were sighted. The *Shenandoah* continued for Cape Horn.

The prow of the *Shenandoah* passed below Cape Horn on 15 September 1865, after passing almost 50 miles south of the exposed rocks of Diego Ramirez the day before. A course that slung them far southwest of the 'turn', now brought them up onto a course of east by south, but with winds beginning to shift towards the northeast. Waddell and Whittle were expecting the fearsome weather of the Horn at any time – and the following day they got it. Gales and strong winds from the north and west, accompanied by heavy seas and heavy rain squalls, exacted the Horn's toll on the fleeing ex-raider. Almost as soon as this weather had had its way with the *Shenandoah*, Waddell's next concern, once again, was icebergs. For the next several days, the ship worked a northeast course, keeping an eye out for the Georgia Islands, Shag Rock, and of course, ice.

Meanwhile, in Great Britain, the prime minister, Lord Palmerston had the seizure order for the *Shenandoah* issued to the colonial governments on 17 September 1865. The *Shenandoah* was running out of places to go and the British government was taking heavy 'diplomatic fire' from the US government. Something, somewhere, had to occur soon.

A doubled watch was mounted on 20 September when the first piece of ice was spotted, and almost before the extra hands could take their positions, large icebergs began to appear everywhere. Surgeon Lining noted that one iceberg was estimated to be nearly 180 feet tall. Waddell was mesmerised by the ethereal beauty of the ice as well, recounting that, 'the icebergs were castellated and resembled fortifications'. Fog then dropped in, hampering the lookouts' efforts and raising anxiety levels once again amongst the dispirited crew.

Having rounded Cape Horn safely, Waddell directed the *Shenandoah*'s course towards the mid South Atlantic Ocean. He was heading north, but still had not told his other officers, or the crew. The *Shenandoah* was now almost on the same latitude as Cape Town, South Africa. Those officers and crewmen who considered Cape Town to be an 'English' port assumed Waddell would turn the ship towards Africa in the next few days. But as they saw the ship head further north, the officers on the ship decided to inquire more formally of Waddell as to their destination. They created a petition stating their view that the *Shenandoah* should make for Cape Town, as the vessel was becoming increasingly lighter due to her consumption of coal. This made her less easy to handle, especially in the bad weather they expected to face in the North Atlantic. They closed their petition by saying that they were not challenging his command, nor trying to interfere with the normal chain of command as it applied to day-to-day operations.

Before Waddell had time to consider the document laid before him, the enlisted ranks of the *Shenandoah*'s crew presented him with their own petition. The young officers had tried to make their document as non-confrontational as possible, inquiring in the most polite tones as to Waddell's course. But the enlisted crew's petition, which also suggested that the *Shenandoah* could land the men who wanted to go to South Africa in one of the remote bays along its north-western coast, was less polite in tone. Waddell did not say so at the time, but years later, in a private letter that was published without his consent, he spoke freely of what he thought and saw at the time: a tired and demoralised group of officers and crew fomenting the most heinous naval crime imaginable, mutiny. The wily North Carolinian had seen this type of behaviour years before on the *Relief,* and of course he had been a young midshipman in the US Navy when the aftershock of the supposed 'mutiny' on the *Somers* occurred. He decided to let the potential spark of mutiny burn itself out. He would call a staff meeting of the officers to let them discuss the issue.

Waddell seized control of the situation immediately, telling the young officers that he would be guided by their opinion but that first they should know his. He had originally considered landing in Cape Town, but had decided to take the ship to England. And once again, he did not say which port, though all believed it would be Liverpool. Waddell then said he would abide by their group decision, and then left the cabin for them to come up with a course of action. He was letting them feel the weight of responsibility. The discussion descended into angry argument as the lieutenants looked over the petitions and debated the points contained within them. For over an hour the debate raged.

Whittle sat in on the debate, but let the other lieutenants, Chew, Grimball, Lee and Scales, take the lead in arguing the various issues. In the end, the case for Liverpool won, as Waddell believed it would, but the debate by the leading officers did little to heal the split in the crew. While Waddell didn't gloat over the fact that his course of action had won the day, he did take satisfaction from the petition signed by the 77 men on the *Shenandoah* who supported him.

On 6 October, Lord Palmerston instructed the Royal Navy to capture the *Shenandoah* if she were found to be carrying mounted weapons, and then to turn the vessel over to the US Navy at the first opportunity. However, Palmerston also clearly stated that the officers and crew of the *Shenandoah* were not to be turned over to US authorities, but were to be transported ashore and set free. Palmerston may have decided that the *realpolitik* of the situation demanded that he cooperate with the angry and powerful American government, but that didn't mean he'd kow-tow to Washington, DC.

Early on the following morning, a ship was spotted to the west of the *Shenandoah*, and close to the speeding Confederates. Whittle reckoned she was English by the cut of her sails, but again no contact was made or attempted, on Waddell's orders. They travelled in silence, except for the fresh winds pushing them along at some 12 knots. But every ship spotted now brought instant anxiety, an ironic reversal of fortune for the ex-raider, now she was the hunted and defenceless prey.

The *Shenandoah* crossed the equator for the fourth time in her circumnavigation of the world on 11 October. This was two days after the anniversary of Waddell and his original crew sailing out from Liverpool aboard the *Laurel* to meet the *Sea*

King, as the *Shenandoah* had been in her former life. It had been a dramatic year, from gales in the South Atlantic's 'Roaring Forties', to fetes in Melbourne, meetings with island kings in the Pacific and drunken whaling captains in the Arctic Sea. There would never be a cruise by a warship like this again. There now came the closest approach of any ship yet to the *Shenandoah*. The vessel, intrigued by the northward-speeding black steamer of the Confederates, changed her course in order to run alongside and exchange information. But Waddell made sure no signals were sent out from the *Shenandoah* and told the helmsman to make way from the vessel. The disappointed crew of the *Shenandoah* were desperate for news from the unknown bark, which they could make out had several women passengers aboard, but knew they dare not give any inkling of their true identity.

Waddell's fears were realised at 4 p.m. in the afternoon of 25 October, when the shout 'Sail!' came down from the top lookout. Every set of spyglasses swung to the north. Waddell ordered another lookout aloft. By the time he reached the crow's nest, the vessel could be seen even by those on the quarterdeck; whoever she was, she had spun on her stern and was closing hard, too hard for Waddell's liking. He knew he couldn't change course immediately. If it were a warship, the game would be up. Instead, he slowed the speed of the vessel as much as possible, even to the point of having the propeller lowered from its well into the water just to create drag. He hoped to make nightfall, when, using the smokeless Cardiff coal they had been hoarding, he would raise steam and proceed on a new course, thus losing the unknown chasing vessel.

The crew of ex-Confederates anxiously watched the sun

descend as the mystery vessel drew closer. Just before nightfall, as the last of the sun's rays bounced off the ocean's surface, the vessel had closed to within three miles. The lookout could now report with certainty that it was a steamer. Waddell was sure it was a warship, but he still had the upper hand. With the disappearance of the sun's last glint, the engine room got the order for full steam up and Waddell instructed the helmsman to put the *Shenandoah* about on a course heading east. For 16 miles she steamed eastward, then turned her prow northwards again, staying on this course for some 100 miles. The *Shenandoah* was under steam propulsion again for the first time in 13,000 miles. Some time later, Waddell would be told that the USS *Saranac* had been operating in that area, searching for the *Shenandoah*.

As the *Shenandoah* steamed northwards the following day, the first crewman to die during the entire voyage passed away. Named William Bill, he was a native of Hawaii, and Surgeon Lining believed him to have succumbed to venereal disease. On 27 October, under strengthening south-westerly winds, the Hawaiian was laid to rest in the ocean's deep. The Confederate flag had been raised in his honour, then dipped to half-mast, then re-stowed lest another vessel came upon them. The *Shenandoah* was around 1,000 miles out from Liverpool now, and Waddell and Ship's Master Bulloch were performing the final navigational calculations to set the ship up for her final dash into what they hoped would be sanctuary.

While the ship sped along with the southwest winds filling her sails, the last breaths of another crewman aboard the *Shenandoah* were leaving his oxygen-starved lungs. Sergeant George Canning, one of the Australian 'stowaways', was dying from the effects of a lung wound that had never healed. The morning watch on 31 October was disturbed by the call of 'All hands to bury the dead', according to Whittle's diary. With the last rites read by Assistant Surgeon McNulty, who was a Catholic like Canning, the body of the last Confederate marine to die while ostensibly serving aboard a Confederate naval vessel, was committed to the deep. Neptune had exacted his last tariff from the Confederate's cruise through his kingdom.

The *Shenandoah* was now some 900 miles from Liverpool. By 3 November, the Confederates were bearing down on Cape Clear on the south-eastern coast of Ireland. Waddell had the course changed so that they would shoot straight as an arrow up the St George's Channel into Liverpool. He planned to sprint through the channel in the least amount of time, hoping to slip past any Union warships that might be lurking off British waters. Even the fact of being in British waters might not be enough for a cocksure Union warship captain to chase them, so no chances would be taken.

Sunrise on 4 November 1865 saw the Confederates gazing upon the soil of Ireland, the first land they had seen in 23,000 miles and for 122 days. Waddell and Ship's Master Bulloch, always proud of their navigational skills, were jubilant. As Waddell pointed out in his memoirs, 'We could not have made a more beautiful landfall', for as he went on to say, 'The beacon in St George's Channel was where and at the time looked for.' This navigational feat, in particular notable since their chronometers had not been rated in months, was one of the most incredible feats of navigation in the history of sailing, and fully comparable to any modern sailing record.

Waddell directed Paymaster Breedlove Smith to pay off the men the following day. He realised that the ship's finances had been reduced greatly by the expenses of repairs in Melbourne and that he could pay only a portion of what was owed. But Waddell promised that once ashore, he would get the men their full pay, as he trusted that Commander Bulloch would have funds set aside for them. Waddell, honest to the last, made sure each man received a certificate stating how much was owed him, of which they – officers and enlisted men alike – received a percentage.

All aboard began to pack their bags and gaze towards the lights from houses and ships on either side of the St George's Channel. A short time before midnight on 5 November, Waddell ordered rockets launched, hoping to attract a pilot boat to come out from Liverpool. A boat finally answered the repeated firings and upon her coming alongside, he inquired as to their identity. Careful to the last, the Confederates said they were the *America*, three months out from Calcutta. The pilot, believing this, tied up alongside and climbed up the ladder. Once he was on board, Waddell revealed the *Shenandoah*'s true identity, and asked the pilot if the Civil War was truly over. The pilot said, 'It has been over so long people have got through talking about it. Jeff Davis is in Fortress Monroe, and the Yankees have had a lot of cruisers out looking for you'. The astonished pilot then blurted out, 'Haven't you seen any of them?' A laconic reply came back, 'Not unless a suspicious looking craft we sighted off the Western Islands was one.'

The pilot took the wheel just as the tides were falling away on the River Mersey. He told Waddell that it would be best if they waited until morning, but Waddell told him to try anyway. They crept forward against the falling tide, only to find themselves aground on a sandbar at about 4 a.m. The *Shenandoah* had reached out and literally touched British soil.

By 7 a.m., the tides had returned, and with the engines raised for steam, the pilot pushed the *Shenandoah* forward over the sandbar and up into the Mersey. The 'Stainless Banner' of the Confederacy was flying from the jack staff, one last time. When the fog came up, the crew of Her Britannic Majesty's warship, *Donegal*, were astounded to see a Confederate warship anchored along behind them. While the Confederates waited upon an officer from the *Donegal* to come aboard, the Confederate flag was ceremonially lowered by the *Shenandoah*'s quartermaster. When Captain James A. Paynter of the *Donegal* arrived aboard the *Shenandoah* he found the entire crew arrayed before him, tears on some cheeks, with Waddell awaiting him. The career of the Confederacy's last commerce-raider and Waddell's only combat command had now ended. What would happen next was anyone's guess.

7

A wanderer on the face of the earth

When the sun began to burn away the fog that lay above the River Mersey in Liverpool on 6 November 1865, the interested onlookers near the Rock Ferry slip were treated to the sight of a strange, sleek, black vessel, anchored near the warship HBM *Donegal*. If they looked carefully, they would have seen a large number of sailors in strangely coloured grey uniforms with weathered complexions, keenly gazing ashore, but making no move to lower boats. The same curious onlookers, if they paused to pick up the *Liverpool Mercury* newspaper the following day, would have been treated to a story that would have been as incredible as if man had just landed on the moon.

The *Liverpool Mercury* breathlessly noted that the steamer *Douglas* had passed the *Shenandoah*, apparently lying at anchor, near the bar that marked the entrance to the Victoria Channel at 8 a.m. But 'knowledgeable' seamen had discounted the story, saying the crewmen of the *Douglas* must be mistaken, for the last news of the *Shenandoah* was that she was still in the North Pacific. The *Mercury* went on to say that all Liverpool was astounded when at 10 a.m. the *Shenandoah* steamed up the

Victoria Channel, flying the 'Palmetto' flag from her masthead. As the *Mercury* glibly pointed out, 'all doubts on the point were set at rest'.

What the *Liverpool Mercury* and the rest of Liverpool didn't know was the dramatic diplomatic story that had begun 24 hours earlier. Immediately upon the arrival of Captain Paynter from HBM *Donegal*, Waddell delivered into Paynter's hands one of the most unusual documents in the history of international law. Waddell's document surrendered the *Shenandoah* to the British government, thus giving a last tweak to the cheek of the Union government, and at the same time throwing the officers and crew before the mercy and justice of the British government. Waddell's surrender letter, showing a firm legal grasp of the legalities of the situation, is printed in full here, due to its extraordinary content:

SHENANDOAH, November 6, 1865.

MY LORD: I have the honor to announce to your Lordship my arrival in the waters of the Mersey with this vessel, lately a ship of war, under my command, belonging to the Confederate States of America.

The singular position in which I find myself placed and the absence of all precedents on the subject will, I trust, induce your Lordship to pardon a hasty reference to a few facts connected with the cruise lately made by this ship.

I commissioned the ship in October, 1864, under orders from the naval department of the Confederate States, and in pursuance of the same commenced actively cruising against the enemy's commerce. My orders directed me to visit certain seas in preference to others. In obedience thereto I found myself in May, June, and July of this year in the Okhotsk Sea and Arctic Ocean. Both places, if not quite isolated, are still so far removed from the ordinary channels of commerce that months would elapse before any news could reach there as to the progress or termination of the American war. In consequence of this awkward circumstance I was engaged in the Arctic Ocean in acts of war as late as the 28th day of June, in ignorance of the serious reverses sustained by our arms in the field and the obliteration of the Government under whose authority I have been acting.

This intelligence I received for the first time on communicating at sea, on the 2nd of August, with the British bark Barracouta, of Liverpool, fourteen days from San Francisco. Your Lordship can imagine my surprise at the receipt of such intelligence, and I would have given to it little consideration if an Englishman's opinion did not confirm the war news, though from an enemy's port. I desisted instantly from further acts of war, and determined to suspend further action until I had communicated with a European port, where I would learn if that intelligence were true. It would not have been intelligent in me to convey this vessel to an American port for surrender simply because the master of the Barracouta had said the war was ended. I was in an embarrassing position; I diligently examined all the law writers at my command, searching a precedent for my guidance in the future control, management, and disposition of the vessel. I could find none. History is, I believe, without a parallel.

Finding the authority questionable under which I considered this vessel a ship of war, I immediately discontinued cruising, and shaped my course for the Atlantic Ocean.

As to the ship's disposal, I do not consider that I have any right to destroy her or any further right to command her. On the contrary, I think that as all the property of Government has reverted by the fortune of war to the Government of the United States of North America, therefore this vessel, inasmuch as it was the property of the Confederate States, should accompany the other property already reverted. I therefore sought this port as a suitable one wherein to 'learn the news,' and, if I am without a Government, to surrender the ship with her battery, small arms, machinery, stores, tackle, amid apparel, complete, to her Majesty's Government for such disposition as in its wisdom should be deemed proper.

I have, etc.,

JAMES I. WADDELL.

Captain Paynter graciously accepted the letter from Waddell and then departed over the side to have the letter taken ashore and telegraphed to the Foreign Secretary's office, now headed by Lord Clarendon. (The British Prime Minister, Palmerston, had died, and been replaced by Earl Russell.) Almost immediately following the British officer's departure, a customs official came aboard. After a cursory look about, the official informed Waddell that the crew could go ashore, but only if they left their possessions aboard, pending a more detailed inspection. Whether the men decided as one not to go ashore without their possessions, or Waddell ordered them not to, is not known, but in any case, all stayed aboard.

Shortly thereafter, Waddell received from Captain Paynter of the *Donegal* a message that all personnel aboard the *Shenandoah* were restricted to the vessel, pending a decision from Whitehall in London regarding their fate. Captain Paynter also sent over Lt. Alfred Cheek from the *Donegal,* who also informed Waddell that a unit of Royal Marines from HBM *Goshawk* would be coming aboard the *Shenandoah* to take over the vessel. The *Goshawk* would anchor alongside the *Shenandoah,* not so much in case the ex-confederates might try to sail away (which Waddell thought was an absurd idea), but so as to give the appearance to the American government that proprieties were being observed, and no materials would be allowed to leave the ship. Surgeon Lining noted in his diary that the Royal Marines would be given 'any assistance that might be necessary', adding laconically that 'all hands were then relieved of duty'. For the first time in over a year, soft Southern accents failed to be heard on the deck of the *Shenandoah* on the night watches.

For Waddell, it was a tense waiting game. He had no way of knowing that the re-appearance of the *Shenandoah*, not only in British waters, but in a British port, had inflamed an already tense diplomatic relationship between the US and Britain. Angry arguments over reparations for damages caused by British-built commerce-raiders, such as the *Alabama* and *Florida*, had been raging since the end of the war. The British had been hoping that the passage of time would gently heal things, but unwelcome reports of the continuing depredations of the *Shenandoah* kept appearing in the press. Proof of rumours that she had been sunk by an iceberg in the Arctic Sea was almost wished for by the British Foreign Service, as that would give some sense of retribution to the furious American government. Instead, here she was, anchored on the Mersey with a full crew and her armaments stowed below. The British government's face and hands were as red as the coats of their soldiers in the American War of Independence, and the Yanks were spoiling for a fight again.

Meanwhile the US consul in Liverpool, Thomas Dudley, was initially dumbfounded at the news, then full of joy. As far as he was concerned the British government had egg all over their faces. He instantly shot a telegram to US Minister Charles Francis Adams in London. Both Dudley and Adams used the strongest diplomatic language to demand that Waddell and his crew be arrested and the ship confiscated, before being turned over to the American government for 'justice'. While the American government ranted, the British newspapers tried to parrot the same line, but the US consuls and other officials of the US government took a cynical view of this sudden 'about face', particularly in light of the unspoken support shown for the Confederate cause in Liverpool during the Civil War.

On board the *Shenandoah*, as Waddell and his crew pondered what was to become of them, all that could be done was to enjoy the fresh food and provisions sent out from Confederate sympathisers ashore, or brought over from the *Goshawk*. As they tucked into the fresh fare and raided the rum locker, still full from the pillaging of the whaling ships, in London Prime Minister Earl Russell and Foreign Secretary Lord Clarendon, newly acquainted with the whole *Shenandoah* saga, were deftly passing US Minister Adams' and Consul Dudley's demands, along with Waddell's letter, on to the Crown's legal counsel.

Once again, the Fates not only smiled upon Waddell and his

crew, but they laughed and tore up the demands of the American government like so much confetti paper. In this instance, the Fates' names were Sir Roundell Palmer, Sir R.P. Collier, and the most important insofar as Waddell's own fate was concerned, Sir Robert Phillimore. Waddell had studied Phillimore's works for years and carried his book on international law on board the *Shenandoah* as his standard reference when dealing with ships of questionable provenance; the prodigal law student now stood before his master. In the end, Waddell had conducted the perfect 'crime' by adhering strictly to Phillimore's precepts. The highest legal authority in the greatest empire in the world had spoken and clearly slapped down the overbearing demands of the American government. Unlike the recently deceased Lord Palmerston, Earl Russell had yet to develop a sense of the *realpolitik* of the situation. Palmerston may have worried about the immense American military might and congressional threats of military action, but Russell was more bullish. The Americans could sulk for a while and calm down, then maybe the British Empire might discuss some reparations for the activities of the Confederate commerce-raiders.

The ultimate irony though, was that James Iredell Waddell, named after one of America's first US Supreme Court justices, had been found not guilty of illegal actions under the accepted precedents of international law by the highest legal body in the British Empire. An even stranger irony was that he had been acting against the government under whose flag he had been born (the United States), for a government that had existed but for a short while (the Confederacy), which had in all but diplomatic terms been accorded the rights of a nation. As the British soldier's lyric from the song of the American War of

Independence said, 'it was a world turned upside down'.

The finding of the Crown's counsel was sent back to the Prime Minister's office and to the Foreign Secretary. Lord Clarendon immediately sent a copy to US Minister Adams, while at the same time sending instructions in parallel with those of the Prime Minister's office to Captain Paynter aboard the *Donegal*. All crew members of the *Shenandoah* were to be freed with the exception of those found to be British, who of course would be charged with breaking the Foreign Enlistment Act. By the end of 8 November 1865, the message had been relayed to Captain Paynter, who, along with Lt. Cheek, once more crossed over by boat to the *Shenandoah*, informing Waddell of the decision by the British government. All were free to go, with the stipulation that those of the crew who were British must remain and be detained for arrest. Waddell, in accordance with Paynter's request to question each man as to his nationality, had Whittle assemble the crew. According to one crew member's account, they stood in formation on one side of the ship's deck, while Whittle called out their name and number. They then paraded before Paynter, who asked each man his nationality. As the crewman humorously noted, all the men from England, Scotland or Ireland claimed to be Southerners. Captain Paynter, having no proof that the men were not the nationality they claimed to be, declared all free to go.

Resounding cheers greeted the announcement of their freedom, and the crew assembled one last time with their baggage before them. Waddell thanked them all for their service and support, and with that, the greatest adventure of their lives was over. Before departing the *Shenandoah*, Waddell gave Paynter, 'my tumblers, decanters, and bedding, with a few

trophies from the islands. . . as a souvenir of our acquaintance'.
All then quickly scrambled over the side into a waiting ferry,
which carried them all across to the Great George landing. The
goodbyes continued, with Waddell promising to see what he
could do to make sure everyone got their full back pay; in
contrast to his own experience with the US Navy and Gideon
Welles, Waddell would honour his word.

By 11 November, Waddell had apparently made contact with
Bulloch, as word had reached the dispersed crewmen of the
Shenandoah that the ship's clerk was paying off at the Liverpool
Sailor's Home. Accounts are muddled, with several crewmen
claiming in affidavits and books that they were never paid any
more funds, while others claimed they were. However, the most
reliable comments from Bulloch and Whittle assert that most, if
not all, of the officers and men received a substantial portion of
the monies owed them.

As for the *Shenandoah*, by 12 November, she had been
officially transferred to the US government. US Consul Thomas
Dudley would take a cursory tour of the vessel, with US
newspapermen in tow, to look over the vessel with an eye to
having her sailed back across the Atlantic to New York. They
were stunned at the amount of 'booty' still aboard the vessel,
leftovers from the whaling ship seizures, and the fact that
Waddell, meticulous to the end in his adherence to law, had left
$828.38 in gold and silver in the ship's safe.

By this time, Waddell appears to have settled in Waterloo, a
small village north of Liverpool at the time, lodging in either the
Royal or Waterloo Hotel. This was of course the same village
that James D. Bulloch, and the small colony of Confederates
directly involved in covert Confederate naval operations, had

inhabited for the last four years. At some point, Waddell was informed by Bulloch of the imprisonment of his wife Anne by US authorities. Whether this news, and the strain of overwork, compounded to weaken his health again, is unknown, but by 18 November, James Iredell Waddell was near death. William C. Whittle, his former executive officer, noted that Waddell had suffered three or four haemorrhages in his lungs, coughing up large amounts of blood. Whittle went on to record that he feared that if Waddell did survive, he would have 'consumption', known today as pulmonary tuberculosis. Now ensconced in the Waterloo Hotel, near the Bulloch home, Waddell would be bed-ridden in convalescence for the next several months.

Meanwhile, US Consul Dudley, acting on instructions from US Minister Adams in London, had been trying to get Rear-Admiral Goldsborough, commander of the US Navy's European Squadron, to find a merchant marine captain and crew willing to take the *Shenandoah* to America. After several days' search, Dudley hired Captain Thomas F. Freeman to take her out. Freeman managed to hire on a crew of 55, only a few more men than Waddell had when he took the *Shenandoah* 'to war' off the Madeira Islands. After a few days' preparation, the *Shenandoah*, flying an American flag, slipped out of Liverpool on the morning tide, the sun glinting on the flat River Mersey.

Only a day out of Liverpool, and upon reaching the open Atlantic, the screw of the *Shenandoah* began vibrating wildly. Captain Freeman quickly had the propeller raised up into its well, and sails let out. No sooner had this been accomplished, however, than a storm of incredible ferocity fell upon the tired ex-raider. Her fore-topsail was broken entirely, right down to the deck mount, while other masts and spars were also damaged.

As the storm raged over the next two days, one by one her sails were ripped from the masts. Freeman was unfortunate in that, unlike Waddell, he did not have an experienced and wise sail-maker like Henry Alcott aboard. Alcott had always been prepared for such a situation.

Another two days of ferocious weather went by. The crew were now on 'iron rations' due to the galley fires being put out by tremendous waves sweeping up, and over, the entire length of the vessel. The weather finally eased somewhat, and the ship's carpenter began to clear away the wreckage, but by the time this was done another winter storm fell upon the beleaguered *Shenandoah*. Freeman was facing another gale with a tired crew and a tired ship; he turned the bow of the *Shenandoah* back to Liverpool. On 6 December 1865 the *Shenandoah* once again floated in on the Mersey's tide, but this time without most of her sails, very little coal, and a combative crew. Upon anchoring, Freeman reported to US Consul Dudley that the crew refused to work aboard her and recommended they be paid off. He went on to say that she needed new sails, over a hundred new tons of coal and another crew if Dudley wanted her to go to sea again. With that, Freeman took his pay and went back to his company.

Waddell would have heard news of the *Shenandoah*'s forlorn return, and strangely her condition matched that of her former commander, sick and tired. Her refusal to sail under a Yankee flag must have cheered him up somewhat. However, the thought that his wife Anne was still, for all he knew, imprisoned by US authorities, outraged him. On 27 December, Waddell penned a letter from Waterloo to a person in Mobile, Alabama, explaining his current situation. Considerable debate has arisen about two issues concerning this letter: first, the identity of the person to whom it was addressed, and second, the identity of the person who obtained the letter without Waddell's knowledge and had it published. Regarding the first issue, it may be that the letter was addressed to one of James' brothers, who was known to have been living in Mobile, Alabama, after the war. It is also possible that in light of the harsh press that Waddell was receiving, both in Britain and America, that he may have been writing to Rafael Semmes. Whoever the recipient, the fact that the letter was addressed to someone in Mobile, Alabama, guaranteed its publication. For although Waddell did not know it, Semmes had been arrested by a group of US marines under orders from the Secretary of the Navy, then forcibly transported to a prison outside Washington, DC, in the hope of wringing a confession of piracy from his lips. All Mobile, and the rest of the South for that matter, was outraged. A letter from the South's last great naval hero, Waddell, would be manna from heaven for a hero-starved South.

Waddell's letter, written from the point of view of a man whose life seemed almost biblical in the Job-like tribulations he had endured, railed against the injustices of the United States government. He thundered, 'I am now in exile, but far from being a ruined man.' He then went on to quote in detail the conduct of Gideon Welles against him upon his resignation from the US Navy, and his refusal to deliver his lawful pay, and the outrageous arrest and imprisonment of his wife. Then, like a warship circling its prey, Waddell refuted, point by point, the allegations by Welles that he had continued combat operations in the *Shenandoah* after learning the war was over. Tired of the constant second-guessing and criticism of his command from every quarter, he also turned his cannons upon his own officers, bitterly noting that after learning of the war's end from the *Barracouta*, 'the officers set a bad example to the crew'. Referring to the constant questioning of his decision to sail to Liverpool and the petitions generated by the young officers, he went on to say that, 'Their conduct was nothing less than mutiny. I was very decided with some of them. I had to tell one officer I would be Captain or die on the deck, and the vessel should go to no other port than Liverpool.' Concluding his diatribe against his former officers, he acknowledged that, 'My obstinacy made enemies among some of the officers, but they now inwardly regret their action in the Cape Town affair.'

The letter exploded into newspapers not only across the entire South, but all of America. James Iredell Waddell might be in exile, he might be exempt from the General Amnesty Proclamation of President Andrew Johnson, Lincoln's successor, but he was unbowed, undefeated and unrepentant. He had been wronged, and he was still being wronged by the US government.

The New Year came, and in Maryland, Waddell's wife Anne, though now only under house arrest, had heard of James' illness, and probably read a copy of his published letter. His Ulyssean cry of despair had been heard throughout America, and though it may have fallen upon deaf ears in the whaling seaports of New England, in Maryland, which sympathised with the South during the war, but suffered under a harsh Union rule, her imprisonment became a hot political subject. Taking advantage of the publicity, on 12 January 1866, Anne Waddell filed a plea for release from her parole and bond with the US Secretary of War, Edwin M. Stanton. Her plea fell on deaf ears, for Stanton, whose energies during the war had been devoted to weeding out officers he thought might have Southern sympathies, was still feeding his blood-lust from the apprehension and hanging of the conspirators involved in Abraham Lincoln's assassination. All Anne Waddell received back in response for her troubles was a tersely worded reply: 'The Secretary of War declines to take any action in the case of Mrs A.S. Waddell for application to be released from the parole and the condition of bond.'

Sometime in the spring of 1866, James Waddell, recovered from his severe illness and anxious over the possibility that British authorities might waver in their determination to stand up to the demands of the US government, made his way to Paris. Waddell was taking advantage of several factors in choosing to go to France. First, although Napoleon III of France had quashed the Confederate Navy's last hopes of ocean-going ironclads by stopping contract orders and construction, he had still been the most sympathetic to the South, of all the major European powers.

This led to the second reason why France was a good place for ex-Confederates. Since January of 1862, both Britain and France had been engaged in military operations in Mexico. By 12 February 1866, President Johnson had had enough of the foreign interference on the territory of his southern neighbour. He ordered US Army units to the Mexican border along the Rio Grande, then instructed the US Navy to take up blockade positions along the Mexican coast. France and Britain were getting a strong signal of the United States' determination to enforce the Monroe Doctrine – which stated that the European powers should no longer colonise or intrude upon the affairs of the newly independent states within the Americas – with battle-hardened troops and sailors to back up the threat. This then was the backdrop to Waddell's journey from Britain to France. The United States, flush with victory from the Civil War, was out to settle scores and willing to push the European powers around if need be. Paris was safer for the moment, and besides, there was still a sizeable number of ex-Confederate naval personnel about the city.

In Maryland, the campaign to release Anne Waddell finally succeeded and sometime in late spring or early summer of 1866, she sailed for Europe, meeting James in Paris. By 1867 the Waddells had returned to Britain, but exactly when and for how long is not certain. It may be that they were there only long enough to say their goodbyes to the exiled Confederate community scattered about northern England and Scotland. This may be the point at which they received word from family and friends in America that the political climate had changed, or that the possibility of a pardon now loomed on the horizon.

For other Confederates though, life overseas seemed more enticing. The Bulloch brothers had thoroughly ensconced themselves in Liverpool business and society. James Dunwoody Bulloch, always discreet and honest in his dealings, had made use of his contacts to become a stalwart member of the Liverpool business community. His half-brother, Irvine, did likewise, with a bit of help from brother James. Other than a secret visit to America in 1877, where they overawed a nephew named Theodore Roosevelt (then at Harvard University) with their naval stories, they never again set foot on American soil. Neither ever applied for a presidential pardon for their war-time activities either.

The Waddells left Liverpool around 1 July 1867, aboard the steamship *Carroll* and arrived in Baltimore, Maryland, on 19 July. A letter, dated 11 September, written by James' brother, Charles Waddell, to their father Francis, says:

We took the steamer at City Point on Wednesday the 21st July and after a delightful trip of 24 hours, reached Baltimore on Thursday about 1 o'clock in the day – it was raining and I thought I would stay all the evening and go by Rail the next morning to Annapolis. I telegraphed brother that I would take the train Friday, but his reply was take the Steamer 'Highland Light' and come that way: so I took the Steamer and missed an accident which occurred to the Annapolis train that morning. We reached Annapolis about 10 o'clock AM and as the steamer approached the wharf I saw him standing with an umbrella waiting for us. We hauled along side and he came on board and you can imagine him so (?) was our greeting – we flew into each other's arms and kissed and hugged much to the amusement of the passengers who seemed to wonder at the strange sight of two men hugging and kissing: I cared nothing for that nor did he and here let me say I found him in full health and vigor – He weighs 198 pounds and is on the increase and is one of the finest looking men in Maryland as any other State. Sister Nell is also in fine health and is much stouter than formerly and is quite pretty. We talked much and enjoyed the visit much. I remained until Friday and took the boat for Baltimore: remained there that night and until 3 o'clock Wednesday, went sight-seeing – took the Steamer at 3 o'clock and arrived in Petersburg Thursday evening – a more delightful trip I never enjoyed – it was too short, that is all the fault I had to find.

Brother is anxious to be at work and I have a plan view which I will tell you of after I get it under way. He says he cannot consent to live on Mr Iglehart *[father of James Waddell's wife, Anne]* and is determined to do something for a living. He has but little means and it behooves him to be at work.

I have not a doubt but that he will pay you a visit shortly, as Mr Johnson *[President Andrew Johnson]* has issued his Amnesty proclamation which embraces him; and places him beyond annoyance. I do not believe he would have been interrupted had he gone to North Carolina at the time he intended. I read with much interest the Log Book of the Shenandoah as also his history of his Cruise in Manuscript about 500 pages. I begged him to finish it and have it put in print, but he would not consent. I am delighted to find him in such good health and looking so well. You can imagine how we talked and laughed – He telling me of his adventures by sea and I relating mine by land: and a nice time we had.

James and Anne Waddell had arrived back home in a re-united and changed America. The last five years of their lives had been traumatic by any measure. They had lost their only child to diphtheria, and had dared to run the Union naval blockade on several instances. James had sailed around the world destroying the commerce of a nation that had wronged him personally, while serving lawfully under the flag of a recognised belligerent nation, only to be called a pirate. Anne had been seized under orders from the US government, imprisoned, then paroled, in violation of the rights of *habeas corpus* guaranteed by the very constitution the US government said it fought to defend. They were almost penniless, and had no place of their own to call home. But James and Anne Waddell had each other. They had wandered across the face of the earth and James Waddell could still sail a ship. He just needed to find a shipping company who would give him a chance, and that was going to be difficult in America, particularly in the years just after the end of the Civil War.

8

Light of Heaven

James and Anne Waddell had returned to an America that had been wholly transformed by the Civil War. The victory of the Union over the Confederacy had wrought such a change in American society that a well-known emeritus professor from Harvard University was moved to remark, 'It does not seem as if I were living in the country in which I was born.' And if America had changed dramatically, so had the city that had figured so largely in the Waddells' lives, Annapolis, Maryland.

After the war, Annapolis enjoyed the benefits of a double economic war boom, one from the influx of Union soldiers and the federal money spent on their maintenance, and one from the black market money that had flowed into the city from the profits created in smuggling and other enterprises. The black market had been a risky business, but the profits, like those involved in blockade-running, had been considerable.

James and Anne Waddell moved back in with her father, James Iglehart, immediately upon arriving back in Annapolis. Again, Waddell moves into the shadows of history and we are reliant on the smallest accounts of his activities from others. As we know from his brother Charles' letter, James' first concern was for employment. But one event that occurred after James Waddell's return to Annapolis is certain, and the details are heart-rending. On a Sunday afternoon not long after settling into his father-in-law's home, James paid a visit to the cemetery where his daughter Annie had been laid to rest in February 1863. He had last seen her in 1862, a vibrant little girl aged three. Annie had been swept away by the ravages of scarlet fever and diphtheria while he was on his run through the Union blockade to Europe. Again, Charles Waddell, who had also lost a child, writes, 'We visited on Sunday the grave of our dear Sarah and his little daughter Annie – no one went with us as I did not desire any one to accompany us: we lingered around it for two hours or more and talked of the past until sadness filled our hearts. I was sorry when the time came for me to return and it was with a struggle I tore myself away.'

Assuming that James Waddell spent the rest of 1867 resting and writing his memoirs, it can be reasonably assumed that his restless nature and drive to find employment for himself and a home for Anne, made 1868 a busy year. The numerous Confederate sympathisers in Annapolis may have provided some assistance in the way of contacts, but these must not have panned out either, for the Maryland Census for 1870 shows James' occupation as 'Hardware Merchant' and Anne as 'Keeping House'. However, James Waddell's name appears on the US census for New York City in 1870, his occupation being listed as 'Master of Ship' and it is known that he obtained a master's license for steamships in New York in that same year.

So did James Waddell work in his father-in-law's hardware business to support himself and Anne while looking for a chance to go to sea again? Waddell had angrily said in his letter from Liverpool in 1865 that he would never go to sea, as his career was ruined, but time and the continued growth of America were healing the wounds of the Civil War, even if the activities of the Confederate raiders was still the subject of an unresolved international dispute between Britain and America. It may be that James Waddell stayed working with his father-in-law, James Iglehart, from 1868 until 1870, out of pure pragmatism.

If James Waddell didn't work on the sea for a few years, it could reasonably be argued that it was not from lack of interest from potential employers, but more as a result of political expediency on the part of shipping companies. They simply couldn't take a chance on hiring the highly qualified and highly unrepentant Waddell, for his presence might cost them passengers, government contracts, or even worse, bad public relations. From 1870, Waddell slipped into obscurity as easily as his former command, the *Shenandoah*, could disappear into an Arctic fog.

But on 21 May 1874, Waddell suddenly appears on US immigration records in New York City aboard the ss *Bolivia*. There is little doubt that it is James Waddell, as the birth date is listed as 1824, but what is interesting is the port of departure, Glasgow, Scotland. This suggests that Waddell may have been doing trans-Atlantic runs and was coming home after the conclusion of a contract.

Yet another possibility exists for the whereabouts and occupation of Waddell, one that dates back to 1870. Waddell's cousin, Alfred Moore Waddell, was a US congressman for North Carolina by 1870 and he had voted affirmatively on a congressional act that would award the Pacific Mail Steamship

Company (PMSSC) the contract to carry the US Mail between Oregon, California and western Panama. Knowing as we do the personal code of honour that James Waddell had, it is hard to imagine him being involved in any form of influence-peddling, though politics in that era were certainly not as clean or transparent as they are in America today. It may be that Waddell was employed by the PMSSC as early as 1870 on a subsidiary route across the Atlantic, and was merely awaiting developments.

The historical trail of James Waddell becomes clear again in 1875, for it is known that the Pacific Mail Steamship Company had made him the captain of its new ship, the *City of San Francisco*. After trials and work-up voyages, Waddell was ordered to sail to San Francisco from New York. What neither Waddell nor the Pacific Mail Steamship Company realised was that they were sailing into a storm – a public relations storm. As soon as the Pacific Mail Steamship Company had proudly announced the forthcoming arrival of the *City of San Francisco* with James Waddell as her captain, the whaling community in the Pacific port exploded in rage. A whaler named Hall wrote vituperative letters to the *San Francisco Newsletter and California Advertiser*, hoping to enrage San Francisco's maritime business community. On top of that, Hall wrote a menacing letter to the Pacific Mail Steamship Company implying that it would not be a very good idea to send Waddell on the *City of San Francisco*'s first voyage from the city. If that wasn't a big enough headache for the company, a ghost from Waddell's Civil War past now rose to torment him.

Ebenezer Nye, who had two vessels sunk by two different Confederate raiders, the *Alabama* and the *Shenandoah*, wrote a scathing letter to the *San Francisco Chronicle* that not only defamed Waddell, but accused the Pacific Mail Steamship Company of having a policy of hiring ex-Confederate naval officers. In fact, Waddell's first officer aboard the *City of San Francisco* was Walter Raleigh Butt, a former Lieutenant in the Confederate Navy. In the face of this furor, the Pacific Mail Steamship Company capitulated and ordered Waddell back to New York. James and Anne made their way back across America to Annapolis by rail.

But now Waddell's luck began to turn and the basic decency of the Californians, who had not felt any direct effects of the Civil War, rose to his defence. A tremendous counter-reaction to the rabid and clearly self-absorbed interests of the whalers developed, with friends, family, and US naval officers flaying the Pacific Mail Steamship Company for their decision to fold in the face of such 'un-Americanism'. Letters poured into the company and the San Francisco newspapers, hauling them over the coals for their lack of reconciliation, common decency and compassion.

The Pacific Mail Steamship Company, realising that they now had a classic American underdog public relations campaign going for them, returned Waddell to command of the *City of San Francisco*, and ordered him out from New York and back to San Francisco with all due speed. Waddell arrived back in San Francisco just in time for her first trans-Pacific voyage in early 1876. His itinerary across the Pacific could not have been better designed if it had been planned as a celebration of his naval triumphs aboard the *Shenandoah*. A stop-off in Hawaii, followed by a visit to New Zealand and Australia, then Japan and back across the Pacific to San Francisco, it would be a return to old hunting grounds, and ironically, a sail across the same shipping lanes from which he had tried to capture Union ships.

The *City of San Francisco*, however, was a far cry from the sleek, but spartan, *Shenandoah*. At just over 3,000 tons, the *City of San Francisco* had an iron hull with her sails rigged as a bark. However, unlike the *Shenandoah*, her primary means of propulsion were her steam engines. The fittings and décor of the ship's cabins, saloon and dining areas were among the finest yet seen on an American trans-Pacific steamer. One later passenger marvelled at the food served aboard, comparing it to that of the finest hotel. Other passengers noted that Waddell and First Officer Butt ran the ship as if it were a warship, insisting on scrupulous cleanliness, discipline and absolute adherence to gentlemanly decorum by all the junior officers and staff at all times. The *Shenandoah* may have been a technical marvel to sail, but the *City of San Francisco* was the finest vessel Waddell would command in his entire career as a mariner.

The *City of San Francisco* sailed out of San Francisco and a few days later reached Hawaii, slipping quietly into port at Honolulu. As the passengers departed in a happy mood and the mail and fresh supplies were brought aboard, Waddell could relax and enjoy a small success for the first time in years. Now aged 52, the tall North Carolinian had endured a turbulent maritime career, by any measure, and a period of calm, evenly paced work was what he needed. Ready for sea again after a short visit, Waddell ordered the anchors raised on the *City of San Francisco* and began to bring her about to head out of Honolulu. But the Hawaiians had a surprise for the ex-Confederate. The local newspaper had got wind of Waddell's arrival, and had written a rather affectionate article mentioning that the famous commander of the *Shenandoah* was now captain of the *City of San Francisco*, the new trans-Pacific mail carrier and passenger steamer. So, on the morning of Waddell's departure, Hawaiians flocked to Pearl Harbor to wave off the *City of San Francisco*. They included the Royal Hawaiian Band – who promptly struck up 'Dixie'! As the crowds cheered, the bemused Waddell ordered the US flag dipped in reply, bringing up yet another cheer. First Officer Walter Butt must have shaken his head in amazement.

As Hawaii fell behind, the *City of San Francisco* set her course for New Zealand and Australia, reaching there, it is assumed, in another week. If the Hawaiians had given Waddell a warm and enthusiastic send-off, his return to Sydney harbour, the scene of the tense stand-off between the Australian colonial government and the *Shenandoah*, was said by one observer to be as if Drake himself had dropped anchor. The newspapers, dignitaries, and society of the city went wild. The *City of San Francisco* barely had time to get her anchor wet before Waddell was dragged off the ship to a week-long series of celebrations and parties. The Australians were ready to forgive and forget, and most of all, to honour a seaman who was not only a gentleman, but a sailor amongst sailors. The Australians, as independent and cantankerous as any American, regarded Waddell as one of their own.

After a lengthy stay in port, Waddell had to get the *City of San Francisco* back under way again, this time sailing for her home port, San Francisco. It was a quick and uneventful crossing, but for Waddell it would have been a time for reflection on the reception he had received all along his inaugural voyage. It seemed that everywhere he went outside the United States, people were willing to forgive his actions as commander of the

Shenandoah, and fondly remember his skills as a mariner and his manners as a gentleman. He must have wondered if he would ever receive the same treatment in America.

Upon reaching San Francisco, and after a short period for rest and the refitting and re-supplying of the *City of San Francisco*, Waddell had the mail ship under way again for the South Pacific. Fortunately, firmer information is available about this voyage and its schedule. According to an advertisement of the period, she departed San Francisco on 25 May 1876 for Sydney, Australia, with an expected departure from there on 2 June for Fiji. (The latter date may be a printing error, as this seems rather a short time for crossing the Pacific.) A departure on 9 June from Fiji for New Zealand was next on the itinerary. Records indicate only a few passengers on this portion of the voyage: only some 19 all told. The advertised schedule shows a port call in Auckland for 17 June, with departure the same day, Napier on the 18th, Wellington on the 19th and Lyttleton (the port for Christchurch) on 20 June. From there the vessel dipped down to near the bottom of New Zealand's South Island to berth at Port Chalmers (the port for Dunedin). Interestingly, the schedule shows a week's stay in Port Chalmers before returning to Lyttleton on 29 June and departing the same day northwards, retracing its journey through the ports already visited before re-crossing the Pacific. It was a busy schedule, to say the least, and according to notes left by one passenger, quite stormy at several of the ports of call.

Waddell made at least one more voyage across the Pacific on this same run, sometime in late 1876. After that, the Pacific Mail Steamship Company began to lose some of its mail contracts and decided to shift the *City of San Francisco* to its San Francisco to

Panama run for 1877. This, ironically, would be the same 'gold run' that the Confederate Navy had dreamed of attacking. Waddell must have laughed to himself over this turn of events. It was a quick, and for a mariner, largely boring run, but not without its dangers. Although the route had been heavily plied since 1848 by gold ships and passenger vessels carrying the hopeful gold-miners, the lower Californian and Mexican coasts were not well charted, on account of the Mexican War and the Civil War. Other factors were the US Navy's budget difficulties and its dispute with the Coastal Survey.

Waddell made three successful runs to Panama from San Francisco, but during his fourth voyage in May of 1877, disaster struck. At 9.10 in the morning of 16 May 1877, the *City of San Francisco* was proceeding along her normal route between Panama and San Francisco. Five minutes later she had run aground, her bottom breached by an uncharted underwater obstacle. Waddell knew the Tartar Shoals were nearby, but his route, at this point some 20 kilometres directly west of the Mexican coast, had always been safe before. No matter, it was only a potential disaster if Waddell didn't manage it right. The *City of San Francisco* was carrying just over 250 people, with 90 of these being ship's crew. Almost half of the 160-odd passengers were Chinese, and it was rumoured the ship was carrying silver bars for the Asian community in San Francisco. What wasn't a rumour was the $750,000 dollars of silk and lace that were stowed below in cargo, and that cargo was already getting wet, as the below deck crew reported to Waddell that three compartments were taking on water.

Waddell's demeanour was as calm as if they had been aboard a small, leaking boat in a duck pond. He quickly ordered the vessel's course changed to head directly for shore with all available speed. For the next 20 minutes the *City of San Francisco* steamed towards the Mexican coast, but rising water caught up with the boiler run, putting out her fires. The boilers had enough head upon them to keep the vessel going for 40 more minutes, but it wasn't enough. Five kilometres offshore the *City of San Francisco* came to halt and began to settle in the water. Waddell ordered all the passengers to the lifeboat stations, telling them to take no luggage with them. Once they were all assembled by the lifeboats, he gave the crew orders to get them overboard and away. Meanwhile Waddell, First Officer Butt, and several other junior officers hurriedly prepared a makeshift raft, which they then piled with emergency rations, before getting on board. Waddell was the last person to leave the deck of the *City of San Francisco*, quite literally with water washing at his ankles.

The surf along this stretch of Mexican coast was substantial, even with the fine weather the survivors of the sinking *City of San Francisco* were experiencing that May morning. One by one, the lifeboats overturned in the near-shore surf. Fortunately, no one was drowned, but they were all wet, tired, stressed and hungry; even Waddell and his officers were swept into the surf. There were now 250 people stranded on a remote stretch of Mexican coastline, with only a small amount of food, no water, and no shelter. And Waddell was responsible for them.

Waddell was more than well-trained in dealing with the situation. Ordering an immediate inventory of their available supplies, he discovered that they had some ship's bread (hardtack), potatoes, whisky, and a small pig that had swum ashore from the sinking ship. Knowing that water was critical, he sent men to search for sources. Fortuitously, they found a small stream almost immediately in a nearby ravine. With this critical issue in hand, and knowing that the burning sun would give way to a very cold night on the edge of the Mexican desert, fires were ordered. They might also help in being discovered by a passing ship.

Waddell, however, was not going to wait to be rescued. Calling forward Third Officer James Dow, Waddell instructed him to take one of the lifeboats and a picked crew and head northwest up the coast towards Acapulco, 150 kilometres away. Dow got his men together in a short time and pushed off along the coast, while Waddell turned to more immediate matters. Though the Mexican coast may have looked desolate, Waddell knew there was a chance that their arrival had been observed by someone who might not necessarily be interested in saving them. With that in mind, he set armed guards around the perimeter of the camp in case shipwreckers arrived on the scene.

Out at sea, Third Officer Dow with his small boat and crew rowed through the afternoon and night. The next day, 17 May, Dow's boat was spotted by a Mexican gunboat out on patrol. Immediately upon pulling alongside Dow's boat and hearing his story, the Mexican captain pulled the exhausted men aboard and headed directly for the beach where the survivors of the *City of San Francisco* were huddled. In short order, the Mexican gunboat transferred Waddell and the survivors of the *City of San Francisco* aboard and then set sail north to Acapulco. Since the port was under assault by Mexicans rebelling against the government, the survivors were placed aboard the USS *Lackawanna*, a sloop-of-war sent to protect American interests and property in Acapulco. The captain and crew of the

Lackawanna were clearly star-struck by Waddell's presence, for they knew his reputation.

The *Lackawanna* had served on blockade duty in the Civil War, slugged it out with the Confederate ironclad *Tennessee* at the Battle of Mobile Bay (even ramming her). She had survived the war, only to be decommissioned, and had only recently been returned to service in the Pacific Ocean. Faster than one could say 'splice the mainbrace', the crew of the *Lackawanna* had a convivial reunion of old adversaries, with food, drink and clothing provided for the shipwrecked passengers. In a remarkable gesture, the officers of the *Lackawanna* even raised $500 amongst themselves for the passengers' benefit. All Waddell and his fellow survivors had to do now was wait for a vessel heading north to San Francisco to stop in Acapulco.

On 20 May, the SS *Costa Rica* appeared in Acapulco and the survivors of the *City of San Francisco* transferred to her for the trip north. The *Costa Rica* was scheduled to stop in Manzanilo, Mazatlán and San Diego before reaching San Francisco, so it would be a leisurely trip north for the traumatised survivors. When the *Costa Rica* reached Mazatlán, Waddell discovered that the USS *Pensacola* was in port. The *Pensacola* was the flagship for Rear-Admiral Alexander Murray, who was the commanding officer of the US Navy's North Pacific squadron, and an old friend of Waddell's from San Francisco. Murray and Waddell frequently met for dinner whenever the *City of San Francisco* and *Pensacola* happened to be in port at the same time. Murray listened to Waddell's story, and knowing what this could do to Waddell's attempt to re-build his maritime career, probably advised him to go ashore at San Diego and take a train north to San Francisco to report to the Pacific Mail Steamship

Company – and get his version of events into the press first. Murray also offered financial assistance to Waddell and his passengers, but the ever-polite North Carolinian declined the generous offer.

When the *Costa Rica* got to San Diego, Waddell quickly left the ship and caught the first train north to San Francisco. It was already two weeks after the sinking of the *City of San Francisco*. Reaching the city, he had a quick reunion with Anne before reporting to the offices of the Pacific Mail Steamship Company. After a thorough debriefing and extensive report to the managing officers, Waddell began to prepare his papers, for he knew there would be an investigation. Within days of his return to San Francisco, agents from the US Steamboat Inspection Service appeared at the Waddells' door, informing him that his master's license to command steamships was being suspended for a year. Furthermore, an investigation and Maritime Board of Inquiry would be convened. The agents' attitude implied that he had navigated improperly by coming too near the Mexican coast. Waddell was devastated and his enemies in San Francisco, the whalers, were delighted at his plight.

Once more, however, the proud but beleaguered ex-Confederate was rescued by his reputation and polite demeanour. Ship captains from the Pacific Mail Steamship Company who had sailed the same route, as well as US Navy captains who also knew the section of Mexican coast where the wreck occurred, rose as one to his defence. Numerous letters poured into both the Maritime Board of Investigation as well as the San Francisco papers. If Waddell was incompetent, then so was the US Navy and the Pacific Mail Steamship Company. The Maritime Board of Investigation, originally confident to the point of arrogance, was becoming nervous at the backlash. The US Navy captains of the North Pacific Squadron, obviously spurred on by Waddell's friend Rear-Admiral Murray, thundered that no detailed hydrographic survey had ever been undertaken for that portion of the Mexican coast, so any charts that did exist could not be trusted. They also went on to note that an earthquake had occurred in the region during early May, so there was no way of knowing if there hadn't been an upthrust in the sea floor that caught the bottom of the *City of San Francisco*. The Pacific Mail captains fired their broadside into the Marine Board, pointing out that this was the same route that had been used by the company since its inception.

Then the outraged passengers of the *City of San Francisco* joined the fray. A letter of support signed by every passenger aboard the mail ship was sent to every newspaper in San Francisco and virtually every major paper in California. In the letter, which was called a letter of 'respect and affection', Waddell was called a 'magnificent officer'. Another passenger, in his own personal letter to a San Francisco paper said, 'The Captain stood at his post giving his orders with such perfect coolness and preserving such an assured demeanour, that seeing him standing there, all idea of danger was displaced by a feeling of confidence.' Yet another passenger said, 'The management of the *City of San Francisco* disaster was of the kind that discloses the true capacity of a commander.' Waddell had a fleet of supporters pummelling the Maritime Board of Investigation now, and they must have begun to see that the winds of political reality were not blowing in their direction.

The San Francisco newspapers that had so strongly attacked Waddell in the past were now trying to back-pedal by printing articles that questioned the wisdom of the Pacific Mail Steamship Company in hiring any ex-military naval officer. The *Daily Alta* carried a small article saying that an attempt would be made by a Clyde wreck removal ship to raise the *City of San Francisco*. The rumours of large quantities of silver bars being aboard her were apparently believed by someone.

Waddell, his spirits buoyed by the overwhelming support he was receiving in the 'court of the press', appealed to have his suspended license returned to him in June 1877. A San Francisco newspaper noted, in its 15 July 1877 edition, that the Marine Board investigators 'believed generally that Captain Waddell had steered correctly'. The Marine Board was trying to haul itself off the rocks of public approbation now. Finally, in what has to be one of the most extraordinary of many examples of irony in Waddell's life, an oceanographic survey vessel, the USS *Hassler*, which had aboard it Prof. Benjamin Pierce of the US Coast Survey (based in Washington, DC), sailed to the rescue of Waddell's career. Pierce noted that, 'the most important [area of the Tartar Shoals] and the portion of which was less accurately defined than any other danger encountered by the steamers on the route [from south Mexico to San Francisco], had now been accurately mapped with recommendations and advisories to all the commercial shipping companies for new routing sent out.' Over a quarter of a century before, Waddell had been seconded to the US Coast Survey for exactly the same type of hydrographic survey work, the US Navy believing then that the Coast Survey was not doing an adequate job. In this instance, the area in question fell outside the Coast Survey's mandate, sparing them another argument with the US Navy.

The Head of the US Steamboat Services, First District, Charles Bemis, waded into the situation now. Seeing that the continued printing of letters from Waddell's supporters was beginning to cast his organisation in a less than flattering light, and agreeing with the evidence provided of his conduct, he overturned the suspension of Waddell's license. The Pacific Mail Steamship Company exonerated him too.

What Waddell hadn't realised, nor had many Californians, was that all across America the story of the ex-Confederate naval officer and the US Navy officers cooperating for the good of the public, regardless of past differences, had captured the nation's imagination. On the east coast, the *Baltimore Daily News* said that all the seamen concerned were 'American sailors, you could recognise the fact all the world over', and they 'were not ashamed to take the hand in peace from which they burned to snatch a sword in the conflicts of years ago'. And on the west coast, *The Daily Exchange*, a San Francisco business newspaper, summed it up best, saying that with 'his cool and superb bearing as the *City of San Francisco* was rapidly sinking beneath his feet, we fancy that Captain Waddell has done much to wipe out the memory of his questionable acts while in command of the *Shenandoah*. . . We are proud of Captain Waddell and are glad he is an American.'

Waddell, who had dreamed of being a naval hero aboard a US Naval warship in the manner of John Paul Jones, had achieved something greater in the eyes of the American public, and something the rest of the world already knew, from Britain to Australia. He was a sailor's sailor, America's Drake. He was an American hero, full stop.

The Pacific Mail Steamship Company was overwhelmed by the outpouring of public acclamation. Seeing an opportunity to generate some good publicity for the company, particularly amongst the Southern states that were still enduring the economically and emotionally painful process of reconstruction, the Pacific Mail Steamship Company decided to send Waddell back to the eastern United States to embark on a public relations tour. Very shortly after the US Steamboat Service returned Waddell's license, he and Anne were on the Trans-continental Railroad, headed across America for the east coast and the beginning of what must have been one of the most unique public relations campaigns to occur after the Civil War. Frustratingly again, the exact dates of their departure from San Francisco are unknown, nor when or where they arrived on the east coast.

What does shed some light on their activities, however, is a letter by James Waddell, dated 14 September 1877, and written from the residence of Alexander H. Stephens, the former Vice-President of the Confederacy, in Crawfordville, Georgia, a small town southeast of Atlanta. In the letter to his father, Waddell writes, 'I have been in Charleston, Savannah, Augusta', then adds in a post-script that, 'I am going as far as Mobile.' Judging by the cities he notes, and the date of the letter, it can reasonably be assumed that the Waddells had arrived back in Annapolis by mid August. From there, they both began their progress southwards. We know Anne accompanied him, for in the same letter to his father, James notes, 'Anne was glad to see you'. It may be that the schedule of visits set up for them by the Pacific Mail Steamship Company was a loop through the South, for Waddell stated earlier in the letter, 'I shall remain a day in Charlotte [North Carolina], and perhaps a day in Greensboro [North Carolina]. I will communicate with you about the time I will reach Hillsborough so that you may not be surprised at seeing me.' James Waddell was truly coming home for the first time in years.

However, it is James Waddell's commentary about going as far south as Mobile that is intriguing, and even more frustrating for the lack of information as to his movements. On 30 August 1877, Rafael Semmes, who had been raised to the rank of Rear-Admiral in the Confederate Navy after his feats as the commander of the CSS *Alabama*, died in his beloved Mobile. (Semmes was also given the rank of Brigadier General after he brought his sailors ashore to help defend Richmond in 1865.) It is hard to imagine that if the Waddells had been in the region, they would not have attended his funeral, for Semmes' passing would have been an epochal moment in Southern culture. He was the greatest Southern war hero after General Robert E. Lee, and he cast a long shadow. In 1905, Theodore Roosevelt visited Mobile and to resounding cheers said that his 'proudest Southern association was through two brothers of his mother who performed service for the Confederacy under Admiral Rafael Semmes on the famous *Alabama*'. Roosevelt was, of course, referring to his uncles 'Jimmy' and 'Irv', or James Dunwoody Bulloch and Irvine Bulloch. So, were James and Anne Waddell in Mobile for Semmes' funeral? At present, the only flimsy evidence is James Waddell's tantalising letter of 14 September 1877.

Upon the conclusion of the Waddells' publicity tour through the South, the record of their life goes quiet yet again. The anecdotal evidence is that James continued as a captain for the Pacific Mail Steamship Company, though what route and what ship, or ships, he may have commanded are unknown. The only evidence of his whereabouts, and that of his wife Anne, lie in the US census records for 1880, which show them as having a household in Annapolis, his occupation listed as 'Mariner' and hers as 'Housekeeper'.

In 1881, James Waddell was 57 years of age. Whether Waddell was tired of long sea voyages for the Pacific Mail Steamship Company, or he was let go from the company as it began to cut back its activities due to the loss of mail contracts, his next employment afloat was in the place that had most affected his life, Annapolis, Maryland. A letter dated 16 July 1881, in his hand, notes that he is writing from Annapolis, but reveals nothing about his employment situation.

Whether friends and associates had alerted James to the possibility of a forthcoming position with the Maryland 'Water Police' (also known as the 'Oyster Navy'), or Maryland Governor William T. Hamilton had contacted him about the calamitous state of the marine fisheries police is not known, but Waddell was needed. Nearly 60 years old, the stern North Carolinian was going into combat again, this time in the Maryland 'Oyster Wars' and in 1882 he became the Commander of the Maryland State Oyster Navy.

Since the arrival of English settlers on the shores of Chesapeake Bay nearly 300 years before, the incredible abundance of shellfish had been coveted, first as a food source, then as a product to be harvested and sold. The Native American tribes that occupied the area originally used the shellfish as food also, but their reliance on the Chesapeake's marine 'bank' extended to the use of fresh-water pearls as a form of currency for trade. Colonial Americans and their ancestors, who pushed out the Native Americans over time, merely followed in their footsteps. But by the late 1860s, over-exploitation of the precious resource had begun to worry Maryland's government, who of course viewed the oysters as not only a source of employment, but a source of taxation too. The problem was being caused by oyster poachers from Virginia,

Delaware, and even as far away as New Jersey.

In 1868, the Maryland state government had formed a State Oyster Navy consisting of 50 men. Charged with keeping the peace because enraged local oyster men were fighting the poachers, sometimes with firearms, the 'water police' were also responsible for the prevention of poaching and harvesting oysters that were too small (a practice known as 'culling'). The Maryland State Oyster Navy was first commanded by Hunter Davidson, a former 1st Lieutenant in the US Navy, native of Virginia, and more recently, a Commander in the Confederate States Navy. His 'navy' consisted of a steam vessel and two tenders. The hiring of the feisty Davidson to head the Maryland State Oyster Navy was a message from the Governor of Maryland – Thomas Swann in 1868 – that he was going to get tough on protecting the state's precious maritime resource. Davidson evidently didn't take long to live up to his reputation, for twice oyster poachers tried to kill him, once shooting through the cabin door of his patrol boat. By 1872, Davidson had either had enough, or had been tempted by better money, for he left the Maryland State Oyster Navy to join the Argentinian Navy as a torpedo expert during the Paraguayan War.

With Davidson's departure in 1872, the Maryland 'Navy' was re-organised and it is unclear exactly who was in command. By 1874 though, the Maryland legislature realised the Oyster Navy needed more vessels and approved the building and purchasing of six more vessels; it also re-organised the service again. But all the while, oyster hauls increased, as did oyster poaching. Throughout the rest of the 1870s and into the first years of the 1880s, the command of the Oyster Navy became a plum political appointment for those who backed the Maryland governor and the other branches of government that controlled it. The quantity of oysters that was being pulled in by 1882 was so great that poachers were shanghaiing new immigrants from Baltimore, and as far away as New York, to crew their boats. Poachers took to wearing boilerplate around themselves when confronted by irate local oyster men, and gunfire often broke out. The situation was clearly out of hand.

The hiring of James Waddell can then be seen in two lights. On the one hand, it was an astute political appointment in that Anne and her family, the Igleharts, were well-known and long-time citizens of Maryland. Anne's incarceration by Union authorities was common knowledge, as was the involvement of the Maryland state government in helping to free her from her federal bond and house arrest. Secondly, like Hunter Davidson, Waddell knew a stern hand was needed to get things in hand in the Oyster Navy and to get the poaching under control. The fact that he didn't mind the smell of gunpowder in his nostrils was a benefit too, as far as Governor Hamilton was concerned.

What Waddell inherited as a 'navy' was a leaky patrol boat named the *Leila*, the same two tenders that Hunter Davidson had used, and a random selection of small sailing vessels that the Maryland legislature had purchased over the last ten years. It wasn't much to work with, but then Waddell had some experience with making do; after all, the *Shenandoah* hadn't been 'specification-built' for war when he commissioned her.

Waddell's appointment wasn't without some criticism. However those grumbles were soon silenced, for over the next four years Waddell turned the Chesapeake Bay coast of Maryland into a no-go zone for oyster poachers and illegal oyster men, while getting the Oyster Navy into fighting form.

One incident in 1882 sent a loud message out to the oyster poaching community. Captain Waddell, as he was now referred to by Marylanders, got wind of a flotilla of oyster pirates operating in Maryland waters. Using the decrepit patrol boat *Leila*, Waddell and his crew managed to ambush the poachers' flotilla and run three vessels aground. Not content with that, Waddell then turned a small-bore howitzer that had been mounted aboard the *Leila* upon a fleeing poacher and sank it with shellfire! When news broke that the ex-commander of the last Confederate commerce-raider was sinking vessels in the Chesapeake Bay with cannon fire, it created uproar, and there was both consternation and laughter, depending on people's view of oyster poaching.

But it wasn't all gunfire at sea for Waddell. The Maryland legislature wanted to know what they were spending money to protect, and the 1882 Maryland Assembly funded a project which would, 'examine the conditions of the oyster beds of this state and report to the General Assembly'. James Waddell was now going to add yet another unique entry to his naval career, that of marine biologist.

Throughout 1883 Waddell rooted out discipline problems and pushed for greater funding, as well as a streamlined organisational structure for the Maryland State Oyster Navy, while engaged in oyster surveys. And while James was clearing the Chesapeake, Anne was busily re-establishing old contacts and making a home for them both after all the years of travel. The Igleharts were an old established family in Annapolis, so the social network was extensive for the Waddells, and James could always expect the occasional admirer from the Naval Academy too.

By the time 1884 rolled around, Waddell's changes and his requests for better equipment and funding were bearing fruit. The Maryland Legislature approved the purchase of an iron-hulled vessel that had been built for the US Navy as a replacement for the barely serviceable *Leila*. She was named the *Governor Robert M. Lane* and came with a 12-pound howitzer fitted on a pedestal mount located on the forward deck. Marylanders already familiar with Captain Waddell's itchy trigger-finger were very concerned about the weapon, and it would be removed in the future.

The Maryland lawmakers, while backing the stern policing of the Chesapeake by Waddell, were also conscious of the fact that the boundaries between the nearby states of Delaware and Virginia, as well as that with the District of Columbia, were contentious issues. Disputed boundaries over the high quality oyster beds beneath the Pocomoke and Tangier Sounds, and on the open waters of the middle Chesapeake Bay, had made relations with Maryland's neighbours touchy over the years. In light of the new patrol boat the legislators were buying Waddell's Oyster Navy, they decided to buy themselves some protection. The 1884 Maryland Assembly voted to, 'provide for the defence and indemnity of Henry Lloyd, J. Frank Turner, John S. Gittings, James I. Waddell and Lemuel Smoot, who have been, or may be, sued in the Courts of the United States, or of the State of Maryland, for certain acts alleged to have been done by them, or any of them, as officers of the State of Maryland, in the enforcement of an act of the General Assembly of Maryland'.

Some earlier and very discreet federal legislative work had been going on on James Waddell's behalf as well. The 14th Amendment of the US Constitution, proposed to the US

Congress in 1866 and approved in 1868, precluded Waddell from holding his office, even though he was appointed. Created by a still angry coterie of Northern states to further punish the 'rebels' of the South, Section 3 of the 14th amendment said:

> No person shall be a Senator or Representative in Congress, or elector of President and Vice President, or hold any office, civil or military, under the United States, or under any State, who, having previously taken an oath, as a member of Congress, or as an officer of the United States, or as a member of any State legislature, or as a executive or judicial office of any State, to support the Constitution of the United States, shall have engaged in insurrection or rebellion against the same, or given aid or comfort to the enemies thereof. But Congress may by a vote of two-thirds of each House remove such disability.

Maryland had refused to ratify the amendment (and would not do so until 1959), but it was no matter, the amendment had been passed by a majority of the states, making it ratified. As such, Waddell's appointment would be in violation of federal law if an application to remove his 'disability' were not made, and approved, by a two-thirds majority of Congress. So while Waddell had been fully pardoned by President Andrew Johnson's last two amnesty proclamations, the 14th Amendment still applied. Maryland Attorney General Charles Gwinn must have pointed this out to the Governor before Waddell's appointment in 1882, but it may be that he knew that the 46th Congress of the United States (3rd session) in late 1881 had recommended passage of an act to remove his political disabilities. In yet another of the great ironies of his life, all through Waddell's first year as commander of the Maryland

Oyster Navy, he had once again been operating in direct 'rebellion' against the US Constitution, and he was still unrepentant about his service in the Confederate Navy.

It also appears likely that 'cousin' Alfred Moore Waddell, in his official capacity as a US congressman from North Carolina, helped sponsor the congressional act. In a letter dated 16 July 1881, Waddell wrote to his father, asking for 'my letter of resignation and a document from the Navy Department proposing to give me the monies due me; on <u>condition</u> I would give my "honor not to go South" – Alfred requires all those papers and if you can send him those and send him those in haste.'

So it was in early January of 1883 that Waddell finally found out if he had been forgiven by the federal government that he had fought against, and which still owed him back pay for service rendered in the US Navy aboard the USS *John Adams*. On 5 January, an Act to remove the political disabilities of James Iredell Waddell was passed by the Congress of the United States of America and duly recorded in the *US Statutes at Large*. He was an American citizen once again. Eighty-one years in the future, this would be of great significance to the United States Navy.

Possibly only James Waddell could have truly appreciated the legalistic morass in which the federal government and the Maryland state government had found themselves mired. The fact that his political disabilities had been removed by the federal government in 1883 meant that the 1884 Maryland Assembly Act to provide funds for his defence, in case of legal action by the federal government, kept the Maryland government out of Constitutional hot water and away from the nasty political repercussions from not having endorsed the 14th Amendment. The mind boggles at the potential further legal repercussions from this paradox.

The year 1884 also saw the publication of the *Report of the Oyster Commission of the State of Maryland*, based on the survey that Waddell had been ordered to carry out in 1882. Co-written with William K. Brooks and William H. Legg, the report is considered to be the beginning of systematic scientific study in the field of shellfish in the Chesapeake Bay. Waddell, in a small way, had become the epitome of the kind of sailor now lost to his own time. Like Cook in the eighteenth century, he had been to the edge of the world and seen its people, its plants and its animals, but being at war, he had not had the time for inspection and introspection about what he saw. Now, near the end of his life, he was able to look down upon one of the most innocuous inhabitants of the sea and observe its life.

The year rolled quietly into 1885, with the 'oyster wars' quietening down, largely due to the fear that Waddell had spread amongst the oyster poachers, and possibly the weather. In April 1885, James wrote a letter to his brother Guion on paper letter-headed with the Maryland State Fishery Force insignia, possibly indicating that it was a tranquil period at work. He appears to have been homesick for the rolling hills of North Carolina, longing for the home and land that he had roamed over as a rebellious young boy. In the letter he wrote, 'I feel sometimes a strong desire to return, but I know of the changes which have taken place and would see only strange faces who know nothing of me or in whom I could feel any special interest. I have been a wanderer on the face of the earth for so many years I feel I am dissatisfied with my life and I think a home on the land would be distasteful anywhere without a blow off occasionally – I wish you would visit me.'

James Waddell was obviously lonely, but it was more than that. He may not have known how to express it, but he was experiencing the same sense of dislocation and loss of camaraderie that many of his fellow Southerners were feeling. Many Marylanders had supported the South, but the state and its people had suffered much less than his home state of North Carolina, both in terms of economic cost and loss of life. But James had seen sights and had experiences that only his fellow crew members of the *Shenandoah* could understand and share. In a way, his sense of dislocation and unease could be compared to that of the astronauts who landed on the moon. He knew he had seen and experienced something unique in his life, but he found that 'something' impossible to define.

The rest of 1885 passed quietly for the Waddells, though James began to experience the occasional bout of dizziness. As the year ended, James was suffering from severe headaches, some so debilitating that they caused him to stagger. But he never missed his work, even though Anne fussed about him over-exerting himself. Privately, he told his nephew that he sometimes felt 'all in'.

The early spring of 1886 was the last for James Waddell. On the morning of Friday, 12 March, James woke with severe nausea and profuse bleeding from his nose. Anne immediately sent word to their doctor, who, instead of rushing over, sent a message back that the nosebleed was a good sign. Throughout Saturday and Sunday Waddell shook violently, pain wracking his entire body. Anne Waddell thought he had a severe cold. Late on Sunday night James felt somewhat better; the doctor, kept apprised of the situation by Anne, said again that he felt no 'uneasiness' about the old mariner's symptoms. On Monday morning, James begged Anne to help him up into a chair beside his bedroom window. She protested vehemently that he should remain in bed, but he responded that he wanted her to 'open the window so that he could see the light of heaven'. After doing so, he gazed out the window for some time, then got back into bed, asking that no one disturb him. He then went to sleep.

After many hours of deep sleep, Anne, worried, demanded that the doctor come immediately. Upon arriving the doctor attempted to rouse James by bathing him with cold water, but he could not be roused. After several hours of deep breathing, he gave a little sigh, and died.

James Iredell Waddell, the commander of the last Confederate cruiser, the *Shenandoah*, the only Confederate warship to circumnavigate the world and the last Confederate military unit to surrender, had passed into the light of heaven. Anne Sellman Waddell was stunned. It had all happened so quickly, it had all been so short. Their life together, the life of their child, their happiness, had been all too short.

Word about the death of the Confederate 'Sea King' spread with the speed of a sea hawk. Newspapers across America had carried a bulletin about his sudden illness over the weekend; now they carried news of his death. Accolades and telegrams began to trickle, and then pour in. Over the next few days, communiqués from around the world arrived. Few could believe the 'Drake of the South' was gone. Anne, too overcome with grief, was grateful for the assistance in organising a funeral ceremony, which, she was gently informed, would be handled for her.

The funeral for James Iredell Waddell was unique in the

annals of American history. His was the only full state funeral given to any Confederate officer who died outside the former states of the Confederacy. Brigadier General George H. Steuart acted as Marshall, and the lead pallbearers were Captain Charles Manigault Morris, the last commander of the CSS *Florida*, General Bradley Johnson, Captain Murray, and a host of other former Confederate officers and dignitaries. William Morris led a procession of the former Confederates to the Waddell residence to escort the body to St Anne's Church for the funeral ceremony. Not only did former Confederate soldiers and sailors attend as escorts, but also US Navy officers and midshipmen from the US Naval Academy. US naval officers and cadets formed on the streets to salute the passing of Waddell's casket. Many of the young midshipmen had seen the old Confederate mariner walking down the streets by the Academy with his easily identifiable swinging gait, his lifelong memento of a long-ago duel. An occasional conversation with Waddell had inspired many of them, just as he had been inspired by older sailors, so many years before.

The US Navy contingent was joined by the entire Maryland State Legislature who adjourned en masse for the day. They formed in front of the Assembly building, then walked in formation to St Anne's Church for the funeral service, led by the Governor and his fellow state officers. Afterwards, the Maryland lawmakers formed up outside the church to follow behind the massed unit of military men, who passed the casket, hand to hand, along the entire route until it reached its final resting-place in St Anne's Cemetery. The city of Annapolis was hushed, for such an honour had never been seen before, nor would it ever again. It was as if the mourners wanted to keep the 'Sea King' from ever touching land. Upon reaching the burial plot, the mourners gathered around as the casket was lowered into the earth. In a spontaneous last show of affection, flowers began to be thrown onto the casket. Soon, so many flowers had been tossed upon the descending coffin that a cascade of brilliant colours filled the air and earth, inadvertently providing a glimpse to the mourners of what Waddell had seen so far away, so long ago, on the islands of the Pacific: a sublime paradise.

9

Once proud and capable

Anne Sellman Waddell lived on for five more years, passing away in 1891. The house James and Anne lived in during their last years together in Annapolis, Maryland, still stands and is inhabited by a descendant.

The house in Annapolis where Anne Waddell was held under house arrest by Union authorities also still stands, a mute reminder that the justice Americans have dealt to their fellow countrymen is sometimes practice for what their government carries out in foreign lands.

The *Shenandoah*, which had suffered through an attempt by the American government to sail her to New York in 1865, was finally sold at auction. Known again as the *Sea King*, she somehow wound up in the hands of the Sultan of Zanzibar to serve as his private yacht. Re-named once again, this time *El Majidi*, she proved either unsuitable, or too expensive for the Sultan to operate. She was apparently sold on again, this time to a German consortium, which put her back into the service she was originally designed for: the speedy transport of cargo. Plying the trade routes between Zanzibar and Bombay, usually hauling cloves or ivory, she was caught in a typhoon off Zanzibar in April 1872. Driven onto the shore by the tremendous winds and waves of the storm, her strong design saved her. A crew of shipwrights from HMS *Wolverine* successfully repaired her, even though her German owners had said she was not salvageable. In 1879, the *Sea King* was caught by another tremendous gale while on a run back from Bombay. This time her William Rennie-designed hull could not save her. Driven upon uncharted reefs off the island of Socotra, her bottom was ripped out. Only a few crewmen survived to make it ashore. Her death was recorded and commented upon in the London *Daily Telegraph*.

In the early 1960s, during the Vietnam War, the United States Navy was building a new type of guided missile destroyer (DDG). The new series of destroyer was to be named the *Charles F. Adams* class in honour of America's Civil War ambassador to Britain. Adams, of course, had plagued the efforts of James Dunwoody Bulloch to build Confederate Navy vessels in Britain. Casting about for a name for one of the new vessels, it was suggested that since the 100th anniversary of the American Civil War was coming, the Department of the Navy should christen a new destroyer for a Confederate naval officer as a sign of final reconciliation. Somehow, James Iredell Waddell's name was put forward. Naval historians and archivists for the Department of the Navy made a careful investigation of his career, as final approval of a new vessel's name resides with the Secretary of the Navy. During their investigation, naval historians discovered, to their amazement, the 1883 Act of Congress removing the 'political liabilities of James Iredell Waddell', signed off under the hand of President Ulysses S. Grant. Thus, even for US Grant, there was a surrender that had no conditions attached.

On 28 August 1964, the USS *Waddell* (DDG-24) was launched in Seattle, Washington, sliding into the ocean where James Waddell gained his greatest fame, the Pacific. In October of 1992 the USS *Waddell* was decommissioned and sold to the Greek navy, where it was re-named the HS-*Nearchos*. In 2003, the destroyer was decommissioned again and is now moored at Souda Bay, Crete, an ironic and fitting epitaph to a ship named after the Confederacy's own 'Ulysses'.

The official US Navy biography of James Iredell Waddell, and an early hand-edited copy of his 'Memoirs', can be found today in the US Naval Historical Center at the Navy Yard in Washington, DC, open to the public by appointment. (This book drew on Waddell's original, unedited memoir.)

As of December 2006, the heirs and descendants of James Iredell Waddell have still not been paid, with interest accrued, the financial compensation due him for his final service with the United States Navy aboard the USS *John Adams*. Somehow, one can believe he still expects to be paid.

Author's note

This book was conceived and written on the Isle of Jura, Scotland at the Feolin Ferry House, with additional work done at Homeleigh House, Crugmeer, Cornwall. The author wishes to thank the Feolin Study Centre and the Lithgow Charitable Trust for their support and assistance, as well as the US Naval Historical Center, the US Naval Institute, NARA, the US Naval Academy, Mr Bob Jones and Mr Roy Rawlinson of Liverpool, the Glasgow University Archives, Mr Bill Kooiman of the US National Park Service, San Francisco Maritime Museum, the North Carolina State Archives and History Department, the British National Library, Her Majesty's Royal Navy of Britain, the Department of the Navy, United States Navy, the Glasgow Maritime Heritage Centre, the National Maritime Museum of Britain (with particular thanks to Mr Andrew Choong and Mr Jeremy Mitchell), the Maryland State Archives, the Georgia State Archives, Dr Lindley Butler (Emeritus), Mr Michael Higgins, Dr Dan Good (Emeritus), the Ulysses S. Grant Association, the President Andrew Johnson Museum and Library, the Museum of the Confederacy at Richmond, Virginia, the National Civil War

Museum at Port Columbus, Georgia, the Bermuda National Museum, and the Museum of the Atlantic in Halifax, Nova Scotia.

Finally, for my wife Becky, whose favourite film as a child was *Gone with the Wind*, here is a story that even Margaret Mitchell could not have imagined, 'as God is my witness. . . '

Bibliography

MANUSCRIPTS AND PAPERS

Barron Family Papers, MSS. 2 B2787a, 1-7, Virginia Historical Society, Richmond, VA

Francis Thornton Chew Diary, in Francis Thornton Chew Papers, University of North Carolina, Chapel Hill, NC

Logbook of the *Shenandoah*, Atlanta Historical Centre, Atlanta, GA

Ulysses Samuel Grant Papers, US Library of Congress, Washington, DC

John Berkley Grimball Papers, Duke University Library, Durham, NC

Alfred Moore Waddell Papers, University of North Carolina Library, Chapel Hill, NC

Anne Sellman Waddell application for release from bond, Union Provost Marshall's File, Record Group 109, War Department Collection of Confederate Records, US National Archives and Records Administration (NARA), Washington, DC

James Iredell Waddell Letters and Papers, North Carolina Division of Historical Resources, Archives and Records Section, Raleigh, NC

James Iredell Waddell Papers (including letters, service record and original memoir manuscript, known as 'ZB' file), US Naval Historical Centre, US Navy Yard, Washington, DC

James Iredell Waddell Scrapbook, Special Collections, Nimitz Library, US Naval Academy, Annapolis, MD

Waddell Family Bible, Maryland State Archive, Annapolis, MD

GOVERNMENT DOCUMENTS

Case of Great Britain as Laid before the Tribunal of Arbitration Convened at Geneva, 3 vols (Washington, DC, US Govt. Printing Office, 1872)

Case of United States to be Laid before the Tribunal of Arbitration to be Convened at Geneva, 3 vols (London, Richard Bentley and Sons, 1872)

Dictionary of American Naval Fighting Ships, 8 vols (Washington, DC, US Govt. Printing Office, 1859-81)

Official Records of the Union and Confederate Navies in the War of the Rebellion, 31 vols (Washington, DC, US Govt. Printing Office, 1894–1922)

Papers Relating to the Treaty of Washington, 6 vols (Washington, DC, US Govt. Printing Office, 1872-74)

Johnson, President Andrew, 'Message from the President of the United States in Answer to a Resolution of the House of Representatives of the 8th Instant, Relative to the Surrender of the Rebel Pirate *Shenandoah*.' US Congressional Record and

US National Archives and Records Administration (NARA)
War of the Rebellion: A Compilation of the Official Records of the Union and Confederate Armies, 128 vols (Washington, DC, US Govt. Printing Office, 1880-1901)

PUBLISHED MEMOIRS

Bulloch, James D., *Secret Service of the Confederate States in Europe*, 2 vols (New York, Putnam, 1884)

Davis, Jefferson, *Rise and Fall of the Confederate Nation*, 2 vols (New York, Thomas Yoseloff, 1958)

Hunt, Cornelius, *The Shenandoah, or the Last Confederate Cruiser* (New York, Carleton & Co., 1867)

Mason, John Thomson, 'Last of the Confederate Cruisers', *Century Illustrated Magazine*, 56 (1898)

Semmes, Rafael, *Memoirs of Service Afloat* (Baltimore, Kelly, Piet & Co., 1869)

Waddell, James Iredell, CSS *Shenandoah: The Memoirs of Lieutenant Commanding James I. Waddell*, edited by James Horan (New York, Crown Publishers, 1960)

Whittle, William C. Jr., *Voyage of the Shenandoah*, edited by D. Alan Harris and Anne B. Harris (Tuscaloosa, University of Alabama Press, 2005)

CONTEMPORARY NEWSPAPERS, MAGAZINES AND OTHER JOURNALS

Liverpool *Mercury*
Illustrated London News
New York Times

New York *World*
San Francisco *Daily Alta*

SUPPORTING SOURCES

Adams, Ephraim Douglas, *Great Britain and the American Civil War*, 2 vols (New York, Russell and Russell, 1924)

Ashe, Samuel A., 'Captain James Iredell Waddell', *North Carolina Booklet* 13 (1913)

Balch, Thomas Willing, *The Alabama Arbitration* (Philadelphia, Allen, Lane and Scott, 1900)

Bennett, Michael J., *Union Jacks: Yankee Sailors in the Civil War* (Chapel Hill, University of North Carolina Press, 2004)

Benjamin, Park, *The United States Naval Academy* (New York, Putnam, 1900)

Bockstoce, John R., 'War at the Top of the World', *Civil War Times Illustrated* 25 (October 1986)

Brett, Henry, *White Wings: Fifty Years of Sail in the New Zealand Trade, 1850-1900* (Auckland, Brett Printing Company, 1924)

Butler, Lindley S., *Pirates, Privateers and Rebel Raiders of the North Carolina Coast* (Chapel Hill, University of North Carolina Press, 2000)

Canney, Donald, *Africa Squadron: The US Navy and the Slave Trade, 1842–1861* (Washington, Potomac Books, 2006)

Chaffin, Tom, *Sea of Gray* (New York, Hill and Wang, 2006)

Cox, Bryan, 'Officers Serve in Three Navies Within US', *Washington Times*, 4 December 2004

Dalzell, George W., *The Flight from the Flag: The Continuing Effect of the Civil War upon the American Carrying Trade* (Chapel Hill, University of North Carolina Press, 1940) de Kay, James Tertius, *The Rebel Raiders* (New York, Ballantine Books, 2002)

Durkin, Joseph T., *Stephen R. Mallory: Confederate Navy Chief* (Chapel Hill, University of North Carolina Press, 1954)

Eisenhower, John, *So Far from God: The US War with Mexico, 1846–1848* (Norman, University of Oklahoma Press, 2000)

Emmons, Frederick, *American Passenger Ships: The Ocean Lines and Liners, 1873–1983* (Newark, University of Delaware Press, 1985)

Feege, Edward H., 'The Rehabilitation of James Waddell', *Naval History*, June 2005

Feifer, George, *Breaking Open Japan: Commodore Perry, Lord Abe, and American Imperialism in 1853* (London, Collins, 2006)

Hill, Jim Dan, *Sea Dogs of the Sixties* (Minneapolis, University of Minnesota Press, 1935)

Graham, Eric J., *Clyde Built: Blockade Runners, Cruisers and Armoured Rams of the American Civil War* (Edinburgh, Birlinn, 2006)

Hutchinson, Thomas J., *The Parana: With Incidents of the Paraguayan War* (London, Edward Stanford, 1868)

Kemble, John, 'The Genesis of the Pacific Mail Steamship Co.', *California Historical Society Quarterly* 3 and 4, 1934

Kemble John, 'Steamships to Hawaii', *Steamboat Bill* 16, 1959

Luraghi, Raimondo, *A History of the Confederate Navy* (London, Chatham Publishing, 1993)

McPherson, James, *Battle Cry of Freedom* (Oxford, Oxford University Press, 1988)

Merli, Frank, J., *Great Britain and the Confederate Navy: 1861–1865* (Bloomington, Indiana University Press, 1970)

Morgan, Murray, *Dixie Raider: The Saga of the* CSS *Shenandoah* (New York, E.P. Dutton, 1948)

Pearl, Cyril, *Rebel Down Under* (Melbourne, William Heinemann, 1970)

Owsley, Frank Lawrence, *The* CSS *Florida: Her Building and Operations*, 2nd edition (Tuscaloosa, University of Alabama Press, 1987)

Plummer, Norman H., *Maryland's Oyster Navy* (St Michaels, MD, Tiller Publishing, 2005)

Thomson, Brian (Ed.), *Blue and Grey at Sea* (New York, Tom Doherty Associates, 2003)

Schooler, Lynn, *The Last Shot* (New York, Harper Collins, 2005)

Spencer, William F., *The Confederate Navy in Europe* (Tuscaloosa, University of Alabama Press, 1983)

Stephens and Sons, Alexander, *A Shipbuilding History: 1750–1932* (London, E.J. Burrow, 1932)

Internet

'When Liverpool Was Dixie':
 www.csadixie.com/liverpool_dixie/index.htm

The Museum of the Confederacy, Richmond, VA:
 www.moc.org/site/PageServer

National Civil War Naval Museum, Port Columbus, GA:
 www.portcolumbus.org/

Confederate States Navy, Mobile, AL:
 www.csnavy.org/

Orange County Historical Museum, NC:
 www.orangecountymuseum.org/main.htm

Bermuda National Trust Museum, Bermuda:
   www.bermuda4u.com/Attractions/bermuda_attractions_
   bermuda_national_trust_museum.html
The Maritime Museum of the Atlantic, Halifax, Nova Scotia,
Canada: museum.gov.ns.ca/mma/index.html
National Maritime Museum, Greenwich: www.nmm.ac.uk/
Merseyside Maritime Museum, Liverpool:
   www.liverpoolmuseums.org.uk/maritime/
National Maritime Museum of France:
   www.musee-marine.fr/
US Naval Historical Center, Washington, DC:
   www.history.navy.mil

Index